Insights into the Dead Sea Scrolls

Encompassing

Society and Religion During the Second Temple Period

Simon Berg

Dedicated to our grandchildren:
Ariel, born November 29th, (the anniversary of the arrival in Israel of the first Dead Sea Scrolls from Jordan), Tali, Tamir, and Emma.

Johannesburg - April 2009

Israel - 20 October 2022. Updated second edition

Available through the publishing group 'KDP Print" of Amazon, Amazon, and Book Depository.

Acknowledgments

My heartfelt thanks to my wife Rhona, who has shown unstinting support for the enthusiasm with which I wrote this book, and especially for her guidance in assisting me to restructure my rather 'informal' style of writing.

To my daughters, Maya and Leora, may this book and its subject remain with them as a reflection of one of the complex facets of their Dad, who is so proud of who they are.

To the late Dr Moshe Natas, former Professor of Jewish Studies, biblical scholar, and doyen in the Dead Sea Scrolls who continued to mentor, inspire, and teach me beyond his age of 105 years and who passed away about four years later. I was most privileged to have known him.

To my friend and inspiration Professor Emeritus Phillip V Tobias, Nobel Prize nominee and leading paleoanthropologist, who referred to me as *"another ardent seeker"*.

To my friend Kevin Richter for his editing suggestions.

To my colleagues and friends of the Christian faith who have taught me so much and presented such wonderful examples of understanding and tolerance towards my views, my appreciation. Especially to Claudia Vogel.

Introduction

I will begin by explaining why I wrote a book about the Dead Sea Scrolls:

I had a strong interest in establishing an understanding and background to Christianity and the New Testament because it has been a long-held belief of mine that the tragedy of the Holocaust was largely the ultimate culmination of Christian anti-Semitism.

Becoming a scholar of the Dead Sea Scrolls has resulted in my developing a new and clearer understanding of the origins of Christianity and the development of Judaism as revealed through the Scrolls.

I have learned to understand even more poignantly the meaning of *'you believe what you want to believe',* and in this book, you will understand that both Judaism and Christianity have *evolved.* Even within Judaism different sects also arose, evolved, clashed, and disappeared. It is hoped that these two religions will eventually become more tolerant towards each other, as more information about our common background becomes revealed.

This is becoming more poignant with the ever-increasing support for Israel and the Jewish people coming from a large sector of the Evangelical Christian movement, particularly in the USA. This will be further accentuated as Christianity more openly becomes the infidel, and *Dhimmi,* which is a second-class status imposed on *both* Christians and Jews by Islam.

The level of anti-Semitism in the world today exceeds pre-Holocaust times. Israel has become the collective personification of the individual Jew and has reached the stature of a country that the world loves to hate and demonize! Now, for the first time, you are about to enter an unknown world that may change and enrich the perception of your roots.

My interest began on my first reading a book on the Dead Sea Scrolls. Although the book held my attention, I often had to put it down as my concentration wandered due to difficulty in understanding its content. Also, I had a limited historical background and had to work my way through a maze of archaeological and religious terminology.

This is often the reason why many interesting subjects are not further pursued. Only dedication and persistence take one to read an additional book on the subject which might even be read several years later. In my case, I began obtaining as many books on the Dead Sea Scrolls as I could. I was able to accumulate five or six books in short succession. In retrospect, they gave me an excellent introduction and foundation to this captivating subject.

As my knowledge grew, I began to develop an illuminating interest in the Jewish society of the time. This led to a greater insight into the development of the Jewish religion. Many teachings that were 'written in stone' now became subject to greater questioning and moved away from dogma and the consideration of other options. Nevertheless, on a personal note, my religious observation and convictions remain unaffected. The insight into the understanding and development of Christianity became an important contributor to my knowledge.

I believe that there are scores of books and thousands of papers and articles published on the Dead Sea Scrolls and related topics. Why then, should there be a reason for yet another book written on the subject?

The authors of such books and papers are researchers and scholars, many of whom have had direct access to the Scrolls themselves. The level of their content is largely beyond the understanding of the man in the street. Many books are written at such a high level that only a persistent few can absorb and plough through them to the end.

My objective is to introduce this subject almost from scratch. Over the course of my 25 years in sales management with a multi-national pharmaceutical company, one of my functions has been to extract salient and usable information from clinical trials on cardiology, psychotropic medicine, and diabetes. The information obtained had to be easily understood by medical representatives and clearly conveyed to the medical practitioners.

This book is focused on the 'need to know' principle, and importantly is written in 'reader-friendly' English, avoiding dogma and one-sided opinions. I have also avoided the use of footnotes, asterisks, and a glossary. I have thus been able to provide 'on the spot' explanations and a continuum of the flow of understandable information. The objective of writing this book is to *guide* readers with minimal knowledge of the subject to a *significantly* higher level.

I have not had the privilege of being a Scrolls scholar but nevertheless, I have been able to write a book on this subject. This began by recording the knowledge gained in a progressive and structured manner. What you now read is the result of six years of research. This research has granted me university recognition to pursue a master's degree in this field. At this time, this remains my next challenge.

I must also mention the aspect of plagiarism when writing a book such as this. It is not only impossible to avoid quoting or extracting from various sources but is in fact essential to do so. Only someone who is in original research might not have the need. I have therefore used many opinions to convey different examples as objectively as possible. In essence, this book can be regarded as a *summary* book. Over the past ten-plus years, there has been regeneration towards *specific* aspects of the Scrolls and their background, for example focusing on the Christian connection.

In the formative years of scroll research, many books focused on the work of a specific scroll rather than interconnecting them. Also, I have noted 'about turns', in theories that upset some of the great fundamental and standard beliefs of earlier times.

All in all, my personal and *prime* reason for writing this book was to ensure that I could systematically upgrade my own knowledge on this subject. This has been a very enriching process.

In addition to references taken from books in my personal collection, I have made extensive use of the Internet. Perhaps I could be also regarded as 'a new generation' (when first researching) researcher/author.

Over the years, I have accumulated a vast quantity of notes using this source. This has allowed me to provide the reader with an even *broader* source of views and references apart from those that the classic textbooks provide. Furthermore, I have been able to provide the most current and up-to-date comments.

Thus, my book has not only been written to present an overview but to add many scholarly points of view as well. Sources are provided at the end of the book.

The reader will come across some repetitions of words and explanations. This has been intentionally done for those who are not familiar with them and who could benefit from such reminders.

This will also assist the reader who opens the book at a particular chapter and reads these words for the first time. To those who suggested that I use an indexed reference, which I appreciate, the reason for its absence is that when I first began collating my information, it was rather for purposes of being an 'informative' book as opposed to a textbook, and so I continued as such.

I have written this book with passion and emotion. I hope some will rub off onto you! It is with this introduction that I now leave you to read this book, hopefully in not too many sessions.

And to those on the African continent who have so demonized the Jewish people and Israel, in an age of 'violence', 'abuse', 'madness', 'injustice', and utter criminality, I am prompted to remind all of these words:

"When your people were still barbarians running naked around this Island, my people were already Priests in the Temple of Solomon!"

(Sir Benjamin Disraeli - Prime Minister of Britain, replying to an anti-Semitic taunt in the British Parliament.)

Table of Contents

PART 1: The Essential Background

Chapter 1: The FIRST Temple

It is believed that because of changes to the worship and sacrificial practices introduced by the priests of the Second Temple, who became more orientated towards their Hellenistic/Roman occupiers of Palestine, some priests broke away, having found the impure worship and corruption within the Temple establishment intolerable.

This led to the formation of the sect known as Essenes, who wrote many of the Dead Sea Scrolls. Speculation exists as to whether, because of the breakaway, they *then* became the Essenes, or whether they were *already* established as a sectarian group *prior* to these changes.

Before I became interested in Jewish history and the Scrolls, had I been asked to explain or describe the following, I would no doubt have been confused:

- The First Temple
- The Tabernacle
- The Holy of Holies
- The Ark
- The Second Temple
- The Temple Mount
- What was kept in the Holy of Holies?
- The Dome of the Rock
- Who built and/or reconstructed the Temples?

- Who destroyed the Temples?

If you correctly described half of the above, you would be placed in the above-average category. I will now continue with the facts as we know them.

At the outset, let me attempt to provide a satisfactory definition of what the Temple means to the Jewish people. In its most simplistic form, I would describe it as the dwelling place for the Divine Spirit (God) and a place where sacrifices were made to Him.

It was the symbol of God's presence amongst the Jewish people. The Temple was to be the permanent resting place for the Ark of the Covenant and thus the Divine presence of God in the Holy of Holies. It has also been referred to in prayers by the Jewish people, as the 'House of Our Life', 'Your Chosen House', the 'Great and Holy House' and 'The Eternal House'.

Yes, sacrifices were made before and after the destruction of the first and last Temples. But I refer to types of sacrifices that were made on specific occasions and under certain circumstances. Furthermore, there was a greater scope in the variation of sacrifices that could be made at the permanent Temple, compared to those that the Jews were able to carry out in the proximity of the Tabernacle which preceded the Temple. Importantly, it was the place where the High Priest could directly communicate with God and receive an answer.

The Temple was also the designated venue for the three annual pilgrimages as commanded to the Jewish people in the Torah - also known as the Pentateuch or the Five Books of Moses. They are, the 'Feast of Tabernacles' (*Sukkot*), the 'Feast of the First Fruits / and Receiving the Torah' (*Shavuot*), and Passover *(Pesach)*. People came not only from Judea or the Holy Land Israel, but also from outside the region. It was during the Passover pilgrimage that Jesus visited Jerusalem just prior to his crucifixion.

Strangely enough, it is also believed by some that God's first dwelling place of His sanctuary was the Garden of Eden. The holiest site is Mount Moriah.

In Exodus 25:8-9 we read: "*And they shall make Me a Sanctuary that I may dwell among them according to all that I will show you after the pattern of the Tabernacle...*" God continues with His detailed instructions to Moses regarding the Temple's furnishings and structure. This was the sacred site of the interrupted sacrifice of Isaac, and the vicinity where Jacob had his famous ladder dream. On the morning following the dream, Jacob said, in Genesis 28:16-17, "*Surely the Lord is in this place, and I knew not. And he was afraid, and said, How full of awe is this place! This is none other than the house of God, and this is the gate of heaven*".

This was followed by the appointment of the first priest Aaron and details of his priestly vestiges. God instructed Moses about the various sacrifices, from live offerings to the burning of sweet spice incense. Then in the book of Deuteronomy 12:11, God said: "*Then it shall come to pass that the place which the Lord your God shall choose to cause His name to dwell there, there will you bring all that I command you: your burnt-offerings and your sacrifices*". So, what does all this mean?

After the giving of the Ten Commandments to the Israelites, God instructed Moses to build a portable precursor to a permanent Temple, the Tabernacle. This was to be set up each time the Israelites settled down to camp in the Sinai on their forty-year journey to the Land of Israel, then called Canaan.

The Tabernacle

The Tabernacle that was constructed at the beginning of the Israelites' 40-year wanderings in the Sinai desert was a portable and collapsible structure that could be re-assembled according to their travels to the 'Promised Land.'

Its design, given to Moses by God (Exodus 25:8), consisted of an oblong, gold-covered wooden fence 50m x 25m, interspersed with hanging curtains, and enclosing a courtyard. Within this courtyard stood a smaller structure, the actual Tabernacle, or *Mishkan* in Hebrew, measuring 15m x 4m, at the far end to the entrance of the surrounding enclosure. Confusion or a misinterpretation surround what could have been a second enclosure referred to as the 'Tent of Meeting' or *ohel mo'ed* in Hebrew.

This tent is possibly where the Ark of the Covenant might have been originally housed before the actual completed and more elaborate Tabernacle. It was set up away from the camp of the Israelites and where Moses could speak 'face to face' with God and receive answers to questions put by an individual.

Another name for the Tabernacle was the 'Tabernacle of Testimony'. The term Tabernacle referred to all its contents, temple vessels, and utensils. The words 'Testimony' and 'Covenant' were used to imply that the Tabernacle housed the Ark containing the 'Tablets of the Testimony' i.e., the Tablets of the Ten Commandments.

A deeper meaning is that there are two Temples - one Earthly and the second Heavenly. This may be fully appreciated by reading the original Hebrew of the Torah.

The Tabernacle had a roof covering, which functioned as a (nomadic) tent, thought to have been made from a unique species of sealskin, eleven goat hair cloths, and rams' skin. In addition, two other fabrics covered the roof. It reflected a genuine desert tradition - similar to the way in which Bedouin tents are constructed.

The Tabernacle was divided into two parts. The rear section was curtained off and was known as the Holy of Holies. In the Holy of Holies, the Ark, also referred to as the 'Ark of the Covenant' was kept. This was a container of specific design and structure as instructed by God to Moses. In it were placed the two stone Tablets of the Law (the Ten Commandments), together with the stone tablets that had been smashed by

Moses the first time he came down from Sinai, after having seen the Israelites worshipping the Golden Calf.

The Ark rested on a bedrock platform in the Second Temple. This rock now forms the canter point for the *Dome of the Rock* on the Temple Mount in Jerusalem, which is Islam's second holiest site and out of bounds to Jews and other 'infidels'.

Other holy artifacts kept in the Ark (it is believed) were a jar of Manna, a jar of oil to be used perhaps for the anointing of the new High priest (Hebrew: *Kohen Gadol*), the staff of Aaron and the Scroll of the Law - the Torah - the first, which was written by Moses himself.

Also present was a jar of ashes from the 'Red Heifer' - used in certain circumstances for purification. These were artifacts from both the Tabernacle and the First Temple. It is not clear whether these artifacts were later kept in the Second Temple or stored and hidden together with the Ark when it was eventually removed from the First Temple for safekeeping.

The Ark itself comprised an outer and inner gold-covered acacia wooden box, with a set of two rings on each side through which gold-covered poles passed, for the purpose of being lifted and transported by members of the tribe of Levi.

On the top of the Ark, and of the same surface size, was placed a solid gold flat cover, about the thickness of a hand. On it were two solid gold cherubs, one male and the other female, facing one another with upward outstretched wings that covered most of the Ark (Hebrew: *Aron*). The Divine Presence rested between the wings of the cherubs. This cover is also referred to by some as 'The Mercy Seat'. The Torah records that the 'Clouds of Glory', which were a manifestation of God's infinite and divine presence called the *Shechinah*, would rest on the sanctuary as a tangible sign that God was with the Jewish people. You will read further on that the Shechinah eventually left the Temple.

Still within the confines of the Tabernacle, but outside the Holy of Holies, were the following as stipulated by God - the solid gold menorah (lampstand) which had six curved branches, three on each side and a central upright stem, all at an equal height of six feet. This seven-branched menorah burned continuously and stood on the south side of the Holy of Holies. In the center was a gold-covered incense altar which also burned continuously.

On the north side of the Menorah stood a gold-covered table with shelving, on which were placed the twelve 'Show-Breads'. These were replaced every Friday. They were in fact unleavened, as is the *matzah* that is eaten during the days of the Passover. The shelves were additionally used to store golden utensils for the showbread (also spelled *shewbread*) and the incense altar.

As this table stood on the north, this meant that the Holy of Holies was on the eastern side. In the outside courtyard stood an altar covered in copper which was able to hold a large animal. Leading to the top of this altar, also known as the 'Altar of the Elevation-offering' was a ramp that allowed the priest to ascend and perform the sacrifice on the top surface. A copper laver or basin to be used for the priests to wash their feet and hands before sacrificing, also made-up part of the basic requisites. The entire area is known as Mount Moriah or the Temple Mount.

The Tabernacle accompanied the Israelites throughout the forty years in the desert. Sometimes it was pitched and set up for only a few weeks and on one lengthy occasion, for as long as twenty years. Joshua finally led the Israelites into Canaan, part of which is Israel today.

The Ark was re-pitched at Gilgal for fourteen years. Then later at Shiloh, near to where Nablus is situated on the 'West Bank' of Israel today. There it remained for three hundred and sixty-nine years. Later, a stone edifice was built around it. During this time the Ark was captured by the Philistines and returned after a plague broke out among them.

A new Tabernacle was then erected in Nov, where it remained for thirteen years. It was then moved to Givion and finally set up on Mount Moriah.

The Temple of Solomon

Tradition has it that God gave the plan for the permanent structure of the Temple to Moses. It was passed down to King David. He was not permitted to build the Temple but purchased the threshing floor of Araunah for the site of the First Temple. This was in Jerusalem, which David declared as his Capital. The actual task of building the Temple was assigned to King Solomon, the son of David.

From 960 till 950 BCE, King Solomon with the help and support of Hiram the King of Tyre - a small island city port just off the coast of Lebanon - built and completed the Temple with the help of 153,600 workers. The laying of the foundation stones and the preliminary work alone took place over four years prior to work on the building itself. King Solomon spared no expense. The Holy of Holies stood over the sacred site on Mount Moriah. It was lined with gold and encrusted with jewels; in fact, both the inside and outside were clad in gold sheeting. It is estimated that about twenty tons of gold were used.

A huge bronze cistern was cast, known as the *yam*, Hebrew for sea, holding almost 40,000 liters of water, and supported by twelve life-sized bronze bulls. This was to supply the priests with all their water. There were in addition ten brass carts to carry the lavers or smaller containers of water. The candelabra, table, gold incense altar, and all the other furnishings from the Tabernacle comprised part of the Temple. It was a wondrous creation that literally stood as a shining symbol for all to see from miles around. God's Divine spirit rested therein.

There were many priests in attendance at the Temple, originally from the tribe of Levi, headed by the High Priest. They rotated on a roster system, varying in shifts from a week to months. Some came from far to the north, leaving their families to carry out their duties.

These priestly tasks were designated to the Tribe of Levi who descended from Tzadok (Zadock), the High Priest of King

David and later of King Solomon. Jewish people with the names Cohen, Kahn, Kagan, Kaplan, and in special cases Katz, are mostly direct descendants of this priestly class. In recent times it has been scientifically verified that up to 80% of Jewish people with these names all have a unique gene in common, proving their lineage. The lineage is visible in two markers on the Y chromosome, transmitted from father to son.

Apart from being the center for prayer and sacrifices, the Temple accumulated the wealth of the Jewish people through the accumulation of gifts and the compulsory Temple tax as instructed by God. This tax was in the form of the famous 'half shekel' collected from every Jewish citizen within Israel and others living outside Israel.

In anticipation of the rebuilding of the (Third) Temple, half shekels have already been minted together with some of the basic vessels and other items that lie in storage and wait for that day.

Within the Temple area were markets where money changers operated, and it was their tables that were overturned by Jesus who saw their presence as a defilement of the holy place. These money changers functioned much in the same way as the foreign currency department of a bank, by converting foreign currencies to that of the local currency.

The money changed was used to purchase the requisites for sacrifice or used for tax or donation purposes. The markets were a hub of activity, with animals being sold for those sacrifices, people going to the ritual baths (Hebrew pl: *mikva'ot*) for purification immersions, and of course the many maintenance artisans involved in the Temple upkeep.

Once a year on the Day of Atonement (Hebrew: *Yom Kippur*), the High Priest, after having undergone purification, went behind the curtain, or veil (Hebrew: *paroket*), which had images of cherubim woven into it, into the Holy of Holies to plead with God to forgive Israel for her sins, and to grant the nation another blessed year. This curtain, as recorded in the

Christian Bible, is said to have been torn in two (Mark 15:38) when Jesus died.

Should any person have entered the Holy of Holies at any time, other than the 'genuine' High Priest, that person would die on the spot

Further on in this chapter, you will read of the enormous difference in the numbers of High Priests during the First and Second Temple periods. When impure so-called High Priests entered the Holy of Holies on Yom Kippur; they immediately died on account of not being 'recognized' by God. This led to a problem because those who entered the Holy of Holies to retrieve the dead body also died. Thus, a safety feature was established, and a rope was tied around the waist or leg of the priest to pull him out if he died!

In 636 CE Israel was conquered by Arab Muslims. Fifty-five years later at the site of the First and Second Temples, the Dome of the Rock Mosque was built. The Jewish people traditionally call this Mount Zion. The famous golden dome is situated over a large rock said to be the site where Abraham was halted from sacrificing Isaac.

There is a particular square-like indentation in a section of this rock which is about 8 feet or 3.5 meters above the surrounding rock surface. This is where the Ark is believed to have rested and is also the vicinity of the sacrificial altar.

In Islam, it is the site where the Prophet Mohammed is said to have left and flown to heaven on his fiery steed, *Al Boraque,* and ascended through the seven spheres of heavenly revelation - with the hooves having made four deep indentations in the rock. This rock thus became known in Arabic as the *sakhra.*

To this day, Jews are not allowed to walk in the proximity of where the Ark was believed to have been, and hence where the Holy of Holies could have been. Another reason is that if an authenticated 'Red Heifer' (Numbers 19:1) has not been designated for sacrifice to obtain its ashes, purification of the holy area as a prerequisite before building the Third Temple cannot take place. This is based on a law in Torah that instructs that only its ashes can bring about purification. Thus, the Jews remain ritually impure.

However certain areas of the Mount are not included in this ban. Currently, the *Waqif*, the Muslim religious trust, that has been allowed to run the site, does not allow non-Muslims to enter the area. This was because of an arrangement with Moshe Dayan soon after the Six-Day War, an arrangement that had disastrous consequences for the Jews / Israelis wanting to excavate there and physically wish to go to the holy area from which they are now banned.

Chapter 2: Chronology of Events

I now continue with events leading up to the destruction of the First and Second Temples. Note that for the most part, I believe that the given dates are relatively accurate. Discrepancies do exist with some of the dates despite my using respected sources. However, some of these dates are in fact 'carved in stone'. Importantly it will serve to provide you with a time-interval sequence and will clarify historical events and names appearing in this book.

First, some 'dry' calculations to assist the reader with an appreciation for the age of the Scrolls:

In 1,312 BCE ('Before the Common Era') the exodus from Egypt by the Israelites took place. This calculates the age of the Jewish people as a nation to be just over 3,300 years. This is also the age of the first written Torah.

The earliest Dead Sea Biblical scroll is dated to around 250 BCE, which means that it was copied (only) about 1,020 years after the Torah's completion by Moses following the 40-year sojourn of the Israelites in the Sinai. Many of the Scrolls were copies of much earlier dated scroll copies. The significance of this will be appreciated when covering the section dealing with the 'Masoretic Text'.

The oldest complete Hebrew copy of the Bible (Hebrew: *Tanach*) is the Leningrad Codex. A codex is a manuscript arranged in leaves (pages) as in a modern book, and not on a scroll. This codex conforms to the official and traditional Hebrew text. It was copied in 1,008 CE ('Common Era') and is thus currently 996 years old. An earlier copy is the famous Aleppo Codex completed in 930 CE. Part of which was burnt/destroyed/removed from its storage place in Aleppo Syria on the day that Israel was declared a state in 1947. The remaining codex is now in Israel.

The biblical Dead Sea Scrolls are thus 1,260 years older than that codex and any known complete Hebrew Bible!

For 385 years, from Moses to Solomon, the Tabernacle served Israel as a temporary structure being moved from place to place.

The First Temple

King Solomon completes the First Temple on Mount Moriah in Jerusalem, 950 BCE

40 Years later - around 910 BCE

The Pharaoh of Egypt plunders the Temple, taking a considerable amount of gold and silver.

10 Years later - around 920 BCE

The Jewish Kingdom divides into North and South during the reign of Rehoboam, son of Solomon. The northern half becomes known as The Kingdom of Israel, made up of ten of the twelve tribes and the Southern half known as Judah, which included Jerusalem.

85 Years later - 835 BCE

King Joash of Judah in 835 BCE repairs the Temple

115 Years later - 720 BCE

Ahaz, King of Judah dismantles the bronze vessels and places a private Syrian altar in the Temple, thus defiling it.

4 Years later - 716 BCE

The Temple is restored once again, this time by King Hezekia of Judah.

5 Years later - around 711 BCE

King Hezekia of Judah is forced to give up Temple treasures to the Assyrian King Tiglathpileser III. The Assyrian territory encompassed what today are parts of Syria, Iraq, and Turkey. Later other Assyrian kings invaded land occupied by some of the tribes occupying Israel stage by stage until the whole northern part of the country ceased to be a Jewish state.

11 Years later - 700 BCE

The Temple is plundered once again, this time by a prince from the great city of Babylon in Assyria.

50 Years later - 650 BCE

During those times of disaster, the Ark is secretly removed for safekeeping, never to be seen since, and the Divine Spirit left the Temple. Idols were placed in the Temple by no less than the King Manasseh of Judah around 620 BCE.

30 Years later - 620 BCE

Around 620 King Josiah of Judah smashes the idols, restores the Temple, and finds the original Torah written by Moses, which was formerly kept in the Ark.

11 Years Later - 609 BCE

Josiah is killed in a battle against the Egyptians at Megiddo and is replaced by Jehoiakim as king of Judah.

4 Years Later - 605 BCE

Judah under Jehoiakim becomes a vassal state (dependent on) of Babylon.

8 Years later - 597 BCE

Babylon attacks Jerusalem after King Jehoiakim rebels against Nebuchadnezzar, King of Babylon, and Jehoiakim surrenders. The first 10,000 Jewish elite are deported to Babylon.

Zedekiah, a puppet king, is installed. He too eventually rebelled, which resulted in Nebuchadnezzar putting down the rebellion (in 588 BCE) and laying siege to Jerusalem.

The First Temple is Destroyed

2 Years later - 586 BCE

On the 9th of the month of Av in the Jewish calendar, 586 BCE, Nebuchadnezzar, who had laid siege to Jerusalem, burns the city, murders the inhabitants, destroys the (First) Temple and carries off the holy Temple vessels to Babylon, (which was in present-day Iraq). He captures most of the populace of Judah whom he leads off as captives for almost 50 years of exile, into Babylon.

The destruction of the First Temple was seen by the Jewish people as a tragedy of cosmic proportions, a return to 'primeval chaos'.

A new era for the Jews began. Three famous biblical quotes commemorate this:

Psalm 137: "*By the rivers of Babylon, there we sat down; we also wept when we remembered Zion*".

And from the book of Lamentations, "*How does the city sit solitary that was full of people!*"

Isaiah 40: "*Comfort ye, comfort ye my people says your God. Speak to the heart of Jerusalem and proclaim to her that in her time (of exile in Babylon) has been fulfilled, that her iniquity (sin) is pardoned, for she hath received from the hand of God double for all her sins*".

The First Temple stood for about 360 years. Over this period, 18 High Priests served the Temple, or on average one every 20 years. During the Second Temple period, which lasted for about 500 years, there were 300 High Priests or one every 1.6 years. This was due to the high death rate that occurred on account of 'false priests' entering the Holy of Holies! About 10 years prior to the destruction of the First Temple which took place in BCE 586, the Babylonians initially took into captivity ten thousand of the best and brightest Jews. These Jews established an infrastructure that absorbed the remainder who were taken captive when Jerusalem was conquered.

The Second Temple

About sixty years later, in 538 BCE, from the time the Babylonians first took capture of the ten thousand, in 597 BCE, the Emperor of Persia, Cyrus II, conquered Belshazzar the last king of Babylon.

Cyrus issued 'The Edict of Toleration' and permitted the exiled Jews to return to Palestine. He ordered the return of all the Temple treasures to the reconquered Jerusalem and issued a decree to rebuild what then became known as the 'Second' Temple'. In the Book of Isaiah Ch. 45 verse 1 it reads: *"Thus the Lord said to Cyrus, His anointed one."* The Hebrew for *'anointed'* is messiah or *mashiach,* incidentally!

There were four major Holy items in the First Temple that were missing from the Second Temple:

1. The Ark
2. The Breastplate of Aaron
3. Ashes of the Red Heifer
4. The Holy anointing oil

Also: The *Shechinah* or *Holy / Divine Spirit* had departed.

No reference, either biblical or other sources had mentioned the return of the Divine presence to the Holy of Holies.

The rebuilding of the Temple took place under the leadership of Zerubbabel and Joshua the High Priests. Only about 50,000 Jews returned from Babylon. The building took place over a period of 20 years, because of a 15-year halting of its construction by protestations from jealous and suspicious Samaritans who hindered all efforts of the returnees.

73 Years later - 515 BCE

Zerubbabel, a descendent of the Davidic lineage, in 515 BCE completes the rebuilding of the Second Temple. The Temple was less modest than Solomon's and reintroduced sacrifices. Cyrus dies and is replaced by Darius the 1st, who continues with Persian support.

70 Years later - 445 BCE

In 445 BCE Nehemiah, a high official in the Persian court returns to Jerusalem to rebuild the walls of the city and to protect the Temple Mount.

About the same time a priest, Ezra, described as 'the Scribe of the Law of God', re-establishes the reading of the Torah and sacred traditions of the people.

113 Years later - 332 BCE

Alexander the Great of Greece conquers the Persian Empire, including Palestine, and spares Jerusalem and the Temple. Thus begins the introduction of the Greek culture known as Hellenism.

5 Years later - 327 BCE

After Alexander's death at the age of 33, in the year 323 BCE, his Generals embark on a leadership struggle, eventually leading to a split rule of the conquered region. Ptolemy rules Egypt and Palestine, with those Greeks becoming known as Ptolemys. Seleucid rules the old Babylonian empire, which includes Syria. Palestine/Israel lies in the middle.

Some Historical Geography

Under Ptolemaic rule, Palestine was not a separately defined administrative district of the kingdom. For most of the third century BCE, the Ptolemaic Syria and Phoenicia (where Lebanon is today), included both western Palestine and Trans-Jordan. A considerable part of the country was defined by its ethnic character, meaning the status of a region was determined according to the nation to which its population belonged - e.g., Judea in the center, Samaria in the north, and Edom in the south. The Galilee was north of Samaria and partially surrounded the Sea of Galilee (H Ben-Sasson). Judea or 'Persian Judea' was at first allowed to retain its traditional system of government until it came under the rule of Antiochus III.

128 Years later - 199 BCE

The Seleucid ruler Antiochus III wins control of Palestine. In the process, Jerusalem is attacked, most of the males killed, and the women and children sold off into slavery. "Then Antiochus attempted to obliterate the Jewish religion by forbidding sacrifices, traditional festivals, Sabbath worship and the rite of circumcision, upon the pain of death". (JD Tabor)

24 Years later - 175 BCE

Antiochus' son, Antiochus IV pillages the Temple and offers a pig on the altar. He then begins a vigorous forced integration into the Greek culture on the Jewish population.

10 Years later - 165 BCE

This leads to an uprising, led by Judah Maccabee, which is successful in repossessing Jerusalem in 165 BCE. He becomes the first Hasmonaean ruler of Judea and his son Jonathan assumes the High Priesthood in 152 BCE. The Temple was cleansed and rededicated. The Jewish people commemorate this by the Festival of Hanukkah. Thus becomes established the Maccabean, or Hasmonaean, kingdom, which lasts until 63 BCE.

Chronology of Events - The Second Temple

102 Years later - 63 BCE

The last two Hasmonaean rulers, who were of Hellenistic background from the line of the Maccabees, are two brothers: Hyrcanus II and Aristobolus. Quarrelling with each other as to who should be king, they ask Rome to mediate in their dispute and invite the Roman Emperor Pompey. In 63 BCE Pompey obliges, sees an opportunity, and moves in with his army. He conquers Jerusalem and entering the Holy of Holies of the Temple, he finds it to be empty! (The Divine Spirit had already left the Temple).

13 Years later - 50 BCE

A slaughter of Jews takes place and Hyrcanus is appointed High Priest and nominal puppet ruler of the country in 76 BCE. He destroys the Samaritan Temple on Mt Gerizim. Thus begins Roman rule, with taxes being paid to Rome. The lands of Israel and Judah are now officially referred to as Palestine, after the former neighboring territory of Philistine.

29 Years later - 21 BCE

Julius Caesar replaces Pompey and appoints Antipater as Roman Procurator (Governor) of Judea. (The infamous Procurator at the time of Jesus' crucifixion was Pilate.) Antipater's son, Herod, becomes military Governor (king) of Galilee in 37 BCE.

51 Years later - 30 CE

Jesus refers to the Temple as 'My father's House'. In the marketplace at the southwestern corner of the Temple Mount, he overturns the tables of the moneychangers who transacted with pilgrims for the animals they bought for sacrifices. He sees these transactions as a defilement of the Holy environment.

Herod and the Second Temple

It has been said that the reign of King Herod the Great brought a second 'golden age' to Jerusalem as King Solomon previously had done. Jerusalem became one of the most beautiful cities in the world. The Second Temple was enlarged and rebuilt to magnificent splendor. The economy boomed and a comparatively peaceful era ensued. *Yet* confusion reigned between the *cultural identity* of the (holy) city of Jerusalem and the *identity of Herod* himself.

During this period the Hasmonaeans, the Pharisees, and the Sadducees were at extreme odds with each other. The lack of national unity created a dangerous situation. Herod was neither 'fish nor fowl'. He was a product of forced conversion to the Jewish culture. The Romans considered him to be a Jew and the Jews saw him as a Roman. This ideally suited his Roman rulers. The rebuilt and expanded Second Temple was also in a sense a Hellenistic palace - "*it glorified Herod as much as it glorified God*".

The rebuilding of the Temple in fact took place over a period of 47 years, being completed in 27 CE, thirty-one years after Herod's death. By way of further comprehending the date, Jesus was born in approximately 3 CE.

In a tyrannical manner, Herod brought stability and prosperity. He built a magnificent winter palace, the fortress of Masada, and the city of Caesarea. In 20 BCE he enlarged and leveled the Temple Mount, and over a ten-year period also rebuilt the retaining walls around it. He totally rebuilt and extended the dimensions of the Second Temple. He also faithfully replicated its furnishings. The Holy of Holies was once again lined in gold, and white marble pillars and floors were added. Josephus (the Roman historian) described the Sanctuary, which was overlaid with plates of gold, as "*reflecting a blaze of fire*" and the marble structures appearing "*like a mountain covered in snow*" when seen from a distance.

In his latter days, Herod became a madman, persecuting and murdering his own family as well as Jews and rabbis who stood up to him. As a result of his interference, and him being an avowed Hellenist, the Temple hierarchy once again became corrupt. There is no apparent reference to Herod in the Scrolls. He reigned from 40 BCE to 4 CE.

The Rebellion against Rome

The Jewish population was divided. Of the better-known groups, there were: the Samaritans, Pharisees, Sadducees, Essenes, Zealots, Ebionites, and the Sicarii or 'dagger men'. All represented one form or another of Jewish ideological or religious beliefs. Then known as Palestine, the area was a seething cauldron of these different groups.

The country was split into two, with one half wanting to co-operate with the occupying Romans and the other half strongly against collaboration. During Herod's reign, all these factions were held at bay. Thirty-three years after his death, all hell broke loose in 37 CE. Steve Manson quoting the historian Josephus: *"those few Jews who recklessly led the nation into revolt were entirely idiosyncratic. Their mad squabbling among themselves and ruthless behavior in Jerusalem proves that they were only out for personal gain"*.

These divisions over the course of time led to the weakness of the people which was aggravated by the hateful presence of the Romans. This continued over a period of about 60 years until the onset of the revolt against Rome, otherwise known as 'The Jewish War'. This became the final explosion between the factions, together with the oppressive legislation, taxation, numerous massacres, and humiliations imposed by the Roman rulers.

29 Years later - 66 CE

The people revolt and rise in 66 CE against Rome and Gessius Florus, the tyrannical procurator at the time. Slaughter upon slaughter ensues. The Zealots, one of the many breakaway Jewish sectarian groups, take the Roman-held fortress of Masada, which was formally Herod's winter palace. This revolt becomes known as the 'Jewish War' which ends in disaster for the Jews in 70 CE.

The Second Temple is Destroyed

4 Years later - 70 CE

Vespasian is appointed the new Caesar. His son Titus is sent to quell the uprising. The culmination is in 70 CE when Jerusalem becomes besieged and after two months the Romans break through its thick walls. This is the start of the greatest massacre of the Jews apart from the Holocaust. The upper city of Jerusalem burns for over a month.

The Second Temple lasted about 490 years

850 Years of actual Temple Worship left this world

Together with the Tabernacle(s)... over 1,200 years

At the peak of the battle, Titus gave instructions for the Temple to be spared. I quote from Josephus (a famed Jewish historian of the time):

"*He (Titus) ran and tried to persuade his soldiers to quench the fire, but they hated the Jews so much that they ignored his order...one of them threw a firebrand into the Temple, and flames immediately burst out from within.*"

Note: Josephus's comments on Titus were not necessarily accurate, as he often wrote in a style appeasing his Roman hosts, as you will read later.

"*While the Temple was on fire, everything was plundered that came to hand, and ten thousand of those that were caught were slain; no pity was shown for age, but children, old men, the secular and priests were all slain in the same manner.*"

"*Yet more terrible than the din were the sights that met the eye. The Temple Mount, enveloped in flames from top to bottom, appeared to be boiling up from its very roots; yet the sea of flame was nothing to the ocean of blood. Nowhere could the ground be seen between the corpses, and the soldiers climbed over heaps of bodies as they chased the fugitives...*"

"*...97,000 prisoners taken. Those who perished in the long siege: 1,100,000...*"

Note: Josephus was inclined to exaggerate details at times; there is, however, no doubt that it was a massacre of genocidal proportions.

Titus victoriously set sail for Rome with 700 prisoners. An arch was erected in Rome to celebrate this victory - 'Titus' Arch.' A carving on the arch commemorating this is seen to this day, showing Roman soldiers carrying the famous Menorah, the Table for the showbread, and other Temple vessels. Speculation has thus arisen as to their whereabouts. Masada fell in 72 CE, when (apparently) the Romans found that they had all committed suicide on their eventual entry to the fortress. This was documented by Josephus, who is the sole individual who accounted for this having been undertaken by the remaining Zealots.

Destruction of the Second Temple

This once again occurred on the 9th of Av - a month in the Jewish calendar - on the anniversary of the destruction of the First Temple. This day has since been a day of mourning and fasting for the Jewish people. The debris from the Temple was used for the foundations of a new Roman Jerusalem which was renamed *Aelia Capitoline*.

The destruction of the Second Temple had an enormous impact on the Jewish people, even to this day. The Sadducees, the Essenes, and Zealots faded away. The beginnings of Rabbinic Judaism became more entrenched since only the Pharisees and the early Christians, known as 'Jewish Christians' or Nazarenes survived.

Both incorporated the Temple into their religious beliefs. The Jewish people were separated from their contact with God. 202 of the 613 commandments (*Mitzvoth*) that were so integral to Judaism could no longer be applied. To many, the destruction of the Temple meant the destruction of Judaism. Jews, for the first time, left the country *en masse* into permanent exile and into what is now referred to as the (Jewish) 'Diaspora'.

To the 'Judeo-Christians', the 'Spiritual Temple' replaced the physical Jerusalem Temple. The former place of sacrifice was replaced by the concept of the 'ultimate sacrifice' of Jesus himself, to atone for human sin.

This is symbolized today in the Mass (Eucharist or Holy Communion) by the sacrificial meal of bread and wine.

An opportunity to rebuild the Temple arose in 614 CE when once again the Persians together with the Jews of Jerusalem, defeated the Christian occupiers. The Persian king, *Chosroes*, gave his permission for rebuilding, but later reneged. Both Judaism and Christianity await the Third Temple. This is a subject on its own and is widely promoted on the Internet and in Jewish and Christian literature.

This is a fleeting overview of Jewish history during a crucial period spanning just over a thousand years. I trust that you are now better prepared to grasp the historical significance contained in the writings of the Dead Sea Scrolls.

Timeline: The High Priests of Jerusalem

BCE 190

Onias III is a High Priest during the rule and under influence of the Seleucid Empire, for 20 years.

BCE 174

Jason is appointed High Priest.

BCE 172

Menelaus bribes the Seleucid king to appoint him as High Priest.

BCE 170

Menelaus has his rival Onias III executed.

BCE 169

Jason the son of Onias III, having fled to Transjordan, returns to attempt to overthrow Menelaus. He was defeated, captured, and dies in Sparta.

BCE 167

The Hasmonean family of priests successfully leads a rebellion against their Greek occupiers under Mattathias and his five sons. The Temple is cleansed. The festival of Chanukah celebrated ever since.

BCE 162

Judas the Maccabee one of the five Hasmonaean brothers overthrows the Greek rule.

BCE 161

Judas is killed. The Greeks re-establish power in Jerusalem.

BCE 153

Judas' brother Jonathan gathers an army and takes back Jerusalem.

BCE 150

Jonathan, Judas' brother becomes the High Priest and later Governor of Judea.

BCE 142

Jonathan is killed and succeeded by Hasmonaean brother Simon.

BCE 134

Simon is killed. His son John Hyrcanus takes charge.

BCE 104

Aristobulus I, king of Judea succeeds his father, John Hyrcanus.

BCE 103

Alexander Janneus is appointed both King of Judea and High Priest.

BCE 88

Alexander crucifies 800 Pharisees. (See 'The Pharisees')

BCE 76

Alexander Janneus is killed. Hyrcanus II appointed High Priest.

BCE 67

Aristobulus II takes by force from his brother Hyrcanus II, the High Priesthood.

BCE 63

Pompey, a Roman general, enforces Roman rule in Judea and makes Hyrcanus II a captive.

BCE 47

In exchange for Julius Caesar's support, Hyrcanus II becomes the Roman representative ruler of the Jews.

BCE 40

Hyrcanus II is captured by the Parthians (Greeks). Romans name Herod king of Judea

BCE 35

Herod's wife's brother Aristobulus becomes High Priest. Herod has him killed.

Chapter 3: Society and Religion during the Second Temple Period

Insight

"The influences of the different divisions of society together with the occupiers of Palestine during that period, resulted in a major and permanent effect on Judaism and is felt even to this day."

Under this heading I have devoted much attention and space to some of the main role players in this book. This will assist the reader to gain a solid foundation of the whys and wherefores as to how those religious groups influenced the development of Judaism in particular. Importantly the reader will be able to grasp the significance of the role of Jewish religious law (*Halachah*), its interpretation and why in some cases there were differences between the population groups. The reader will find it easier to grasp why a split occurred in mainstream Judaism, between the Essenes and possibly other Jewish groups. I will also attempt to provide a basis and greater clarity of how religious thought and belief developed throughout the period following the destruction of the First Temple until the end of the first century of the first millennium.

The Pharisees

The name Pharisees may have been designated to them by the people from whom they were separated, possibly the Temple cult who were under the influence of Hellenism which was an off shoot of the occupying Greeks and their culture. An alternative suggestion for the name is from the Hebrew word *peirat*, meaning 'specify', because they proceeded to specify the correct meaning or interpretation of the law. In Hebrew they were the *peirushim*.

In rabbinical references, the Pharisees are sometimes referred to as the *sages*, because they were the inheritors of their tradition. Although they numbered only about 6,000 during Herodian times, they grew steadily until they eventually came to dominate the religious life of the Jewish people.

According to the Jewish historian Josephus (first century CE), they were said to have had seven subdivisions, ranging across a spectrum from conservatism to liberalism. They were essentially representative of the middle and lower classes and consequently were minimally influenced by the Hellenistic culture of the time.

During the Hasmonaean period, many Pharisees were also priests, usually of the lower ranks. Their views were dominant in the Temple, regarding procedure and protocol during the festivals. You will further on read how this led to an uprising with disastrous consequences.

Most importantly, the Pharisees scrupulously observed the tradition of the 'Oral Law', of which originally there were 613, a series of (Divine) interpretations of the Mosaic Law, in contrast to its rejection by the Sadducees. Although traditionally they are regarded as the 'Fathers of Rabbinical Judaism', this connection is doubted on the grounds that they preferred to be known as *talmidei halachminim* or very wise students who were versed in Jewish law.

There were two important schools of thought or interpretations amongst the Pharisees: one of Hillel, and one of Shammai. Jesus took to task the Shammai, as they were "*far more rigid and unforgiving in their outlook*". Tragically, the distorted image as portrayed of the Pharisees in the 'New Testament' (Christian Bible), significantly contributed to prejudice against the Jewish people at large. This was exploited and virulently criticized in the Gospel of Mathew, Chapter 23, which led to hatred, discrimination, and the murder of Jews throughout the millennia.

I will be covering the next prevailing political and influential group, the Sadducees, but it is relevant at this stage to add an important differentiation, namely the belief in 'life after death' or the immortality of the soul and divine interference.

These were some of the significant beliefs of the Pharisees, as well as belief in divine providence, reward, and punishment after death, and the belief in angels. None of these were part of the Sadducean teaching.

The Pharisees first appear by name in about 150 BCE during the reign of Jonathan the Maccabee. Rabbinical sources record their origins even further back, to the time of the *Men of the* Great *Assembly*, of rabbinic tradition and forerunners of the Sanhedrin, who could have been made up of the *scribes.*

This would mean that the *scribes* in fact were the forerunners to the Pharisees. Most famous was the influential religious leader of the 5th century BCE, Ezra the scribe. He was designated that title due to his knowledge of the laws of Moses. He also taught the Torah to the returnees from Babylon.

After the Babylonian exile, and now finding themselves surrounded by idolatrous enemies, the Scribes and men of the Great Assembly began expounding the Torah (the 'Five Books of Moses') to strengthen the nation's individuality by way of laws and practices unique to Israel. Only a handful (about 50,000) of people returned to their homeland from the formerly great nation that had existed before the destruction of the First Temple.

The term *scribes* (criticized in the Christian bible) was a generic term but essentially, they were interpreters of the bible and experts in the way the Law should be understood and observed. However, there exists another form of identification, which I will delay describing. I first want the reader to have graduated through the essence of the book, which of course relates to the Essenes and the Dead Sea Scrolls. This interesting option and speculation will be found in the section 'Christianity and the Dead Sea Scrolls' towards the end of this book.

Following the Hasmonean victory, the Talmud records: "*the mantle of the Scribes passed onto the increasingly flourishing sect of the Pharisees*". Thereafter came the development and contributions of the great Jewish sages, culminating in *Rabbinical* Judaism throughout the first 200 years after the destruction of the Second Temple.

During the Hellenistic Hasmonean period 138 BCE - 76 CE, the Pharisees became more prominent as an opposition group in control of political affairs. It has since been established that they were partly instrumental in establishing the Oral (rabbinical) Law, later recorded in the work known as *Mishnah*.

Previously the Mishnah was regarded as having been taught by the Tanna'im or Rabbinic sages who flourished 50 BCE - 200 CE which was compiled around 200 CE. Later, around 400 - 600 CE, it became an integral part of the Talmud when it was compiled and redacted.

The Pharisees were largely made up of laypersons who developed the skills to interpret the laws of the Torah. Some took this a step further in their interpretations and stipulations on how the Temple priests should perform their sacred duties. This often led to a clash with the establishment. Most Jews took a more conciliatory approach towards legal issues, whereas the Essenes demonstrated a far greater challenging and expansive approach to Halachah.

The assumption that the Pharisees had represented a kind of mainstream Judaism is outdated. Even though they numbered only around 6,000 and even with their popularity over the last two centuries BCE, the devotion *they* showed to the Jewish religion was not the same as the mainstream Jewish people. Such devotion also did not come from the Sadducees, whom you will read about later. Most of the Jewish people did not belong to any religious party or have an affiliation to the laws as explained by the Pharisees. These included Jews living outside Palestine - known as the Diaspora. The Jewish masses upheld the basic core practices and beliefs, relating to God and the Torah, with Israel being the land of the Jewish people and the Temple in Jerusalem. Their loyalty was demonstrated by the numerous times they revolted against the Romans and Greeks for violating their beliefs. After the destruction of the Second Temple, religious chaos and despair ensued. A small group of rabbis proceeded to reshape the Jewish religion over the ensuing 100 - 150 years. One of the important consequences of the breakdown of the official infrastructure was that it resulted in divisions between the Jewish-Christians and the Jews. This concluded in a parting of the ways and the formation of Christianity.

The precise historical origin of the term rabbis is unclear but has been designated to those regarded as leaders, teachers, or principal spiritual leaders of the Second Temple era.

There were also several comments, usually against the writings of the Pharisees by the Essenes. Their criticism confirms that the Pharisees had already developed rabbinical laws as early as about 200 BCE. This fact will later be better understood when I cover the 'MMT' Dead Sea Scroll.

The Pharisees were divided on the matter of how to respond to the Hellenists. One half wanted to be tolerant if the practice of Judaism was allowed to continue, and the other half said that no government was acceptable. This dispute became one of the central issues eventually leading to two Jewish revolts against Rome.

The first occurred in 94 BCE. At the Temple, during the Feast of *Succoth* (Tabernacles), the self-appointed High Priest Alexander Janneus, a Hellenized Sadducean Jew, showed his contempt for the Pharisees' strict observance when he poured the water offering over his feet instead of over the altar as prescribed by Law. I quote from the *Adler Machzor,* a description of part of the age-old ceremony: "*At daybreak, the procession left the Temple and proceeded in a triumphal march to the pool of Siloam. A golden ewer was filled from its waters and brought back to the Temple. Its contents were poured upon the altar simultaneously with the libation of wine. The libation of water and its attendant ceremonies were opposed by the Sadducees*". (A 'libation' is a liquid offering, usually wine.)

The outraged people in the Temple pelted him with citrons (*etrog* in Hebrew), a citrus fruit that is traditionally used as part of the symbols of Succoth, for the Feast of Tabernacles. This resulted in Alexander Janus giving the order for his troops to attack the worshippers. 6,000 people were killed. It precipitated the outbreak of a six-year war costing 50,000 Jewish lives. At the end of the war Janneus crucified 800 Pharisees in front of their families. He then cut the throats of the wives and children who had been watching.

Later, after the destruction of the Second Temple, Pharisaism will be seen to become the basis for Jewish life and civilization up to the present time.

The Pharisees occupied both the presidency and the vice-presidency of the Jerusalem Sanhedrin and were a relatively small, but learned and pious group within Jewish society. Despite their numbers, they exerted much influence through their expertise in biblical interpretation and biblical law. Amongst their great teachers were Gamaliel the Elder, and Hillel.

Even the Sadducees adopted some of their rulings to have themselves accepted by the masses. The Pharisees had appeal and support from the middle and lower classes, whilst the Sadducees were essentially the upper classes of that time.

Some of the Pharisees formed themselves into closed fellowships into which new members were admitted following a trial period. They were particularly zealous in the observation of the laws of purity and diet (keeping kosher) and certain professions were considered dishonorable, such as tax collecting. They kept themselves apart to preserve their holiness and purity. Despite this, they were popular among the common people. Some belonged to priestly families, but this was the exception rather than the rule. The priestly class as we shall see further on belonged to the Sadducees.

The Pharisees despite these devout and unique observations also stressed the principle of 'love thy neighbor' as being the essence of the Torah. However, many pursued arrogantly a level of strict observance and hair-splitting arguments focusing on ritual and observance, to the neglect of its ethical and moral doctrine.

This was later commented on in the Talmud and referred to as the "*wounds of the Pharisees*" and decried religious types who drew attention to themselves by exaggerated embellishments.

However, and this needs to be stressed, when one is confronted by this level of extremism, one tends to portray all the people in this light. The fact is that the great contributors to the Talmud, the Tannaim, admonished religious hypocrisy and emphasized the importance of moral behavior. The Pharisees were not all cast in the same mold as these extremists.

When the Roman legions were passing through Judea, the nation was filled with a deep and burning faith to preserve their religion and identity. The Pharisees instructed the people in the Law (Torah) and the Prophets, and their teachings led to the purest form of God-fearing piety and the most elevated morality. Therefore, the words that Jesus is said to have delivered in Mathew 23, as covered in the ensuing section, are a tragic *distortion* of the truth.

Later, when I deal with the society during the Second Temple, you will gain further insight into the composition of the population. However just to touch on it, I need to mention the ordinary inhabitants referred to in Hebrew as the *amei ha'aretz, 'the people of the land'*. They were simple and coarse and hated the Sadducees and the scholarly Pharisee classes, who in return also hated their boorishness.

This mutual antagonism was by no means universal, as shown by one of Judaism's greatest sages, the Pharisee called Hillel. His most famous quote recorded in the Talmud was when a man asked him to briefly explain what the Torah is about, said: "*What is hateful to you, do not do to your fellowman. This is the entire Torah. All the rest is commentary - now go and study.*" His essential purpose was to admonish the wicked and to bring God's comfort to the "*meek of the land*".

Negative and Prejudicial Portrayals of the Pharisees

In an article on anti-Semitism published by the 'Philadelphia Church of God', the following quote from historian RS Wistrich is used: "*Nazi anti-Semitism could never have aroused the response it did, had it not been planted in groundwater poisoned by Christian theology...*"

The International Standard Bible Encyclopedia states "*The New Testament evidence shows Jesus in agreement with the beliefs and practices vitally important to the Pharisees. The conflict between Jesus and the Pharisees was essentially the understanding of his mission*".

Dr Young, in his contribution to the encyclopedia writes: "*While Jesus disdained the hypocrisy of some Pharisees, he never attacked the religious and spiritual teachings of Pharisaism*". He then continues in a similar vein by explaining what Mathew 'implied' when criticizing the Pharisees in Chap. 23 below.

Dr Young writes that it was rather a case of the Pharisees not practicing what they preached, and not about *what* they preached!

He continues by writing "*Unfortunately, the image of the Pharisee in modern usage is seldom, if ever, positive. Such a negative characterization of Pharisaism distorts our view of Judaism and the beginnings of Christianity... The theology of Jesus is Jesus, and is built firmly upon the foundations of Pharisaic thought...(!)*"

Mathew 23 Verses 13, 15, 23, 27, and 29 all begin with a shocking diatribe: "*How terrible for you, you teachers of the*

Law and Pharisees! You Hypocrites!" They are also referred to as "*You snakes and children of snakes!*" One needs to understand how these inflammatory statements influenced Christian attitude towards the Jewish people over the past 2,000 years and their subsequent outcome!

In Mathew 23:2-3 Jesus is recorded as having said:

"*The scribes and the Pharisees sit upon the seat of Moses. Whatever they might say, therefore, do and observe; but do not act according to their behavior, for they say and do not perform*"!

The element of hypocrisy was not to tarnish all Pharisees, but a call for the masses of the poor and disaffected at not having their needs attended to. This is the reason why Jesus castigates. The Judaism of Jesus and the Jewish heritage of Jesus recognize and respect the teachings with which he himself was taught. In fact, it is these teachings of morality incorporated in the Christian Bible that led to Christian morality. Where else but from its Jewish roots and the teachings of the Pharisees do the messages of morality and spiritual lessons draw their sources?

Who Controlled the Temple?

It is widely believed that it was unlikely the Pharisees were the dominant influence in the Second Temple period, particularly the era following the Maccabean uprising. This is despite later rabbinic literature endorsing their overwhelming influence. That influence was predominant even before the Hasmonaean dynasty and despite the strong presence of the Sadducees in the Temple. The transmission of the 'Oral Law' (613 identified commandments in the Torah and their interpretations) throughout that period by the Pharisees continued even into the immediate post-Temple destruction era. This ultimately led to the Judaism of the Mishnah and the Talmud. This former early rabbinic Judaism continues to this day.

Now we come to the famous 'yes, but' the Hellenists could still have controlled the Temple even though the Pharisaic belief was the one to be ultimately accepted. Control meant that which was accepted; was to be observed as being the correct halachic (Heb.) or legalistic protocol. Thus, if there were usurpers in the priesthood and because they were in charge, it by no means meant that they were accepted by the masses as having the correct observance in their practice of Judaism.

You will learn when covering the Dead Sea Scrolls further on, that the Pharisaic views dominated the Temple. You will read about the all-important 'MMT' Scroll, wherein it was written that the Essenes broke away because the laws of the Pharisees were not being observed at the Temple.

The Hasmonaean shared a common cause with the Pharisees to cleanse the Temple of excessive Hellenism which they recognized was due to *Sadducean* priests who had become too Hellenized. The Qumran scrolls revealed the Pharisees as being allies of the Hasmonaean during their *early* period. Here because of the MMT, we could have substantiation from the Scrolls themselves proving that the Pharisees controlled Temple ritual.

The Mishnah, which epitomizes Pharisaic or rabbinic maxim, is shown by another example from the *Damascus Scroll*. In the section referred to as the 'Admonition', there are those who are "*builders of the wall*" and those who shift the boundaries of the wall who are seen as sinners.

The concept of putting a fence around the Torah is recorded in the Mishnah as being necessary to protect the Torah by creating additional laws, ensuring that the Torah is not transgressed. The prophet Hosea in chapter 5:10 chastises the leaders for removing the 'boundary' that protects the Torah.

In some of the Essene or Qumranic literature, the Pharisees are referred to as 'Ephraim' and the Sadducees as 'Menashe'. These names originate from the twelve tribes that Israel was divided into and are names of the sons of Joseph. Today these names are incorporated in the blessing a father gives to his son.

The Sadducees

The Sadducees were the aristocratic and essentially the priestly class of the society at the time. Their name is derived from Tzadok, who was the high priest in the Temple of Solomon. The Sadducees are called *Tzadokim* (pl.) in Hebrew.

The Tzadokite family lineage of high priests served at the head of the priesthood throughout First Temple times and was assigned to this task by Ezekiel the prophet. Their lineage was also continued by intermarriage into the high-priestly families hence the name *Cohen,* from the Hebrew for a priest. They were partly influenced by the prevailing Greek culture of Hellenism, but primarily their loyalty was to the religion of Israel, or Palestine as it was later renamed. Their priestly duties continued throughout the First Temple times, except when worship was brought to the Temple by several foreign and local invasions. They also continued their priestly functions in the Second Temple period from 515 BCE until their power was taken from them during the Hasmonean dynasty, in the remaining 150 years before the first millennium. At large they continued to play a key role in supporting the Hasmonean aristocracy and their priestly kings.

When reading about the Sadducees, it is usually in comparison to the Pharisees, rather than who they are.

I too will have to be drawn into this, firstly as I have already covered the Pharisees and am now able to differentiate the two thus with greater meaning. Secondly, it will allow the reader to appreciate these differences and their significances. There will be some repetition about what was previously discussed under the Pharisees.

As mentioned earlier, the Sadducees rejected the Pharisees' interpretations of the Torah's laws, due to their (Sadducean) literal application. Hence the laws of purity including certain aspects of keeping kosher, physical and spiritual laws, were regarded as applying *exclusively* to the Temple and priests, and they refused to extend those laws into the daily lives of the Jews. They believed strongly in the concept of 'free will' and the fact that God did not exercise His influence in the earthly realm. This did not however conflict with their belief that God punishes individuals during their lifetime. In the writings of Josephus, essentially three Jewish 'philosophies' are identified based on their interpretation of the divine hand in fate versus free will.

He writes that:

- "*The Pharisees believe that in some things human beings have free will, while in others they do not.*" They believed in the 'hereafter' and 'immortality of the soul' and uniquely that the righteous are destined to revive and live again. This conceptual belief continues as a belief both within Judaism and Christianity - with a 'conditions apply' clause and some fine print.

- Whereas "*the Essenes deny human freedom and attribute everything to God's sovereignty*" i.e., fate. "*Fate governs all things, and that nothing befalls men but what is according to its determination.*" This showed their belief in predestination.

- On the other hand, the <u>Sadducean</u> belief was the rejection of fate and holding that man had free will: "*all our actions are in our own power so that we are ourselves are the causes of what is good, and receive what is evil from our own folly.*"

- The Sadducean belief that divine punishment was metered out during earthly life and not after death, was seen as the reason for strict literal observation of the law as laid out in the Torah, and not by interpretation.

Whereas the Essenes also believed in 'the immortality of the soul' i.e., the 'afterlife' and its subsequent reward or punishment, as did the Pharisees.

Also, another source of a *major* dispute between the Pharisees and the Sadducees were the differences in the calendar dates for the observation of certain festivals. Later we will read of the consequences of some of the Sadducees having moved away from their priestly duties towards Hellenism, which resulted in the Maccabean Revolt. Yet large numbers of them, in particular the so-called lower clergy, remained loyal to the Torah, and they stood firm by the written Law and resisted any re-interpretation. They were also a major influence in the high court and senate in Judea. They did not regard Jesus as a radical, but rather one whose zealousness fitted the image of the Pharisees. They formed the upper tier of Jewish society, of the highest standing and wealth. Nevertheless, throughout the Talmud, strong arguments appear against the Sadducees, referred to as Tzadokites.

The Sadducees were not seen in a favorable light. They did not believe in resurrection and angels. Therefore, according to Christian belief, the rising up of Jesus three days after his death on the cross, and Mary's visitation by an angel, were in direct contradiction to what they believed, and hence their negative portrayal in the New Testament.

Many scholars think that it was from these remaining Sadducees that a breakaway group eventually became the Dead Sea sect now known as the Essenes. Their grief and anger at seeing their traditional role of the high priesthood being replaced and usurped by a Hasmonean in 152 BCE and disagreement with him on points of Jewish Law, could have led to their formation and retreat to Qumran. There is much speculation as to who this High Priest was at the time.

The Sadducees did however remain in Jerusalem - other more moderate ones playing a key role during the Hasmonean period and being part of the governing council with the Pharisees.

It needs to be mentioned that a (sub) group called the *Boethusians* existed. They too held similar views to the Sadducees and opposed the Pharisees. Certain similarities were present in their writings and those of the Essenes. There is speculation around the meaning of their Hebrew name which is *Beit'ysin* or House of the Essenes.

The end of the Sadducees as a prominent class came when the priests decided to stop the daily sacrifices at the Temple on behalf of the Roman Emperor. This in turn, also contributed to the revolt against Rome in 66 CE and lead to the destruction of the Second Temple. In 70 CE after its destruction, they too disappeared, with the conjecture that some of their traditions influenced a Jewish sect known as the Karaites who became established in the eighth century CE. The fact that nothing was left behind in writing could also have been a contributing factor to their disappearance.

The Hellenists

Hellenism can be briefly described as a reference to the cultural background of mainly the Greeks, and to a lesser extent the Roman influence on a people whose own beliefs and culture were different. Hellenization is the inculcation of that culture into the lives of a people. It involved Greek ideas and practices promoted by the Greek civilization, with the objective of assimilation of the known world into a single nation sharing its culture. It thus also resulted in the assimilation of all who came under its influence. For example, those Jews who became Hellenists began to lose their Jewish heritage as they adopted the Hellenistic culture and beliefs. This threatened and weakened the Jewish people. Throughout the ages, assimilation has been regarded as the *prime threat* to the continuation of Judaism. To this day 'intermarriage' is strongly fought against by the Rabbinate and 'conscientious' Judaism.

To place the adoption of Hellenism in a modern-day context; an analogy can be made by seeing the influence of American culture, from the sixties until at least the nineties, on some Asian and some Middle Eastern countries - to the dismay of many religious state cultures.

Today we can expand that example by the inclusion of hedonism, as being the culture of some. This no doubt plays a role in the precipitation of the rise of Islamic fundamentalism and in the extreme right-wing seen in Judaism today.

Nevertheless, some of this Greek philosophy and Greek wisdom was adopted and or adapted into Jewish teachings, particularly from the masters, Aristotle and Homer, into the teachings of the Talmud.

The Hellenistic influence was however much more of cultural assimilation than religion. Even the Essenes were heavily influenced: "*Among the sect's fundamental beliefs and practices - determinism (incorporating the influence of background on behavior), dualism (the principle of good and evil), the solar calendar, communal property, angelology (belief in angels), celibacy, the desire to create a utopia and many of the organizational patterns*" (Lee Levine). The association of Essenism with these concepts, which are *contrary* to Judaism, will become clear to you as you progress through this book. One percent of the Scrolls found were written in Greek.

Under the command of Alexander the Great, the Greeks conquered the Persian Empire in 312 BCE and occupied Israel/Judea as well. It is recorded in the Talmud that when Alexander arrived in Jerusalem, he met with Shimon HaTzadik, (The Righteous), the last of the men of the Great Assembly. To the amazement of everyone, Alexander bowed down before him. The explanation given is that before every battle (which he never lost) he dreamed of a strange man and regarded the dream as an omen of victory. Shimon Ha Tzadik was that man in the dream. The outcome was that he did not destroy the Temple as was the expected course of the conquest, and he allowed Israel to be peacefully absorbed into the Greek Empire. As a tribute to him, the rabbis decreed that the first-born sons of that generation be named Alexander. To this day Alexander remains a popular Jewish name, Sender being the shortened form derivative.

At first, the Greek authorities did not interfere with the Jewish religion, and the Jews flourished for 165 subsequent years. It was over this period that the Hellenistic influence took hold of part of the Jewish population. Hellenism placed much value on education and intellectual pursuits and in particular the body beautiful, with all the aspects leading to the development of the perfect human form.

Archaeological evidence of this is found in the design of synagogues, both in Palestine and in the Diaspora. Furthermore, and what is regarded as being contrary to Judaism, Hellenistic pictorial symbols (or icons) e.g., mosaics were found on the floors and walls of these synagogues and in cemeteries, tombs, and ossuaries. The Greeks regarded the unique Jewish rite of circumcision with horror. Operations were developed to reverse this 'disfigurement' by those Jews wanting to be fully-fledged participants of this culture.

The Sadducees developed an affinity for Hellenism. They were already in part estranged from their rivals the Pharisees because of their 'free interpretation' of the Torah, and by not accepting the all-important Oral Law which guided the Pharisees. One of their mistakes was to believe that their own perceived enlightenment could allow them to absorb what they chose to be as the best of the Hellenistic culture without jeopardy to Judaism *per se*. Today one can compare Jews becoming 'Jews for Jesus' for similar reasons.

This was the beginning of the end. The Sadducees as priests in the Temple, introduced Greek tainted sacrifices into their rituals - so breaking a cardinal Jewish law - as decreed in the Torah given by God to Moses and the people of Israel. The honeymoon came to an end in 169 BCE when Antiochus Epiphanies IV the Seleucid (the Greek dynasty ruling Syria), attempted to destroy Judaism, removing the High Priest, and replacing him with his own Hellenized puppet, so leading to a total corruption of the Temple. During this period as described in the Book of Maccabees, the persecution of the Jews took place, which lead to the Maccabean uprising.

The Samaritans

We have read about the two tiers of society i.e., the Pharisees and the Sadducees. Now I come to a third, the largest, known as *'Am ha'aretz'* or *'the common people'* when translated literally from the Hebrew. The Bible in the Book of Kings II refers to them as 'the people of Israel'. 'Plebs' would be today's derogatory slang describing such people. The *'Am'* term in fact describes a class similar to the peasant class of medieval times. 'Boor' is another description that has been linked to them as individuals. Many scholars regard them as the descendants of Jews who remained in Judea after the destruction of the First Temple when the people went into exile in Babylon. Much of the remaining nation went into spiritual, religious, and cultural decline. This was aggravated by intermarriage and thus dilution of the Jewish people. Some historians have identified these people as the Samaritans. I must add though, that not all scholars agree about their origin or history.

The theory based on the *'Chronicles of the Samaritans'* themselves, states that they are direct descendants from the tribes of Ephraim and Menashe.

They had a High Priesthood directly from Aaron who was the first High Priest appointed by God, and lived in Samaria, central Israel. Later the Jewish High Priest, Eli, either fled or went to Samaria; attracting northern Israelites to his newly established 'headquarters' in Shiloh, which was previously based in Shechem. This is recorded as being a split of the Samaritans.

Some of them went into exile in Samaria in the north. They had their own Temple on Mt. Gerizim, which was destroyed in the second century BCE by John Hyrcanus. Mt. Gerizim was their Jerusalem. Their High Priest was expelled and thereafter they suffered a life of persecution. They had their own version or variation of the Torah. Later their persecution increased, and they were forbidden to read their Torah, their synagogues were burnt, and many were crucified.

All this took place under the rule of the Romans 180 BCE - 92 BCE. The Samaritans also fared badly during the Christianization of Palestine. They are still a people and a practicing religion to this day in Israel. Their annual pilgrimage on their Passover still takes place to Mt. Gerizim where they sacrifice the lamb in the traditional manner. They are not recognized as Jews.

A variation to the preceding theory is as follows: They were thought to have been the Israelites of a district of Samaria who had intermarried with Cuthiteans or Cuthites and other tribes brought into the conquered territory. They were rough, uncouth, and alienated from Judaism. They despised both the elitist Sadducean class and most of the Pharisees, typifying the boor's hatred for the scholar.

It has thus become clearer to me in understanding why the term the 'Good' Samaritan was given to that individual who helped Jesus. They were the poor and destitute, referred to as the 'Ebyi'onim' in the Scrolls, who were unlearned and illiterate - and the *meek*, humbled in spirit and without hope of salvation. They saw themselves depicted in the psalms.

Jesus, who could well have been a Pharisee, reached out to these Amei-ha'aretz (pl.), presenting himself as a healer to the broken in spirit and a teacher to the simple and humble. He introduced a doctrine suited to the needs of all who sought personal salvation.

After the return of the Jews from Babylonian exile, the Samaritans were excluded from participating in Temple worship. They separated themselves and built their own Temple on Mount Gerizim. Today the Samaritans live in Shechem, in Israel which they regard as *their* holy city, and still look upon Mount Gerizim as the 'sacred' Mountain. They have their own version of the Torah, with numerous differences to the Masoretic biblical text.

The Samaritan Pentateuch

Used today, the Samaritan 'Torah' contains only the five books of Moses. They reject the Prophets and Writings, which make up the balance of the Hebrew Bible. The Oral Law is also rejected by them.

Written in Hebrew, it essentially follows the original. However, there are about 6,000 differences between the so-called Masoretic (original) texts, with many having only minor spelling differences or 'scribal' errors. Of the 6,000 'differences', 2000 of them are the same as in the *Septuagint*, which I will cover in detail further on in this book.

Other differences pertain to the religious ideology of the Samaritans, for example, added to the Ten Commandments a commandment to build an altar on Mount Gerizim. It would be more accurate to be regarded as *one* of the versions instead of a variation of the original Torah. It needs to be added that recent opinion no longer looks upon these textual differences as being peculiar to the Samaritan version, but in all probability that it was the text of the day. By this, I imply that it is considered a Torah by some leading academics and was widely used and regarded as authentic by many, <u>even outside</u> the so-called Samaritans. More on the importance on the various textual differences of the Tanach (per se) will be dealt with in this book.

Chapter 4: The First Discovery of the Scrolls

Insight

"The Scrolls are unquestionably Israel's *greatest* cultural treasure."

Shuka Dorfman, Director of The Israel Antiquities Authority.

The Dead Sea region where the Scrolls were discovered is a unique part of the world. It is due to these geographical and climatic features that the Scrolls were so wonderfully preserved for over 2,200 years!

The Dead Sea, having ten times the salinity of sea water, receives its main source from the River Jordan, draining out of the Sea of Galilee, also known as Lake Tiberius in the north. It is the lowest region on earth, being about 400 meters *below* sea level. We then add the climatic conditions, the average temperature range from about 24 to 38 degrees Centigrade, with an extremely low humidity level - an important factor in accounting for the minimal degradation of the Scrolls. Rainfall in this Judean desert area is about 1 - 2 mm per annum. It is virtually uninhabitable, has no significant wind or corrosive breezes and is the closest on earth to a lunar landscape. On the East Side are desert mountain ranges folding out into Jordan, and on the West are smaller hills and plateaus undulating towards Jerusalem about 40 kms as the crow flies. The Romans called the sea the Asphalt Lake and its Hebrew translation is the 'Salt Sea'.

The Scrolls were found in a total of eleven caves on the sea-facing side of the cliff, about two kilometers west of the Dead Sea. The discoveries of scroll fragments and other Jewish artifacts took place over approximately a ten-year period and concluded with Cave 11, discovered in 1955.

Since then, no other relevant fragments have been found. Not all the caves along this escarpment were natural, only Caves 1, 2, 3, 6, and 11 - the rest were man-made, i.e., cut into the clay-limestone escarpment.

Situated on this plateau or escarpment about 60 meters above the Dead Sea, are the ruins of Qumran, or as it called, Khirbet (Arabic for ruin) Qumran. These were once the place of habitation of the Essenes, who were responsible for writing and accumulating many of the Dead Sea Scrolls. Two ancient roads met at Qumran, one from Jerusalem and another from Jericho. These ruins were known to nineteenth and early twentieth-century explorers and were regarded as a fortress used for defense during the Roman occupation. During their time, they were twice destroyed or damaged by earthquakes and fire and finally destroyed in 68 CE by the Romans in their rampage during the uprising.

In Hebrew, the Scrolls are referred to as the 'Hidden Scrolls' (*Hamegilot hagenuzot)* whereas other scholars now use the terms 'Qumran Scrolls' or the 'Library of Qumran.' 'Dead Sea Scrolls' is more accurate as other scrolls have been found in the region of the Dead Sea such as those at Masada and the 'Bar Kochba' documents. The Scrolls can be described as a collection of selected works from a specific region and are regarded as a religious library.

The discovery of the Scrolls is always a wonderful introduction to the subject. Some books devote an almost disproportionate amount of space to this, filled with detail encompassing both speculation and the authors' own investigations. Essentially there is now an established background, which I will briefly cover.

It took place in late 1946 or the beginning of 1947. The region was then part of the Jordanian kingdom. Following the 'Six-Day War' in June 1967, that area again became part of Israel. In the Judean desert, a Bedouin goatherd said to be called Muhammad Ahmed el Hamed (the Wolf), made the first discovery whilst looking for a lost goat. He tossed a stone into a cave hoping to scare out the goat, and instead he heard breaking pottery. His interest aroused, he and a friend went into the cave and found ten large jars, nine of which were empty, and one which contained three scrolls. It has been established that the design of these jars was unique to Qumran. Two of these scrolls were wrapped in linen.

For the first time in two thousand years, they saw the light of day.

These were amongst the best-preserved scrolls, having been stored in jars and protected by linen wrappings. They were also some of the most important scrolls found. It is quite remarkable that in the very first cave since designated the code 1Q, that such a quality find occurred. The Bedouin then later discovered four additional scrolls in Cave 1.

The first three scrolls found in the tenth jar were:

- The Isaiah Scroll.

- The Habakkuk Commentary or Pesher Habakkuk.

- A partial second copy of an Isaiah scroll.

The four additional scrolls were:

- The 'Manual of Discipline' also known as 'The Community Rule' or the 'Rule of the Congregation.' It also had an additional section designated the name 'Messianic Rule' which was separate from the main scroll by way of the theme of its content, although it was copied on the same scroll.

- Collection of Psalms and Hymns known as Hodayot (for Thanks giving).

- The 'War Scroll'.

- The 'Genesis Apocryphon' or 'Genesis Narratives'.

If these were the only discoveries, the world could have considered them a wonderful and complete treasure on their own, as so much of what is known about the Essenes and the period, appear in these seven scrolls. Yet we were to be given an additional collection of works in various lengths, which almost overshadowed these in their revelations.

The Scrolls form a collection of material that gave the world information about the many other Jewish groups that existed during the Second Temple period and were not only about the Essenes, around whom much of this book focuses.

In fact, some of the Scrolls are pre-sectarian and thus represent the heritage the Dead Sea sectarians brought with them when they established the group.

This period is recognized as a critical moment in Jewish history. After the destruction of the Second Temple, the observance of the Judaism we practice today had become established and became known as Rabbinic Judaism.

Certain scrolls have helped provide a clearer picture of the theologies of the Pharisees and the Sadducees. This is based on the commentaries from the Essenes in their works, together with a blending of their beliefs into various attitudes and judgments. Thus, we read of the development of *Halachah* (Religious Law) by its incorporation into related Essene scrolls, whether modified based on their inspired interpretation, or representing the generally accepted Halachah by most of the Jewish populous. This was further accentuated by how these laws were recorded. They represented the attitude towards the authority of the Torah by both the Pharisees and Sadducees and the Essenes themselves.

Those Dead Sea Scrolls attributed to the Essenes incorporated their beliefs and thus their legal texts reflected *their* interpretation of the Torah. Scholars have been provided with an opportunity to uncover missing links between Torah and Talmud by way of noting the development and established interpretation not previously seen in recorded works. Until their discovery, there was virtually no documented evidence between the Maccabean Dynasty and the period when the Oral Law was eventually beginning to be committed to writing in about 200 CE.

The rabbinical culmination in the written redaction of the Oral law was what later became part of the Talmud, circa 400 CE. Its study and the discourse of these laws are an integral part of Judaism and its practice today and over the past 1,600 years.

In fact, it has been noted that the Essenes developed their own form of legal argument, some of which later developed in parallel to, and were incorporated into the Talmud. Qumran material showed that there was an alternative system of Jewish Law. There were thus competing trends between Priestly/Sadducean and Pharisaic/proto-Rabbinic halachic traditions.

We now come to the beginning of the intrigue that followed over the next forty years.

The first part was to be the permanent possession of these treasures, which incidentally are described as the "*Greatest archaeological discovery of the century (20th) and rivaling Tutankhamen's Tomb*". A series of fascinating events unrolled until the first scrolls came into archaeologists' hands. There are certain differences in their recording, so I will rather present the generally accepted sequence of events.

The Bedouins, having discovered the two jars, took them and the first three discovered scrolls to Bethlehem to be sold. They eventually were sent to a dealer in antiquities called Kando. He bought them for five Palestine pounds (then $20). Kando, a Syrian Orthodox Christian then took them to the archbishop of his church Mar Samuel, who recognized them as indeed being genuine and valuable. Mar Samuel offered to buy these but wanted any others that the Bedouin had found. Eventually, he purchased four of the seven for $250.

They were:

1.   The (Great) Isaiah Scroll
2.   The Habakkuk Commentary
3.   The Genesis Apocryphon
4.   The Community Rule

At this stage, I need to mention that an authoritative sequence of events leading to the sale and acquisition of particular scrolls to the various intermediaries has proven frustrating. This is due to at least half a dozen authors on the subject, each having their own version. In some cases, personal investigations took place, to the dispute of others. Nevertheless, I will continue with what I regard as accurate a description as possible, leading to the eventual official possession of the first set purchased.

It was through the connections and efforts of the Syrian Orthodox Archbishop Mar Samuel, that these first purchases came about. At the suggestion of Anton Kiraz, a scholar at the famous *Ecole Biblique* in Jerusalem, Samuel agreed to show them to the professor of archaeology at the Hebrew University of Jerusalem, Eliezer Sukenik.

Sukenik was the father of Israel's most famous archaeologist, Yigal Yadin, who performed the first study on the Scrolls and later excavated Masada and documented his findings. He was Chief of the General Staff of the Israeli Army (*Haganah*) during the War of Liberation or Independence, 1947 - 1948.

The meeting was set up with Kiraz to make the introductions with Sukenik, as the archbishop did not want to become politically involved, especially with the idea of selling the Scrolls directly to Israel. This would have greatly upset Jordan. It is relevant to know the political and historical background of the times. Briefly, they are as follows:

Modern Zionist History can be regarded as having started at the beginning of the Twentieth Century as a movement to establish a homeland for the Jewish people. This was through the efforts of Theodore Herzl and began with the first Zionist congress in August 1897 in Basle Switzerland to advocate a large-scale migration of Jewish settlement in Palestine.

Both Arabs and Jews had always lived in the land in varying numbers according to political domination. Until 1917 Palestine was part of the Ottoman (Turkish) Empire, which was followed by the British forces' conquest of the Turks towards the end of the First World War. Palestine was then declared by the League of Nations a British mandate.

From about 1905, Jewish immigrants started to arrive, bought land, and began to develop the country. This ultimately led to rival conflict with the Arab inhabitants. Arab workers now came *en masse* to seek work opportunities, since the Jewish immigrants had built up the land and the economy had improved. Today, these migrant workers refer to themselves as the dispossessed 'Palestinians'.

The situation markedly deteriorated when the League of Nations declared Palestine a British mandate in 1918 after WW1, and declined further because of British bias towards the Arabs - which is still practiced today.

During the Second World War, the greatest tragedy was inflicted upon the Jewish people, known as the Holocaust or *Shoah.* This resulted in the murder of 6 million Jews and in a massive displacement of the remainder of European Jewry.

Following this, a new dawn arose. The United Nations on November 29, 1947, voted for a Partition of Palestine between Jews and Arabs. The Arabs rejected the Partition - and so began the War of Independence (or Liberation) which was eventually won by the Israeli forces.

The State of Israel was declared on 15 May 1948. Because of this war, Jerusalem became a divided city. The eastern section came under Arab control, which included the Western Wall and the 'Dome of the Rock' mosque.

It is with this thumbnail sketch that the reader can appreciate the tension between Jordan and the Jewish people of Palestine at the time. The Scrolls were discovered in Jordan. They were now being offered to Sukenik, who met with a Jordanian antique dealer referred to as 'X' on November 23, 1947. The two were separated by a barbed-wire barricade. A trusted Armenian friend of Sukenik, Faidi Salahi, also an antique dealer, acted as an intermediary and showed him a few scroll fragments.

Sukenik immediately recognized their importance and authenticity and offered to buy the document. It was arranged that they meet in the Jordanian side of Jerusalem.

This was to be a most dangerous yet significant mission on the part of Sukenik - significant in that the date set for the collection was on the same day that the United Nations was to vote on the partition of Palestine thereby recognizing an independent Jewish State to be called Israel. It was also a highly dangerous decision, in that if he was caught by the Arabs, certain death would follow. Both his and his sons Yigal Yadin were consulted. Despite them being against the undertaking, he went ahead.

Again, there are some discrepancies between the exact sequence of events and the acquisition of the first set of scrolls. I have used sources of known reputation for the following set of events:

On the 29th of November 1947, Sukenik and his Armenian friend returned by bus to Bethlehem. They were shown two jars, inside which were two wrapped scrolls. The dealer brought them out, and with trembling hands, Sukenik unrolled the first scroll - which we now know as the 'Thanksgiving Scroll' or 'Hodayot'.

He offered to buy all three scrolls brought in for the occasion. The two others were the 'War Scroll', and a second, poorer copy of the Isaiah Scroll. The first copy of the Great Isaiah Scroll was still with Mar Samuel.

It appears that Sukenik was allowed to take back to Jerusalem two of the scrolls for further inspection, after which he would then purchase them. He took a bus back to Jerusalem, this time with a treasure in his hands. On the very same day, came the announcement that the United Nations had voted by a majority for the partition of Palestine. This was a declaration that the Jewish people had again been granted their own homeland for the first time in almost two thousand years. 'Partition' meant that Palestine was geographically divided up between the Arabs and the Jewish people. During the 'Six-

Day War' in 1967, Israel re-occupied and reclaimed its historical land, including the Eastern half of Jerusalem, which had become a divided city. I will repeat some of these details a little further on with relevance to the Scrolls.

It then followed that apparently a few days after returning with the two scrolls, Sukenik telephoned the Armenian to say that he would buy all three scrolls. A meeting was arranged, and the agreed sum of money was handed over. Again, there are variations in the details on how the third scroll was given to Sukenik. The probability is that it took place also following a monetary exchange.

This was a birthday gift to the Nation and the Jewish People throughout the world! The symbolism and the timing of the return of these scrolls to Jewish hands that were hidden before the destruction of the Second Temple cannot be overlooked!

This I regard as the *first* of three miracles.

The next day, 30 November, seven neighboring Arab States declared war and set out to destroy the newly formed Jewish State. Almost six months later, on 15 May 1948, after having defeated the Arab armies, the State of Israel was finally liberated. The rest of the Scrolls and others still to be discovered, were in Jordan, the enemy on her border!

Six years later Yigal Yadin was to obtain the remaining four original scrolls, discovered in Cave 1. How that came about is also a saga on its own. Yadin, incidentally, was his code name as Chief of Operations of the Jewish Defense Force and which he later adopted.

Once again, here is a brief description of events leading up to the State of Israel possessing the balance of the seven original scrolls that were first discovered:

Mar Samuel still had in his possession:

1. The 'Great Isaiah Scroll'
2. The 'Manual of Discipline'

3. The 'Habakkuk Commentary'

4. The 'Genesis Apocryphon'

He tried several times to sell them to raise funds for the Church, eventually taking them with him to the USA where he had permanently settled.

On 1st of June 1954, not wanting to draw the attention of Jordan, he placed a modest advertisement in the *Wall Street Journal*:

> **"The Four**
>
> **Dead Sea Scrolls"**
>
> **Biblical Manuscripts dating back to at least 200 BC are for sale. This would be an ideal gift to an educational or religious institution by an individual or group.**
>
> **Box F 206, The Wall Street Journal**

Again, destiny would have it that at the time of this advert, Yigal Yadin was in New York on a lecture tour of the Dead Sea Scrolls. An Israeli journalist accompanying Yadin spotted the advert and alerted him to it. Of course, Yadin knew exactly which scrolls were being referred to, and began to carefully plan the steps to acquire them.

This was critical, as (a) Israel was in conflict with Jordan, (b) he did not want the Mar Samuel to be aware of the purchaser's identity, and (c) because of the known anti-Semitic sentiments of the Greek Orthodox archbishop of New York. Any one of these could easily have sabotaged or complicated the outcome.

Yadin arranged that an expert Dr Harry Orlinsky, professor at the Hebrew Union College in Cincinnati, would act as the go-between on behalf of a 'client' under the assumed name of Mr. Green.

Identification took place in the vault of a branch of Chemical Bank at the famous Waldorf-Astoria Hotel. After identifying them as genuine, he phoned an unlisted number and used the code word *'Le'chaim'* to confirm. Negotiations then followed, and on the day of purchase, Yadin telegraphed Teddy Kollek, who was then Director-General in the prime minister's office, to obtain permission and funds to purchase. Teddy Kollek, who was later to become the famous mayor of Jerusalem, agreed that $250,000 was to be sent to purchase the scrolls - which would then become a national treasure. It is difficult to fully appreciate the enormity of the amount, even though the price was to be considered a 'bargain' for these were critical times in the history of the newly formed state - immigrants were living in *ma'abarot* - temporary settlements or shacks and tents and in were in dire poverty. Extrapolated to some sort of value, it would surely have amounted to hundreds of millions of dollars today! The Jordan government wanted to sue, but couldn't do so, as it would have meant recognition of the State of Israel.

Prof. Sukenik, who died in 1953, could never have imagined that the balance of the scrolls were to be reclaimed by his son a year later! This was the second miracle.

A major part of the cost was contributed by the New York industrialist and benefactor, Samuel Gotzman. After his death, his children established the 'Shrine of the Book' in Jerusalem, the famous dome-shaped structure - shaped like the lid of the pottery jar in which the scrolls were found. Today this museum is open to the public, who can view 13 original scroll fragments or manuscript parts permanently displayed. The central display in the museum is a *copy* of the Great Isaiah Scroll, magnificently encased in a round glass cabinet resembling a giant one-half of a scroll with a handle grip at its top, passing through its center. It was the longest scroll found.

I had the opportunity of seeing the original scroll on display in 1967. Of course, it then lacked the 'wow factor' for me at the time! It was later seen to be deteriorating despite the special conditions in which it was displayed and replaced by a copy.

The consequence of this purchase led to an even more feverish search by the Bedouins, resulting in further discoveries during the ensuing four years. Waiting for Yadin was another treasured scroll, later to be obtained following a middleman culminating in purchasing the scroll from an antique dealer in Bethlehem. This was to be the *Temple Scroll* considered by many as the largest and most important Dead Sea Scroll. But before discussing how this came about, more background is needed as to the other discoveries and behind-the-scenes activity to result in eventual possession of the entire known collection by the State of Israel.

Later additional scrolls were found at various sites within the Dead Sea region, including Masada and the Bar Kochba caves in the Judean Desert. In all, there were about 25 scrolls found outside of Qumran which were identical to or very similar to the texts found at Qumran.

Scandal, Deception, and Intrigue

In 1991 one of the most sensational and popular Dead Sea Scroll books was published and became a best seller. In fact, it was through this book that I became enthralled by the subject of the Dead Sea Scrolls. This was 'The Dead Sea Scrolls Deception' by Michael Baiggent and Richard Lee.

It had a red 'slash' across the cover and imprinted in white were the intriguing words "The Sensational Story behind the Religious Scandal of the Century". The gist of the book related to the implication of the Vatican withholding scrolls that were threatening to Christianity and could possibly have toppled Christian belief. For me it was my first introduction to the Scrolls.

With hindsight, it is exactly due to a book of this nature why I have written this book, particularly in an 'open to options' format. If you are not acquainted with the 'other side of the coin', people can take advantage of you, or put you into a corner and thus be unable to defend yourself knowledgeably. The book covers the discovery of the Scrolls and the background to the scholarly cartel's interpretation, which according to the authors, was the reason for withholding publication for decades and the Scrolls themselves being jealously guarded and being exclusively confined to them.

As the Professor of Biblical Studies, University of Sheffield, Philip Davies, so aptly stated in a BBC 2 Horizon TV documentary:

"Imagine, Protestant Christian scholars, translating these commentaries, and out of these commentaries emerges a story - a story of a Leader, whose given name of 'Teacher of Righteousness', he is persecuted by a 'Wicked Priest', he is opposed by a 'Liar', his followers are telling of his life out of biblical texts where it is prophesied; the things that happened to him, persecution, exile, possibly death. The death of his opponents is also foreseen. Now all of this takes place against the background of an oppressive foreign ruler. The writers of these commentaries were the followers of this now dead 'Teacher of Righteousness'....and for them, faithfulness to that Teacher was the very essence of their being. Now, imagine, in the 1950s Protestant scholars, are thinking to themselves..." Have we read something like this before?"

The Vatican, having been kept up to date, was believed at the time to be the instigator in withholding the release of these potentially explosive discoveries. As it turned out there were other reasons for the 'scandalous delay.' This theory has since 'been thrown out of court' by academics. Today many research institutions have a concordance of the words of all the Qumran manuscripts, and it has been open season for scholarly research for over ten plus years. Nevertheless, a seed has been planted!

Then came the books 'Jesus the Man' and 'Jesus and the Riddle of the Dead Sea Scrolls' by the Australian Scrolls researcher and lecturer in biblical studies, Barbara Thiering, who gave a new interpretation.

She presented her view that early Christianity had developed out of the Essene community, identified the *Teacher of Righteousness,* a prophet-like leader, as being John the Baptist, and the *Wicked Priest*/Man of the Lie, a break-away rival, as being Jesus. Her usage of the pesher (a form of interpretation) in the Scrolls was for code names and descriptions that could be applied to the Christian Bible.

This was based on her interpretation that the Gospels could be read on two levels.

The first level conveyed the literal understanding. The second level, based on the pesher technique gained from her scrolls background, conveyed their 'true' meaning. This has also been attributed to the Essene technique in their application of pesher. John the Baptist is identified as the 'Teacher of Righteousness' and Jesus as the 'Wicked Priest', also known as the 'Man of the Lie'. In particular, she provided (logical) examples to explain the miracles performed by Jesus. She disputed some of the important dates which had been attributed to the age of certain scrolls.

'The Dead Sea Scrolls Uncovered' by Prof. Robert Eisenman and Michael Wise, inter-alia of co-authoring 'Dead Sea Scrolls - A New Translation' is the third popular book I wish to refer to. Published in 1992, it continues to this day to be a best seller. Wise, an evangelical scholar, and authority on translations and the Aramaic language, is said to have later 'apologized' for his involvement. Eisenman, whom some scholars regard as a 'maverick' gave the world a pre-emptive publication on fifty key documents, which had been withheld from hungry scholars for over thirty-five years.

This is speculated to have been the result of photographic copies of the Scrolls being secretly delivered to his house from the Huntington Library. Its publication caused a sensation in the academic world.

This is a story on its own. However, to add to the controversy, he too disregarded the then-current dating as being accurate. Based on his dating and interpretation he designated the Teacher of Righteousness as being James, the brother of Jesus. If this were correct, then the Scrolls would have taken on a significantly different meaning. Although he is highly regarded, this theory too has been thrown out of court by most scholars.

If you are prepared to read books on the DSS, then I recommend that you also read these three books - in particular, the last mentioned, from which much is to be gained.

Chapter 5: How it all began

The Cairo Genizah

> ### Insight
>
> "Surprisingly, there were many known references to the Essenes, but only following the scroll discoveries were the evaluations of Essenes placed under the microscope."

The *first* Dead Sea Scroll *text* discovered was 50 years earlier in Cairo in 1896 and not in the Dead Sea region. That year, Solomon Schechter, a Cambridge University scholar and Reader in Talmud and Rabbinical literature, set sail for Egypt. This was under the sponsorship of two rather eccentric, wealthy Scottish ladies Margaret Gibson and Agnes Smith, who were dedicated to biblical scholarship. They wanted to obtain old manuscripts for his university His destination was the thousand-year-old Ben Ezra synagogue, in Fostat (or Fustat), a suburb of old Cairo. Although it was a Rabbinic synagogue it was given access to Karaite 'Jews' who stored their works there, used its burial ground, and even intermarried into the rabbinic community.

These Karaites appeared to have had a relationship and similarity in some of their beliefs to a sect of Jews known as the Essenes, whose way of life, beliefs, and literature will form the basis of this book. The Karaites in turn are believed to have been a revival of the Sadducees who disappeared after the destruction of the Temple in 70 CE and were again established as a sect in Baghdad around 765 CE by Anan Ben David. They followed similar beliefs to the Sadducees, acting on the literal instruction in the Torah, and did not follow the Oral Law as did the Pharisees and rabbinic Judaism. They are not accepted as Jews by Orthodox Judaism. Today there are about 17,000 Karaite Jews in the Middle East and in the USA.

This synagogue, as was common to many, had what is called a *genizah,* a storage area where old or damaged holy books are temporally stored before being buried - it is considered highly disrespectful to throw them away.

The term genizah, is from the Hebrew *ganaz*, hide. In fact, the Hebrew term for the Dead Sea Scrolls is *Hamegilot hagenuzot,* the 'Hidden' or 'Concealed Scrolls', a more correct name, as yes, the Scrolls were found in the Dead Sea region, but did not all originate from there, as we shall learn. Some scholars have proposed that the caves themselves were used as a genizah.

With a letter of introduction from the Chief Rabbi of Britain to the Chief Rabbi of Cairo, Schechter obtained permission, and with some financial inducement, worked at gathering documents from this genizah over a two-month period of stay. He worked in a horrific environment - with dust from many centuries and had to take breaks for days at a time to recover from this terrible ordeal.

Eventually, he managed to gather up thirty large bags, almost all of the contents of the genizah. He eventually became threatened with ill health and had to leave.

This is now a famous document collection of over 140,000 pieces or fragments, detailing Jewish life in medieval times. They currently remain in storage at the Stefan Rief, Taylor-Schechter Research Unit at Cambridge University UK.

By the year 2002, only one thousand manuscripts had been collated and recognized. Of course, they were mostly incomplete. Out of this enormous treasure trove, two of these were the texts that are referred to as 'A' and 'B', which have relevance to this book. They were called 'Fragments of a Tzadokite Work', on account of the frequent mention of the 'sons of Tzadok.'

These texts/documents were from the tenth and twelfth centuries CE respectively. The first and more complete work was written in the tenth century and the second, two hundred years later. Both the works were written in a biblical style and neither reflected the development of Hebrew following the destruction of the Temple in 70 CE. In other words, they were written in a similar style to the Scrolls.

Schechter was the first person at that time to identify that these 'Tzadokite' works belonged to a group of Jews who had broken away from the mainstream Jewish people and appeared to have been led by a priestly lineage! Later, after the discovery of the Dead Sea Scrolls, they became known as the 'Cairo Damascus Documents' or 'CD'. More about this further on when I will be covering the Damascus Document scrolls found at Qumran.

Fifty years later Protestant scholars, who at the time had exclusive access to the then discovered Dead Sea Scrolls, came across at least ten copies in Caves 4 and 5, of what was to become known as the 'The Damascus Document', dated 100 BCE. These were one of the most important works of the Essenes. They were the same or similar to those previously discovered by Schechter who had correctly recognized them as belonging to a sect who were later identified as the Essenes.

I should mention that prior to his departure to Cairo, Schechter was asked to identify the book of Ben Sirach (a Jewish sage) that was written in Hebrew and originated from the second century BCE. Previously only Greek copies existed. It is also known as The Wisdom of Jesus (Yehoshua) Ben Sira or Ecclesiasticus a 'Wisdom Text (not to be confused with Ecclesiastes - Kohelet). It is now part of the Catholic bible and is referred to as Sirach and classified as a work of the Apocrypha. This form of Hebrew work will be covered in the book. His sponsors, Gibson and Smith had brought this back from Cairo on an earlier trip. It was the first Hebrew version seen in a thousand years and dates to around 190 BCE. A fragment discovered at the excavations of Masada by Yigal Yadin from 1963 to 1965, was the next time a piece of the same work was found.

And to add some comparative background:

Prior to the discovery of the Dead Sea biblical scrolls, the oldest (incomplete) bible copy in existence was the 'Cairo Codex' of the Prophets, correctly known as the Aleppo Codex dated 895 CE.

Thereafter the oldest known copies of the Hebrew bible were dated to around the end of the first millennium....... a thousand years ago. The first printed bible, written in Latin, was in 1448 by Gutenberg who was one of the first principal inventors of the printing press. The earliest Hebrew-type printing took place in 1483, by the Soncino family, who had fled from Speyer, Germany to Italy. Interestingly, the Soncino Press is still in existence to this day, based in London, Jerusalem, and New York.

Who Else Knew?

Josephus

The existence and background of the Essenes have been known for almost two thousand years. As mentioned earlier, Solomon Schechter was the first person to correctly identify texts derived from their writings. Knowledge about them and the era in which they lived has been made available by well-known historians. Scholars of worldwide repute have referred to these historians when writing about the Dead Sea Scrolls. I shall therefore briefly go into their backgrounds and in the course of this book, will also be quoting them.

The most remarkable historian was Josephus. Some of his work is regarded as hearsay, that is, he recorded events as they were related to him, together with his own experiences and observations. As the reader will appreciate from his personal history there were at times embellishments in the way he portrayed certain events to make his Jewish approach and origins more palatable to his benefactors, the Romans. He has also been described as a Jewish turncoat!

Controversy aside, he is still enormously admired, largely accepted, and much quoted by the world's greatest scholars. Because Josephus was writing for a Greek educated audience, he described the various Jewish parties as "philosophies" focusing on philosophical and social matters rather than religious law. Four of his works, all voluminous, have survived for over 1,900 years and are essentially our only source of history of the late Second Temple period until the end of the first century.

I never cease to wonder how he produced such a record. Each time I reach out and page through the 'Whiston' edition, I am over-awed by the 812 pages of small, printed text on large pages. It is the equivalent of at least 1800 pages in a regular book. To think that it was handwritten and encompassed minute historical details is astounding. Furthermore, he wrote other works which have been lost over time.

The known works of Josephus are made up of the following books:

The Jewish War: A history of the Jewish revolt against the Roman Empire as experienced by Josephus himself, recording the period 66 BCE - 74 CE.

Antiquities of the Jews: A history of the Jews prior to the revolt, based on the Bible, other writings, and the works of previous historians.

Against Apion: A defense of Judaism. Answering an attack by a Roman author.

Josephus: A Brief Sketch of his Life

Born Joseph Ben Mattathias in Jerusalem in 37 CE, he was the son of a priest. His mother was of Hasmonaean lineage. Josephus, in his sixteenth year, took upon himself to experience three of the sects of his era. He became a practicing Pharisee, then a Sadducee and finally he lived with the Essenes. Not content with that, he also became a student of the desert monk, Bannus, for 3 years, living with this semi-naked hermit in the desert and learning his ways. He held Bannus in the highest regard.

In his early twenties, he was sent to Rome to negotiate the release of several priests held by Emperor Nero. Following his return, he served as a General of the Jewish forces in the Galilee during the revolt against Rome in 66 B.C.E. He was eventually captured by the Roman legions. When taken captive by Vespasian, he presented himself as a prophet and predicted that Vespasian was destined to become the Emperor of Rome. As it happened, his prophecy came true. For this he was rewarded by being given his freedom and eventually adopted into the Flavius' family - he was given the name Flavius Josephus.

Josephus assisted the Roman commander Titus (Vespasian's son) with the understanding of the Jewish people and how to negotiate with them. The Jewish people called him a traitor as he tried to persuade the defenders of Jerusalem to surrender to the Roman siege.

He witnessed the destruction of Jerusalem, vividly recorded in his famous book 'The Jewish War' on his return to the court in Rome. His works, written in the style of the Greek historians, are regarded as factually correct but were presented in a way as to flatter his patron. At first, he wrote in his native tongue Aramaic, later it was translated to Greek. He wrote his massive work Jewish Antiquities in Greek for the general non-Jewish reader. After his death, a statue was built in Rome in his honor.

The answer to the question of how such a historical work (uniquely) survived till today is provided by Steve Manson, one of the world's authorities on Josephus. In his book 'Josephus and the New Testament' he writes:

"*First, his writings provided extraordinary background information for the reader of early Christian writings, especially the Gospels.*

They filled in a vast amount of history between the close of the Old Testament and the birth of Christianity". Their survival was further ensured as they contained the only written evidence of the existence of Jesus (other than the Christian

Bible) which is now regarded to have been an early (false) insert to provide credibility to his existence and divinity.

It is with this background, that I mention that he was the first recorder to document the name 'Essenes' in his works, having spent some time with them during his youth. It is from *his* works that scholars draw much of their information.

Philo

Philo Judaeus, a slightly earlier Jewish contemporary than Josephus, also described the Essenes.

He was a Jewish philosopher, who came from a wealthy Hellenized family that lived in Alexandria Egypt circa 20 BCE until 50 CE. Fluency in Greek and Latin, and being a disciple of Plato, combined the best of the Jewish religion with the best of Greek philosophy in his writings that had an influence on both Jewish and Christian theological development.

He is also well known for his figurative interpretations of the Torah, based on the Septuagint translation, and the doctrine of the Logos which has influence to this day on Christian theology. There is doubt whether he wrote factually about the Essenes based on personal observations. Rather, it appears he received his information on a hearsay basis.

Pliny the Elder

Pliny was a Roman geographer (23 - 79 CE) who in his work *Natural History* written 77 CE wrote detailed accounts of places throughout the Roman Empire. Included in this work are details on the lifestyle and geographical details about where the Essenes lived, and the surrounding areas. He too is always quoted with reference to the background of the 'solitary tribe' of Esseni. *"To the West of the Dead Sea, the Essenes have put the necessary distance between themselves and the insalubrious shore. They are a people unique of its kind and admirable beyond all others in the world, without women and renouncing love entirely, without money and having for company only palm trees."*

The First 'Real' Discoveries

It is documented in a letter written in the 8th century CE, by a Bishop named Timothy, addressed to Sergios, Bishop, and Metropolitan of Elam, that 'books' had been found in a cave in the region of Jericho - this time by an Arab hunter who had followed his dog after it had chased an animal inside. Sound familiar? He then went to Jerusalem and informed the Jews there, who came *en masse* and found the books of the Old Testament (I am in part indirectly quoting from his letter) and others in Hebraic writing.

Bishop Timothy, the Nestorian Patriarch of Seleucia, later enquired of the Jews whether there were any references in the Prophets, Jeremiah, which could be of relevance to the New Testament - The Bishop believed that it was not uncommon for the writers and Prophets to have their divine revelation works hidden in such caves. The finding apparently was that those 'books' were made up of more than two hundred 'Psalms of David.'

The bishop expressed concern about other books that could have been deposited in caves in the region, that they should not be plundered. It has been realized that prior to the exile to Babylon, holy books (scrolls) were hidden, which were subsequently re-discovered on their return some 70 years later by the prophet and scribe Ezra in particular.

Other early recorded discoveries include:

In the 3rd century CE, a Christian theologian, Father Origen, found a Greek version of the book of psalms in a jar near Jericho. Much later, in the late nineteenth century, Moses Shapira, a Jerusalem antique dealer, purchased what he believed to be biblical fragments said to have originated from the Dead Sea region. These were later disputed by Dr C Ginsburg resulting in Shapira committing suicide on account of the apparent shame and loss of credibility.

One can only imagine how many works from the Babylonian exile have been hidden in that region, as well as scrolls from the Essene era that have been plundered, stolen, destroyed, or lost in time since their discovery.

Another reference to the Essenes:

In 1864 a British scholar Dr Christian David Ginsburg (unusual!) published a monograph *The Essenes: Their History and Doctrines*, which was dismissed as speculation.

Archaeological Remains

In February 1949, Harding, the British director of antiquities in Jordan, authorized Roland de Vaux, a French Dominican monk from the *Ecole Biblique in* (east) Jerusalem to direct the archaeological excavations. The full report on de Vaux's excavations has never been published, and thus an in-depth detailed report on the archaeology has been withheld from the world. It is a universally accepted custom that the material belongs to the excavator. Access was denied because de Vaux died before publishing. There still is speculation surrounding the history of Qumran. It is also interesting to note de Vaux's bias from a Christian perspective, by his use of associated monastic terms such as 'refectory' and 'scriptorium' in his description of some of the rooms.

Pottery was found in the caves and at the ruins of Qumran. In particular, the pottery helped to establish the time period more accurately. Artifacts including inkwells, arrowheads, and coins were found at Qumran. The pottery jars, in which some of the scrolls were found, were particularly relevant to their dating. The scrolls that were stored in them, however, were not necessarily from the same period.

About eight to ten ritual immersion pools or *mikva'ot,* were found at Qumran. Laws pertaining to their structure, content, and maintenance closely corresponded with the halachic stipulations as recorded in the Mishnah. The Mishnah is a collection of rabbinic laws originating from the Oral Law (Hebrew: *halachah*) that were put into writing circa 200 CE and is the basis for Jewish observance and interpretation of the Torah Laws. Ritual immersion was an essential part of their way of life, leading to a constant state of purity. The related quote in support of the 'pools of purification' will appear when covering the relevant scroll. The theme of purity will be noted throughout the book

Then we have the ruins themselves which covered a time span from around 800 - 700 BCE when they were first built as an Israelite fortress. They continued to be used until the occupation by the Essenes around the time of the Maccabean uprising 168 - 164 BCE, and thereafter.

The site was twice occupied by the Essenes, the second time following a fire and an earthquake in 31 BCE. It was abandoned thereafter till about 60 CE and finally destroyed in the last stages of the first revolt in 68 CE against Rome when Qumran was besieged and then destroyed with its inhabitants. The Roman forces then occupied it for another three years with the military purpose of policing the region. Roman coins were found there dated to between 67 - 68 CE, possibly indicating the times when the Romans killed the remaining Essenes in the period occupied by Rome during the First Jewish Revolt until its conclusion in 73 CE with the siege and fall of Masada.

It is estimated that the Essenes inhabited Qumran over a period of 150 to 200 years. Calculations are based on the number of graves found on the site - around 1,100. Based on the archaeological reconstruction of the ruins and considering the size of the community room and sleeping quarters, it was estimated that between 60 and a maximum of 200 individuals could be accommodated; however probably around 80 people lived there. Recent research seems to indicate that the original residential site could occupy only about 40 individuals.

Theories still abound today on the origin or purpose of the site, whose functions probably differed over the centuries.

These included:

- A 'villa rustica', a resort for rich Jerusalemites.
- A Judean military fortress.

- A halfway house or rest-stop.
- A perfume 'factory'.
- A pottery factory

If in fact, Qumran was a military fortress with proximity to Jerusalem, surely its inhabitants would have needed the approval of the Roman authorities? This consideration leads one to wonder about 'isolationist outcasts' being allowed to occupy such an important and strategic site. I don't have an answer to this.

Cemeteries

The cemeteries close to Qumran are of much archaeological interest and debate. There are around 1,100 graves. And it was there, that the first zinc coffin was found. A debate has centered on whether they are the graves of Essene inhabitants exclusively, during the 200 years of their occupation of the site.

Furthermore, due to limited excavation of these graves, one could question Essene celibacy - since female skeletons were found amongst them. However, these female graves have been since considered to be Bedouin.

There is a 'main cemetery', and graves outside of it. On excavation of the main cemetery, only male skeletons were found, but outside, were graves containing skeletons from adult women and children. To date, 37 graves have been exhumed, revealing 40 individuals. Scientific investigation has indicated that 21 are male, 10 are females, and 5 are children. Three are undetermined, and one is still in dispute.

This has led to some different interpretations by various scholars, which include:

- The Essenes who lived at that site had ceased cohabiting with their wives.
- Only the celibate sect of that sectarian movement lived there.

- Women and their children also lived at Qumran or in the vicinity.

The graves of children could have come from those who were 'adopted' at an early age to be taken into the Essene community. Some or many of the graves were of Bedouin origin. The ratio of 21:10 is not exceptional and reflects the biological sex ratio found in other ancient gravesites.

The most recent theory is that they are graves of Bedouin.

More Caves, more Scrolls, more Revelations

The Qumran Caves are a series of caves, some natural, some artificial, found around the archeological of Qumran in the Judean Desert of the West Bank of Israel. Of the eleven caves to be covered in this book, five occurred naturally and six were dug.

Cave 1. Discovered November 1946 - February 1947 by Bedouins. Yielded the 7 scrolls acquired by Yadin, about 500 Scroll fragments, and one tefillin case.

Cave 2. Discovered in February 1952, by Bedouin, found 33 fragments including Jubilees and Ben Sirach in the original Hebrew.

Cave 3. Discovered in March 1952 by archaeologists contained the Copper Scroll.

Cave 4a. Discovered in September 1952 by Bedouin and *further* excavated by archaeologists Roland du Vaux, who discovered a *second section* to the cave, now referred to as Cave 4b. A total of 80,000 to 100,000 fragments, which made up about 550 manuscripts of biblical scrolls, Apocrypha compositions, sectarian writings, economic documents, 7 *Mezuzot* (Heb. pl for mezuzah), the 'Halachic Letter' otherwise known as 'Miksat Ma'aseh Ha-Torah' or 'MMT', Thanksgiving hymns, Torah, psalms, proverbs, Prophets, Mishnah - Rabbinic Texts. The Damascus Document, inter alia.

Cave 5. Discovered September 1952 by Jozef Milik. Manuscript fragments, 5 tefillin.

Cave 6. Discovered 1952 by Bedouin. Fragments of 31 manuscripts, and well-preserved texts including the Psalms Scroll.

Caves 7 - 10. February - April 1955 revealed by archaeological excavations, yielded a small number of texts, Tefillin and mezuzah.

Cave 11. Discovered in February 1956 by Bedouin. The Temple Scroll and 38 additional fragments of a second Temple Scroll, Targums.

There is a 'second' *twin Cave 11* that is also classified as 11. In it were found containers that held the remains of anointing oil and spices used in sacrifices.

Cave 12 (Discovered 2017) contained a fragment of a scroll that still needs to be studied.

What did come as a surprise to me was that there were in fact "*over 1,000 caves*" (according to J. Charlesworth) *but* only 11 held scrolls! All of which need to be investigated.

Chapter 6: Research and Publication

Insight

"These treasures conferred enormous academic power and prestige upon the scholars who controlled them and could divulge exciting new discoveries at scholarly conclaves in learned journals."

The first professionals to have access to the scroll fragments were G. Harding, a director of the Department of Antiquities of Jordan, and a French Dominican archaeologist and biblical scholar, Father Roland de Vaux.

From Cave 1, they took back with them hundreds of the remaining scattered fragments to the Palestine Archaeological Museum in Jordan, later called the Rockefeller Museum in Jerusalem.

Interestingly I came across a snippet of information in Baigent and Leigh's book (which will be covered further on) - that in a conversation with the then Major General Ariel Sharon, it was revealed that he, together with Moshe Dayan, had planned an underground raid via the sewers of Jerusalem into the Rockefeller Museum to take the Scrolls into Israeli custody. This plan never materialized.

The Kingdom of Jordan, together with the surrounding Arab states were all declared enemies of Israel. The scroll fragments thus remained in Jordanian control until June 1967. The dramatic changeover to them being in Israel's possession took place from the outcome of the Six-Day War.

Despite Israel promising Jordan they would not attack, and requesting they do the same - Jordan decided to attack Israel. Within three days, Israel had conquered their forces and retook East Jerusalem, where the Scrolls were held.

While the battle for Jerusalem was at its peak, Yigal Yadin, seizing the opportunity, requested a company of Paratroopers to be sent to capture the Rockefeller Museum with its scrolls. After an intense firefight between Israeli and Jordanian troops, the museum, together with its scores of thousands of Dead Sea Scroll fragments, fell into Israeli hands and returned once more to the independent state of Israel. This was the *third* miracle!

As more discoveries were made in the early 1950s, a team was assembled to decipher, collate, and report on the mounting material. The fragments lay under glass on long tables in a room, which became known as the 'Scrollery'. Conditions under which they were kept and examined have been described as shocking. The environmental and climatic change of the fragments now, compared to their original state of preservation, took its toll as deterioration set in. Many of the pieces were found to have Sellotape over them, which had to be painstakingly removed years later. Mildew and direct sunlight also resulted in the total disappearance of letters and words, whilst the smoke from cigarettes that were blown over the fragments didn't help either!

By 1956, over one hundred thousand fragments had been collected, together with complete and incomplete scrolls in varying sizes, many from one square centimeter to an average size of fifty to seventy centimeters. When it was realized that payments for these fragments depended on their size, the Bedouins tried to stick them together!

Some of the world's greatest detective work was ready to be undertaken - to piece together, match letter with a letter, parchment with parchment, word with word until the message or contents could finally be read and understood.

I say understood with some hesitation, as in the ensuing fifty years, many interpretations were fought over until the strongest school of academic prowess prevailed to establish a *standard* interpretation.

In all, it is estimated at the current time of writing this book; the collection is composed of what could have amounted to around 1,000 scrolls or manuscripts, with thousands of fragments remaining for compilation.

Almost all estimations on the actual number of scrolls hover around 950. I mention 1,000 as that was the number given in mid-2002 at a ceremony marking the final compilation and translations.

Interestingly, I have come across estimations that the collection of scrolls discovered, represents only six or up to sixty percent of the original total number hidden! Various calculations are used to substantiate this estimation.

By now, the reader may well have a picture in his mind of a giant jigsaw puzzle needing to be pieced together. That is an oversimplification. Many of the fragments appeared to have nothing written on them and many were in a crushed, crinkled, or shrunken form, or impacted upon each other so that they were nigh impossible to separate. Some even had the dried remains of urine or bat droppings embedded in them.

If you imagine the impact that two thousand years could have, you might come close to appreciating the formidable task that the team had in putting it all together. Many scrolls appeared to have been torn or purposely twisted, like wrung out washing, others formed a single unit because the roll was tightly stuck together. Only when the unrolling took place, under carefully controlled conditions, could the words or letters be deciphered.

This took years to prepare. Some words could only be deciphered from the imprints made on the back of the parchment touched - but this was only part of the challenge. Techniques such as ultraviolet lighting, when shone on a seemingly blank piece of the fragment at times faintly revealed sometimes only part of a letter, which was then confirmed when it was shown to match up with an identified adjoining piece.

This could take place for example if the yet unidentified letter was at the edge of a fragment. Once identified it could then be matched to another fragment and thus continuing the now recognized line of words by the joining up of the pieces. Even the matching by chromosome technique was used in more recent times.

These *fragments* or pieces and or sections of scrolls were photographed, and a complete set of negatives were fortuitously then taken to the Huntington Library in San Marino California, under the care of a Mrs. Bechel, where they were kept in vaults to control humidity and temperature. These were to play a prominent role in later years in pre-emptively revealing to the world their hidden contents. More about this later!

In addition, a *concordance* was developed of which 30 copies were made. The concordance was a *directory* made up alphabetically of the entire individual words appearing in the Scrolls showing where and how they were used. A Bible concordance is a list produced by a computer that shows all the *examples* of the usage of individual words in a book or in our case, the Scrolls. Thus, it helped the scholars to connect words missing from the fragments and to match sections. I have shown examples of this being applied by the usage of the [square brackets] when presenting examples of scroll texts.

In later years with the help of a computer program, this resulted in a 'stolen' and illegal pre-emptive publication, subsequently leading to a court case.

A team was first put together because of King Hussein's government's support which approached the Ecole Biblique et Archeologique Francaise, in Jerusalem. The team consisted mainly of Dominican monks, some better-known members being:

- Father J. Milik (Catholic)
- John Allegro (an agnostic who later converted to Catholicism)

- John Strugnell (at first a Presbyterian, later becoming a devout Catholic)

- Roland de Vaux, director of the Ecole Biblique.

Other members of the team included Frank Cross and Maurice Baillet.

Most of the team, of which Strugnell was appointed Editor in Chief, were virulently anti-Jewish and anti-Israel. This was later to also play an important role in the way the contents of the Scrolls were promulgated and their ultimate revelation to the world.

The team or cartel's history can be broken up into essentially three periods. The first was prior to the 'Six-Day War' in June 1967. The second was post-war. Remarkably, they were allowed to continue with their translations and compilations. However, during the third period, their output virtually dried up and the world began to wake up to the frustration of other scholars not having access to the Scrolls.

Even more remarkable was the fact that even though the Scrolls were in the possession of the Israelis, they exerted no influence or pressure on the team and did not insist on bringing in their own Jewish scholars. The third stage came about with exposure, scandal, and publicity, leading to the overthrow of the cartel and the entry of additional scholars into the team. This is the briefest of overview, simply to provide a sequence and insight into what was regarded as an enormous scandal.

The editors of Biblical Archeology magazine played an important role in putting pressure on the team, and on one of its monthly covers a picture of Strugnell was posted with the following quote: "It seems we have acquired a bunch of fleas who are in the business of annoying us". (Strugnell to ABC Television News)

Strugnell himself disclosed at an interview (second period) with a journalist of the prominent Israeli newspaper *Ha-Aretz,* that he was 'anti-Judaist'. He also said, "*The correct answer of Jews to Christianity is to become Christian". "The Zionists based themselves on a lie".* He also described Judaism *as "a horrible religion...and that it should never have survived".* Furthermore, he stated *"the solution for (Judaism) was mass conversion to Christianity"* - such statements having been emitted from an 'erudite' professor of 'Christian Origins' at the eminent Harvard School of Divinity! In self-defense, he later admitted that he had been diagnosed with alcoholism and manic depression. This shortly afterward led to his professional demise, and he was removed from his position.

The Israel Antiquities Authority despite a 'Jew-free' team and long delays in publication, continued to allow the cartel to have their exclusivity to the Scrolls.

The situation improved following a series of events that occurred, including the famous statements from Geza Vermes, who publicly described the goings-on as *"...the greatest and most valuable of all Hebrew and Aramaic manuscript discoveries is likely to become the academic scandal par excellence of the twentieth century"* (1977).

In addition, Hershel Shanks in his magazine 'Biblical Archaeological Review' (BAR) put further pressure on the scandal of these restrictions and delays...*"Those who hold the scrolls have the goodies - to drip out bit by bit. This gives them status, scholarly power, and a wonderful ego trip. Why squander it?"* (1985) and again published in BAR, *"The team of editors has now become more of an obstacle to publication than a source of information"* (1989). All these outpourings of anger resulted in the eventual access to the Scrolls for the many prominent scholars who had been waiting in the wings.

To add fuel to the fire, in 1991 Baigent and Leigh published a best seller 'The Dead Sea Scrolls Deception', with a sub-title 'The Sensational story behind the Religious Scandal of the Century'. The central theme of the book was their assessment and conclusion that the Vatican was withholding unreleased scrolls that were considered to be a threat to Christianity. Most of the scholarly world threw this theory out of court, but a *seed was planted* and remains to this day.

By 1991, Emanuel Tov had been appointed to the position of Editor-in-Chief of the Dead Sea Scrolls publishing project, and the editorial team had increased to about fifty scholars - the third period.

I need to provide some additional background: The Ecole Biblique was in 'East' Jerusalem, the geographical portion that was retained by Jordan because of the outcome of the War of Independence of Israel in 1948. The Ecole was established by the Vatican to deal with archaeological discoveries and scientific theories pertaining to biblical history. Its function was also to take control and or withhold impending threats to Christianity by way of discoveries. Today the Ecole, while financed by the French government, is still composed largely of Dominican priests. The Ecole has been described as "*an adjutant of the Pontifical Biblical propaganda machine*" (Hershel Shanks).

Here are some theories that may have contributed to delays in publication:

Roland de Vaux and J. T. Milik wanted to prevent certain perceived or considered interpretations they arrived at, thought to be early Christian discoveries and which appeared to contradict or threaten the current Roman Catholic Canon.

Dominicans may be attempting to steal the heritage of the Jewish People of Palestine by hiding or distorting the 'true meaning of the Scrolls.'

Even the Israel Antiquities Authority "*wanted to suppress certain unflattering commentaries concerning early Hebrew practices*".

The contents were threatening to the Christian and in particular the Catholic Church.

When research was first undertaken by these Dominican monks, they saw the Essenes almost as their early counterparts - a group of peaceful, pious, and celibate monks living in a retreat and sharing their possessions.

Furthermore, much emphasis was placed on the so-called scriptorium discovered where the Scrolls were believed to have been written. This is part of the monastic way of life, by way of having their own scriptoriums and thus they imposed the notion that Qumran was a monastery.

In response to this misrepresentation, one of the greatest works on the Scrolls was written by the *doyen* Lawrence Schiffman called 'Reclaiming the Dead Sea Scrolls' and proved that the Essenes and their literature were exclusive of Jewish origin and background.

Dating...a Crucial Requisite

It is critical to reach an agreement on when the Scrolls were written. The time span ranged over a period of around three hundred years, from 250 BCE to 50 CE.

If it could be established that certain scrolls may be dated 100 or even 50 years later, its impact could be enormous for the following reason - the years 4 - 3 BCE marked the birth of Jesus, with the ensuing thirty-plus years covering his life and death in about 31 - 37 CE. This was followed by the birth of Christianity together with its first documentation. The last scrolls were written and hidden at the time of the uprising against the Roman occupation - which began in 66 CE, ending with the destruction of the Second Temple in 70 CE. If it could be shown that certain scrolls, which will be covered in this book, were written during this period, they could then take on an entirely different meaning in their interpretation. For no longer would the New Testament be the *only* reference to that period.

The world would now have other historical information which could significantly alter the way Christianity originated, drew its references and teachings, and used phraseology and customs. The role of the disciples in the life of Jesus would then predate him to the times of the Essenes who could be regarded as the true forerunners of the religion. On the surface, nothing has really changed, and Christianity is much the same now as has been for over a thousand years. Some readers might dispute the statement that the New Testament is the only (official) known reference to the life of Jesus. Josephus also made valuable references to the history of that era. In his works, we also read of his references to James the brother of Jesus, John the Baptist, and even Jesus himself. On the other hand, these references are considered to have been later inserted into his writings to provide further 'evidence' of the authenticity of the New Testament. One of the reasons provided for this dispute was that the language and style of writing appeared to differ from Josephus' writings. There is also a possible reference or inference to Jesus in the Talmud, but this adds very little meaning towards historical insight.

The generally accepted dates as to when the various scrolls were written and the cryptic references to individuals, together with interpretations of the themes of their contents have largely placed them in a matching or identifiable period of history. However other important techniques were applied for more accurate dating.

Paleography

This is a method for studying the style of the script. Over time, the shapes of letters have changed, and the way in which fonts have developed, also have a history of their own. The important starting point is to have verified time baseline criteria, usually where a known historical event is freshly documented so that the style/script would reflect the period.

Even though numerous scribes wrote these scrolls, and writing styles varied with individuals, the paleographers were able to put a relatively accurate date to them, and they claim to note the changes that took place within 25-year intervals! Their dating of the Scrolls has been accepted with relatively minimal discrepancy by many scholars. In fact, to date, there have not been any significant differences between other scientific findings and those of the paleographers!

Other Scientific Methods Used

The best known is the Carbon-14 (C14) method. A more developed method is Mass Accelerator Spectrometry, having the advantage of requiring less material. These methods were applied to *some* of the materials tested, however, there is dissatisfaction that only a relatively few specimens were submitted. Furthermore, those specimens were not always regarded to be important. Aside from some dispute about the degree of accuracy of the C14 dating, it was discovered that many of the tested samples had been contaminated by castor oil. Apparently, castor oil, when applied with a fine brush, was used to enhance the clarity of the letters, to clean off any dirt, and to make the dried parchment suppler. Usage of this method to influence the correct dating of the tested material has in recent times become something of an academic debate. Testing was also done on the material that had been wrapped around certain scrolls which may not have been the same age as the Scrolls themselves.

An example of Accelerator Mass Spectrometry dating was the testing of the *Turin Shroud,* believed to have covered the body of Jesus. Yet it was dated between the periods 1260 - 1390, from samples sent in 1988 to three different universities both in the USA, Switzerland, and the UK. The revelation of the result of that test was delayed to the public by six months. Perhaps when historians don't like or agree with an outcome, the accuracy is then disputed. Nevertheless, one does question why only a few pieces of scrolls were tested. At this stage of scientific development, because a relatively large amount of material is required, one can understand the reluctance to sacrifice valuable fragments. I am sure that in the not-too-distant future, improved methods will be used, and perhaps then certain standard theories could be significantly altered.

References - Cryptic and Identifiable

In some of the Scrolls, several identifiable names are mentioned, for example in the 'Nachum Commentary', the king of Greece, Demetrius III, and Antiochus the Seleucid king. Reference to the *Kittim* who were the Romans also frequently appears. Alexander Jannaeus, who crucified 800 Pharisees is referred to in scroll 4Q169 known as the Nachum Pesher.

Chapter 7: The Essenes of Qumran

In a publication from Arutz Sheva, a religious radio station in Israel, a cleverly titled 'Jewish Fundamentalism or Fundamentally Jewish', article appeared. What also struck me was a definition of 'Fundamentalism' that followed, which to my thinking rather appropriately described the Essenes:

"*A usually religious movement or point of view characterized by a return to the fundamental principles, by rigid adherence to those principles, and often by intolerance of other views and opposition to secularism*" (Non-religious way of life).

Robert Eisenman described them as a 'God-intoxicated group'. They carried out their interpretation of the laws (halachic) and recorded God's covenant for the Jews, with their meaning and implications. 'Religious zealots' and 'separatists', also describe them. As startling as this may be, I do wish to place Essenism in its perspective and not on a religious Jewish pedestal. They have been "*totally disconnected and out of step from the wider Jewish society*". Whatever the reader draws from this book about the Essenes and their writings, can only serve to enrich their knowledge of Judaism and Christianity. We will read about the associated history of the period and its influences, which have reached out even to this day.

Even today, extremist sects exist in Judaism. Group such as the 'Khomeini' Jews and the Naturei Karta are examples of this. Also in segments of extreme Orthodoxy among the

Haredi Jews, who are further examples of dissociated extremism.

The coming of Rome was seen by many as the 'End of Times', also known as the *Apocalypse*. During these times, famous biblical personalities including Enoch and Baruch became the themes of apocalyptic works in what became known as the books of the Apocrypha.

Many, including the Essenes, withdrew to prepare for this 'End of Time' apocalypse. They saw themselves on the threshold of an apocalyptic era, and thus also representing the *true form* of the Jewish religion. Their lifestyle and belief were to hasten the end of injustice and the eradication of evil.

At the 'end of time', together with the arrival of the Messiah(s), they saw themselves as the *representatives of God*, who would be living with Him, whether in Heaven or on Earth. Hence many of their literary works were of an apocalyptic nature.

These sectarians believed that only they knew the true Law and thus the rest of the Jewish people were not correctly observing the laws of the Sabbath and festivals. They were thus the *true* believers. They often interpreted the bible differently resulting in large discrepancies between themselves and others.

Core to their being was their belief in the coming of principally two messiahs at the end of days - one being a Priestly Messiah of Aaron, who would restore the Temple to its proper purity, and the second Messiah would be from the House of King David who would come to lead the war against evil. This would bring about the 'Kingdom of God' as is recorded in their writings.

On reaching the section dealing with 'Christianity and the Scrolls' in this book, you will have achieved a greater appreciation of the figure of Jesus, who could also be portrayed as an apocalyptic firebrand, preaching about the coming Kingdom of God.

The 'Library of Qumran' is a discovered documentation of one of *many* sects that existed during the period between the two Temples, albeit a very significant one. Therefore, and this is important to appreciate, only some of the discovered scrolls in the region of the Dead Sea or Qumran are recognized as belonging to the Essenes.

Also included and recognized were scroll fragments found in Masada as belonging to the Qumran community. It is appropriate at this stage of the book to give other names or terminologies that are used in place of their popular designated name, Essenes. They are *Qumranites* and Qumran *sectarians* from the word 'sect'.

The balance of this library was part of the cultural heritage of the Jewish people, particularly from the very latter era of the Second Temple. Different authors composed the balance of the scrolls found. The theory for this vast collection being stored and in fact hidden was the impending feeling of being overwhelmed, and even largely destroyed by the Roman occupiers, especially during the 'Jewish War'. The Jewish heritage was placed there for safekeeping and perhaps even posterity.

Josephus on the other hand, in his compilation of Jewish history, consistently placed the Essenes at the highest level when relating to the Pharisees, Sadducees, and Essenes. His descriptions categorized them as being exemplary and unmatched in virtue.

The name Essenes is an enigma. Speculation abounds as to its meaning and origin and there has not yet been a universally accepted answer. All three of the earliest recorders of their lives, Josephus, Philo, and Pliny, referred to them as the Essenes. Philo suggests that it originated from Greek words implying 'saintliness', 'holy' or 'pure'. Another theory is that the name is derived from the Aramaic word *asayya,* meaning 'healers', and adapted by the Greek pronunciation, Essainoi. The Essenes were known for their healing abilities, using their own special blend of herbs to treat illness.

Another theory proposed by Professor Robert Eisenman of 'The Dead Sea Scrolls Uncovered' fame, suggests that Essene comes from the Hebrew word *Yishiyim* or Jesse-*ites*. This could be, as they write in the 'War Rule' Scroll... *"But a shoot shall grow out of the stump of Jesse".* This is interpreted in 'Pesher Isaiah'.... *"The interpretation of the text concerns the branch of David who will arise at the end of days (an apocalyptic Messianic belief) to save Israel and destroy its enemies...".*

A related phrase in the Jewish daily afternoon prayer service (*Minchah*) is also stated: *"the offspring* (the Hebrew word *tzemach* literally meaning plant) *of your servant David..."* refers to a call for the Messiah to come/reveal himself in our days.

Even in the scrolls attributed as being Essene, there are almost no personal references by name to anyone, let alone reference to themselves by a specific identifiable name. Yes, there are references such as *Bnei* (sons of) *Tzadok,* the *Yachad,* that scholars use, but that is the extent of what is known.

In some of the scrolls, they also refer to themselves as '*Judah'.* This movement could also be called 'the Community (*Yachad*) of those who enter the new covenant'. The Essene hypothesis was first developed by Sukenik and later by prominent scholars including Frank Cross and Andre Dupont-Sommer.

Josephus mentions the name Essene a total of thirteen times in three of his works, along with his description of their way of life and beliefs, based on his personal contact with them. As to Philo or Pliny's contact, this is questionable as hearsay could have played a significant role in their writings. Speculation is open regarding any reference to them in the Talmud and New Testament, as quotes from one or two passages have been bandied about as possibly being related to them.

Much of what the world knows comes from writings attributed to them in certain scrolls. In particular: The *'Damascus Document'*, the *'Rule of the Community'* and the *'MMT'* Scrolls which will be covered further on in this book. These scrolls reveal to the greatest extent the reason for their being, way of life, and beliefs.

More recent theories suggest that they originated from the Samaritan priesthood and later joined up with the 'Tzadokite' priests of the Jerusalem Temple. Just to "throw a cat among the pigeons", another theory is that they were the 'Rechabites' mentioned in the book of Jeremiah, who himself led an ascetic life.

They differed from the Pharisees and the Scribes. In the original Greek text known as the 'Epsilon', Rechabites are referred to as *Essainoi* meaning 'sitters', implying that they were 'contemplators'. Both the latter theories are the result of much research. I have mentioned these should you later pursue an interest in this field and come across these proposals. In addition, other theories also exist. Nevertheless, for the rest of the book, I will remain with what is known as the *'Standard Theory'*.

A History of the Community

Confusion might well enter at this stage, for surely the breakaway Essenes were influenced by their leader Teacher of Righteousness? However, it is implied in the Scrolls that the 'Wicked Priest' was the first to break away and establish the sect, and later, on account of his beliefs, he split the group and became the 'bad guy' to the remaining members.

Here we arrive at a situation of dispute. Once scholarly research was opened from the early nineties, it sometimes deviated from the 'standard model' i.e., that which is generally believed or accepted. Recently it has been proposed that in fact Hyrcanus II, the High Priest 76 CE - 67 CE, was the Teacher of Righteousness!

This is based on one of the scrolls known as Pesher Nachum. Scholar and author Greg Doudna, through his research, concludes that Hyrcanus II who broke away in 67 BCE from his position as a High Priest, took with him part of the Jerusalem (scroll) library to Qumran. Others propose the High Priest Jason, the brother of Onias III, was the Teacher of Righteousness. Doudna's latest theory is quite sensational for it radically upsets the standard theory. Firstly, the date that the Teacher of Righteousness broke away and joined up with the Essenes, is up to one hundred years after the date as regarded in the standard theory.

Secondly, according to the new proposed date, the Wicked Priest would then be Aristobulus II who wrested the kingship and high priesthood from Hyrcanus II.

I have essentially followed the standard theory in this book, but on this occasion have chosen to broaden that theory to illustrate for the first-time reader that many alternative theories are in existence and will continue to be.

The community came into being 390 years after the fall of Jerusalem in 586 BCE referred to as 'the age of wrath' in the scroll the Damascus Document. This places its inception in 196 BCE.

During the second quarter of the second century BCE, the Zadokites lost their monopoly over the office of the High Priest in the Jerusalem Temple. Afterwards, with the establishment of the Hasmonean dynasty (because of the Maccabean Revolt), the Hasmonean Kings took the role of the High Priests.

Their actions had largely the support of the Sadducees in the Temple. These events not only contributed to the formation of this sect but caused its members to do the most radical thing a Jew could do at the time - they rejected the cult in the Jerusalem Temple. Both the Essenes and later the Early Christians (Christians accepted Jesus as the sacrifice) found ways of dispensing with the Temple cult as a means towards achieving personal holiness and still attaining the Divine reward.

From the Damascus Document Scroll, which will be extensively covered further on in this book, you will learn hints about their origins. It intimates that the earliest history of the community can be separated into two periods: one, *before* the arrival of their leader the '*Teacher of Righteousness*', and the other, *after* his arrival.

The second period is thought to have been during the reign of either of the Hasmonaean princes, viz. Jonathan (160 - 142 BCE), or his brother Simeon (142 - 134 BCE), usurped the office of the High Priest to the shock of the practicing Jewish population. The most accepted date of their existence is 196 BCE, during the reign of Antiochus Epiphanes III, the Seleucid (Greek) king or ruler based in Syria, who deposed Onias III, the High Priest. Onias is also thought to have been the Teacher of Righteousness. Antiochus stepped up an intense program of Hellenism including within Palestine, partly to overcome the threat of a takeover by Rome.

This period is referred to in the Damascus Document scroll as the 'age of wrath', as it was the time when many Jews flirted with and even renounced their religious traditional connections in support of the new and 'attractive' Hellenist culture of the Greeks. It is critical to be aware of what took place during this period. The Maccabean priesthood fell under the influence of Hellenism, resulting in the beginning of the end of the traditional and holy observance of the Temple worship and sacrifice. As to whether these Hasmonaeans (Maccabean) were Tzadokites (Sadducean) is still debatable. This has resulted in one of several speculations that proposed that the Essene roots established themselves from the pious Hasidim communities, breaking away from the desecrating and corrupting Maccabees. As an insert at this point, the Temple High Priest Caiaphas who supposedly condemned Jesus was also a Hellenized priest.

The Teacher of Righteousness

The principal influence, leader, and re-founder of the Essenes during a period of their history was an individual known as the *Teacher of Righteousness.* He made his appearance to the community in 176 BCE.

Recorded as *Moreh Tzedek* in Hebrew in the Scrolls, this can be translated as the Teacher of *Justice.* The word *tzedek* is also related to Tzadok (can be spelled Zadok) the first High Priest of the Temple, who was a forerunner to the Sadducean or *Tzadokim (*Heb. pl.) class.

The Teacher is believed to have been a priest who broke away from his role in the Temple, because of defilement having taken place, to lead the Essenes. He is described in the Damascus Document scroll*: "And they perceived their iniquity (sin) and recognized that they were guilty men, yet for twenty years they were like blind men groping for the way. And God observed their deeds, that they sought Him with a whole heart, and He raised for them a Teacher of Righteousness to guide them in the way of His heart"*

His designation as the Teacher of Righteousness occurs 17 times in the Dead Sea Scrolls. He was not *just* a priest according to the Scrolls, but one who claimed to have the correct understanding of the Torah, and through whom God would reveal to the community *"the hidden things in which Israel had gone astray".*

He also claimed to be an inspired interpreter of the prophets, as the one *"to whom God made known all the mysteries of the words of His servants the Prophets"* as recorded in the Habakkuk scroll. He thus claimed to find new and inspired interpretations to the prophets for the *final* generation nearing the End of Days, as recorded in the Essene (eschatological) literature. After his death, his leadership of the entire community appears to have been replaced by the *mevaker* (examiner) and *maskil* (instructor) who took over the responsibilities of his teachings.

He is specifically mentioned in the following scrolls that you will read about further on in this book: 'Pesher Habakkuk', in certain of the Psalms or 'Hodayot', and the 'Damascus Document.'

There is also possible inference to him or directly from him, in the 'MMT' Scroll.

In Pesher Habakkuk, it states ..."interpreted this concerns the Teacher of Righteousness, to whom God made known all mysteries of the words of His servants the Prophets". For he was regarded as the supreme interpreter of the biblical tradition.

Other references to him in the scroll are: 'Teacher', 'Interpreter of the Law', 'Priest', and 'The Priest'. He was never given the designation of 'Prophet'. However, in terms of what are considered attributes of a Prophet, he had visions through the 'Divine revelation' of scripture and the ability to describe the mystery and interpretations of the writings of the prophets. With these abilities, the 'Teacher' could thus also be considered to be a prophet to the Essenes.

In the scroll Pesher Habakkuk, just as Moses received the Law directly from God, it is also implied that he obtained his knowledge in the same way. It is recognized that the Teacher was a priest, but not likely that he was a 'High Priest' because he would not have then observed the solar but rather the lunar calendar.

He devoted his teachings to the preparation of the 'Sons of the Covenant', for the coming of the two messiahs; you will read about this in the 'Damascus Document' scroll.

In the Damascus Document, it is mentioned that a breakaway occurred from within the original community. Their former leader and subsequent persecutor, his nemesis, was referred to by certain coded and derogatory names. 'The Wicked Priest' is the most well-known, and the person around whom there have been volumes of recorded speculation. There is a Hypothesis (Groningen) - that term did not pertain to a particular individual, but rather a title applied to various Hasmonaean Priests.

Other names associated with him are *the Scoffer*, the *Liar* and the *Spouter of Lies*. It is generally believed that this person was the High Priest himself, by virtue of all the wrongdoings carried out by one who wielded the power of that rank. The Wicked Priest was associated with those who did not recognize the Teacher nor the Covenant.

Several candidates have been suggested to be the Wicked Priest, the most popular one being the High Priest Jonathan (the) Maccabee, and another option being Hyrcanus II. Ben Zion Waacholder writes that a number of scholars identify the Teacher of Righteousness as the High Priest in Jerusalem who officiated from 163 to 152 BCE.

Once the community broke away from the corrupt High Priesthood, they withdrew into the Judean wilderness and settled at Qumran to study the Law and to prepare for the coming of the kingdom of God. Their way of life demanded they follow certain strict rules of legal and religious behavior as documented in the Scrolls. It is estimated that this took place around 150-140 BCE.

An Overview of the Essenes Based on Josephus

Both Josephus and Philo recorded that the Essenes numbered about four thousand in their time, including both at Qumran and those scattered throughout every village. Josephus, however, wrote that there was another 'order of Essenes', who were "*at variance in their opinion of marriage*". It is on this group that the book focuses on the 'monastic' Essenes of Qumran. It needs to be added, however, that Josephus does mention in one of his works that he included other sects under the heading 'Essenes'. Nevertheless, the scholarly view is that his works are the first and foremost in obtaining background to them.

Josephus' recording of the Essenes played a major role in assisting scholars to grasp more easily the message conveyed in the discovered scrolls. His work formed a base on which to develop theories. If he had never have written about them, I wonder to what extent scholars would have made the same comments and reached the same conclusions. Speculation would have been rife, and divisions between schools enormous!

According to Josephus, the Pharisees had seven subdivisions, ranging from conservatism to liberalism. In an academic work by Marcus, it has been proposed that the Essenes formed 'the third left wing', and one rung on the ladder below the Zealots.

He introduces in his work 'War'... *"and a third sect, which pretends to a severer discipline, are called Essenes............they reject pleasure as an evil, ...and conquest over their passions to be a virtue. They neglect wedlock.... but do not absolutely deny the fitness of marriage..."*

It is interesting to draw a similarity to the ascetic and monastic lives of the Essenes with what Jesus advises in the New Testament in Corinthians 7:8-9, where he implies that marriage is an unfortunate necessity in order to prevent a man and woman from entering into a sexual relationship; *"Now, to the unmarried and to the widows I say that it would be better for you to continue to live alone as I do. But if you cannot restrain your desires, go ahead and marry - it is better to marry than burn with passion."* Leading a chaste, unmarried life is implied to be the highest level an individual can attain.

Josephus also wrote: "*Accordingly, there is in every city where they live, one anointed particularly to take care of strangers and to provide garments and other necessities for them.*" It is also recorded by him names of Essenes of prominence including Menachem, who worked in the court of Herod; Judas, who taught at the Temple; John, who was given the governorship of a province; and Simon who prophesied and led an attack in battle against Rome in which he died in 66 CE.

He writes about a 'pure meal' that only the initiated may eat after a year of probation. *"And when he hath given evidence, during that time he can observe their continence, he approaches nearer to their way of living, and is made a partaker of the waters of purification* (mikvah); *yet he is not even now admitted to live with them; for even after this demonstration of his fortitude, his temper, he is tried two more years; and if he appears worthy, they admit him into their society."*

"They are long-lived, also, insomuch that many of them live above a hundred years, by means of their simplicity of their diet". Now that's something to take note of! Josephus writes in much detail of their beliefs and lifestyle, which need to be read in his works or in summaries of his works that can be found on the Internet.

He describes them as living in villages, only with healthier social values, working either in agriculture or in crafts that contributed to peace within the communities. They were scornful of marriage and preferred to adopt children and teach them their ways. To them, women were impious, immoral, and not capable of a monogamous relationship.

Comparisons have been made to both forms of communism and early Christian beliefs, regarding money and communal sharing. They despised riches. Once having been accepted into the community, money, and possessions were surrendered to a common fund at the group's disposal so that no member could feel humiliation or pride associated with wealth or the lack thereof. Every morning at 11.00 am they took off their standard white garments, changed into loincloths, and immersed into ritual purification water in one of their cisterns. Baptism has often been compared to this and considered by some to have originated from this ritual. There has been reference by scholars to John the Baptist, whom it is believed had lived amongst them for several years.

After this, they entered a hall and partook in a communal meal wearing a sacred garment. They were given only enough food to satisfy their needs (no wonder some lived beyond one hundred) and ate in silence. They went back to their work, and the same communal meal and its format was followed in the evening. There are certain similarities with Communion and the way some orders of monks partake of their meals to this day. Whist at their own discretion, the Essenes were allowed to be charitable to strangers and with their own families, however, they needed permission from their superiors. In the important scroll 'The Community Rule', behavior within the community was strictly laid out. This will be covered in greater detail when reviewing it together with other scrolls.

Josephus however comments on their behavior, thus providing validation of that scroll's contents. He mentions that they did not take oaths - their word was their bond. Exhibiting anger was forbidden. The keeping of secrets from each other was forbidden, as was lying, blaspheming God, and stealing. Interestingly, there is no mention by Josephus in his description of the Essenes, of their all-important leader 'The Teacher of Righteousness'.

As is written in Deuteronomy 23:14, the commandment for the Israelites to dig a hole before defecating, and to cover afterward, was also a rule with them. They were each issued a hatchet to dig a hole for this. These self-same hatchets can be seen on exhibition at the *Shrine of the Book* in Jerusalem. Josephus writes about their belief in cleanliness, together with the bodily and spiritual cleansing that was a daily act carried out in the purification baths.

They forbade the use of oil as it was believed that oil transmitted ritual uncleanliness. Cleanliness was taken to the extreme by even refusing to defecate on the Sabbath! Josephus wrote additionally "*and covering themselves round with their garment, that they may not affront the Divine rays of light*". Rules for observation of the Sabbath were many and scrupulously kept.

Importantly, Josephus mentions the Essene belief in the immortal soul and that the souls of the wicked are taken to a 'dark' place for continuous punishment. In rabbinic Judaism (today) this is known as *gehonim.* This belief differed from the Sadducean belief - and is a significant difference, as many scholars believe the Essenes originated from the Sadducees, who did *not* believe in an 'afterlife' of the soul.

Their bravery, scorn of danger and pain due to their faith and convictions are written up with much admiration. In their final days of being overcome by the Romans, they suffered terrible torture and yet were said to have died with 'a smile on their faces', refusing to give in. "*Smiling in their agonies and mildly deriding their tormentors, they cheerfully resigned their souls, confident that they would receive them again*" (Josephus: 'War').

It was noted in 1991 that there are 27 parallels between Josephus writings and what scholars have determined from the Scrolls. An additional ten have no support. Additionally, there could be another six discrepancies between them. I doubt that a significant difference has been found in the ensuing years.

Extracts from Philo and Pliny

Philo

Philo records in his work 'On the Contemplative Life', that the Essenes did not offer animal sacrifices (which took place only at the Temple), but rather focused on "*rendering their minds pure and holy*". The honoring of the Sabbath was carried out with great respect.

Their rules had to be obeyed and focused on piety, holiness, justice, and the knowledge of good and bad. "*They honor virtue by forgoing all riches, glory and pleasure*" and "*The belief that God causes all good and cannot be the cause of any evil. Their 'trinity' was the love of God, the love of virtue and the love of man.*" "*They do not neglect the sick on the pretext that they can produce nothing. With the common purse there is plenty from which to treat all illness."*

In his book, Philo refers to them as *ascetics* who were named *Therapeutae,* probably due to their healing abilities using herbs. *"They lavish great respect on the elderly. With them they are very generous and surround them with a thousand attentions."*

Philo also recorded that *"they do not enlist by race, but by volunteers who have a zeal for righteousness".* There are no children, adolescents, or young men. Rather older men *"who have learned how to control their bodily passions".* They shared the same way of life, food, tastes, and even their clothing. References to women were certainly in the negative and intimated those men were in fact their slaves and under their spell. It is also recorded by him that the Essenes found favor in the eyes of Herod. It is believed this was due to their passive obedience to the ruling political authority, however tyrannical it was.

It is interesting to read that in the writings of the 3rd century churchman Jerome, he declared that Philo had contact with members of the church at the very beginning of its existence. These could have been the Essenes as recorded in Philo's work that Jerome was referring to, who he regarded as *proto-*Christians. Philo was sanitized and Christianized to Philo *Christianus* from Philo *Judaeus.*

This legend had its origins from bishop Eusebius, who told it at great length in his Ecclesiastical History, from where it then passed into Jerome's work. You will read about references to the connections between Essenism and Christianity in the chapter covering the Scrolls and Christianity.

Pliny

"To the west (of the Dead Sea) *the Essenes have put the necessary distance between themselves and the insalubrious* (unhealthy) *shore. They are a people unique of its kind and admirable beyond all others in the whole world; without women and renouncing love entirely, without money and*

having for company only palm trees..." This is a much-used quote to describe the Essenes in numerous articles and books, as it so aptly describes them in a nutshell. It is possible that Pliny's source antedated the fall of Qumran but nevertheless is regarded as being credible.

The popular concept remains of a monastic and ascetic Jewish sect living in the barren, Judean desert. Qumran, their break-a-way headquarters, high above and overlooking the Dead Sea and source of the discoveries remains as their domain in the public eye.

Sadducean Origins of the Essenes

The most widely accepted proposal of the Essenes origins and roots comes from Prof. Lawrence Schiffman. In his opinion, they were of Sadducean background. Very often scholarly conclusions are arrived at for something 'that is', because 'it is not'! Whilst respectfully I am not implying this over-simplistic reasoning to Schiffman and others, it sometimes is the core for the deduction. According to the Essene scroll contents and Josephus' records, their belief in the afterlife, and reward and punishment applied to this and the next world. This could imply they were of Pharisaic origin. Here then are the reasons given by Schiffman, which carry wide and respectful support for his Sadducean theory:

First and foremost is the belief that the sect broke away from the Temple on account of the Maccabean dynasty replacing or reducing and defiling the traditional Tzadokite/Sadducean high priesthood that dominated all Temple affairs.

The writers of the famous MMT Scroll state: *"You know that we have separated from the mainstream of the people and from all their impurities..."* specifically, the resulting adulteration of the sacrifices and a decline in the upkeep of its holiness. The Essenes also referred to themselves in their writings as *Bnei Tzadok* or Sons of Tzadok, the Tzadokites being the Sadducees.

There are also derogatory references by the Essenes against the Pharisees in some of their writings. A long history of division existed between these two influential groups within Judaism. The coded term 'seekers of smooth things' is believed to have been designated to the Pharisees as a way of denigrating them. Smooth, as in smooth speech, implying that they sought an easy way out by their interpretation of the Law. It could also have meant false things and therefore false teachings.

This is very different from the strict obedience with which the Essenes had to carry out the Laws and they believed that the Pharisees interpreted the laws to their convenience. Furthermore, as mentioned early in the book, a more moderate and traditionally pious group of Sadducees existed who were greatly disturbed by the Hellenistic influences that were taking place, and they could have been the originators of the Qumran sect.

Another very specific area identifying the Sadducees sect from the Pharisees was in the interpretation of the calendar and the consequently designated dates for festivals.

The Sadducees and the Essenes followed a calendar based on solar months and a 364-day year. Pharisaic and subsequently Rabbinical Judaism followed a calendar of lunar months, with adjustments to comply with the solar year.

For the Essenes, this was to ensure that the Festivals or Holy days as designated in the Torah would always fall on the same day of the week. For example, they took the literal meaning of "on the morrow after the Sabbath" (Lev.23:11) as meaning on a Sunday, as being the first day of the Passover, and it would always take place on that day. By interpretation through the Oral Law, the Pharisees, and rabbinic Judaism today interprets Sabbath in this instance to mean that the first day of the Passover is to be a day of rest.

This in turn by interpretation designated the date for the first offering of the Omer, and subsequently the counting of 49 days (of the Omer) from the second day of the Passover to the eve of the festival of Shavuot. The Sadducees always celebrated the festival of Shavuot (similar to a 'harvest' festival) also on a Sunday. Shavuot is also known as 'Pentecost', from the Latin for fifty. Its name in this regard is unrelated to the Christian holiday by the same name. Shavuot also celebrates the receiving of the Torah at Mount Sinai and when the first fruits harvested were brought to the Temple.

As pedantic as this may seem to non-Jews, the observations of the festivals and fast days on the specific dates are *absolute*, as they are carried out according to biblical and consequently rabbinical law. It would be the same as Christianity changing the dates of Easter and Ascension Day to mid-week, or Christmas to perhaps the 24th June?

Nevertheless, it is interesting to note the usage of the astrological cycle by some of the Jews of that era. Mosaics of the Capricorn symbol have been found in several ancient synagogues. They symbolized the Hebrew month of Nissan. Capricorn was placed at the top, implying that the solar year began with Nissan, as is stated in the Torah. Scholars have interpreted this and other records to there being more than one Jewish calendar.

The most solemn day on the Jewish calendar is Yom Kippur, the Day of Atonement. The Essenes also kept it on a different date. An attack on the Teacher of Righteousness took place on that day by the Wicked Priest, as documented in the 'Pesher Habakkuk' scroll, thus implying that the perpetrator had a different date on his calendar designated for that Holy day.

About festivals, it is opportune to mention that the Essenes kept additional religious holidays on account of their biblical interpretations. They were the 'New Wine Festival', 'New Oil Festival' and 'Wood' Festival.

Several scrolls used by the Essenes, including the Damascus Scroll, the Temple Scroll, the MMT Letter, and the Community Rule, all by way of interpretation, seem to reflect the Sadducean theory.

'The Dead Sea Scrolls' by Wise, Abegg, and Cook, steers away from dogma and suggests that the Essenes were not of the stereotype Sadducees as portrayed by Josephus or in the New Testament, but rather 'Sadducees with Essene theological tendencies'.

On the other hand…

It's not all black and white, otherwise known as 'bifurcation', meaning that only two alternatives/options exist. Of the Scrolls mentioned in the previous paragraph and in other scrolls, a reasonable case could be put forward to dispute the Sadducean proposal. Firstly, there are important basic differences between the Sadducean belief and those of the Essenes, namely:

(a) The belief in angels. The scrolls have numerous references to them, whereas the Sadducees were said not to believe.

(b) The Sadducees were the wealthy, aristocratic class, whilst the Essenes referred to themselves as 'the poor'.

(c) The belief in the resurrection of the dead by the Essenes was contrary to the non-believing Sadduceans.

(d) The 'free interpretation' of the Torah by the Sadducees was in stark contrast to the rules regulating the religious way of life of the Essenes, which were closely tied to Mishnah.

(e) Some of the rulings (legal) were similar to rabbinical law and even written in Mishnaic (legalistic rabbinical) style.

In the words of one of the world's greatest Dead Sea Scroll scholars, Prof. Geza Vermes: *"It is safe enough therefore to assert that the Qumran sectarians were emphatically not Sadducees".* As to the question of whether he believes they are Pharisees, he states *"the answer is no"*. Learn more about this subject and draw your own conclusions.

The Groningen Hypothesis

The Groningen hypothesis was developed by scholars at the University of Groningen in Holland. It accepts the main tenets of the Essene hypothesis but regards the Qumran sectarians as a breakaway sect from the Essenes. In other words, the Essene movement originated before the Maccabean uprising in 165 BCE, whereas the Qumran sect came afterward. The theory supports the belief that the Teacher of Righteousness was persecuted by the (Wicked) High Priest John Hyrcanus the First (134 - 104 BCE) based on 'archaeological evidence.'

According to Garcia Martinez, who proposed this hypothesis at a symposium of Spanish Biblical Scholars in Córdoba in 1986, it could be summarized by the following points:

(a) To make a clear distinction between the origins of the Essene movement and those of the Qumran group.

(b) To place the origins of the Essene movement in Palestine and specifically in the Palestinian apocalyptic tradition before the Antiochian crisis, that is at the end of the third or the beginning of the second century BCE.

(c) To place the origins of the Qumran group in a split produced within the Essene movement in consequence of which the group loyal to the Teacher of Righteousness was finally to establish itself in Qumran.

(d) To consider the designation of the 'Wicked Priest' as a collective one referring to the different Hasmonaean High Priests in chronological order.

(e) To highlight the importance of the Qumran group's formative period before its retreat to the desert and to make clear the ideological development, the halakhic elements, and the political conflicts taking place during this formative period and culminating in the break which led to the community's establishing itself in Qumran.

Jerusalem Origin Theory

Some scholars have argued that the Scrolls were the product of Jews living in Jerusalem, who hid them in the caves near Qumran while fleeing from the Romans during the destruction of Jerusalem in 70 CE. Karl Heinrich Rengstorf first proposed that the Dead Sea Scrolls originated at the library of the Jewish Temple in Jerusalem. Later, Norman Golb suggested that the Scrolls were the product of multiple libraries in Jerusalem, and not necessarily the Jerusalem Temple library. Proponents of the Jerusalem Origin theory point to the diversity of thought and handwriting among the Scrolls as evidence against a Qumran origin of the scrolls.

Chapter 8: The Language and Writings of the Time

Insight

"Prior to the discovery of the Dead Sea Scrolls, there were (only) few examples of text from the region of ancient Israel, much less dated ones."

Before the discovery of the Dead Sea Scrolls, it was a belief that Hebrew, both as a written and spoken language, had essentially ceased following the destruction of the First Temple. Other than the known 'Writings' and 'Prophets' of the so-called 'Old Testament' (Hebrew Bible), in addition to the 'Five Books of Moses' or Torah, it was thought that the only usage for Hebrew was to record these books.

With the discovery of the collection of the Dead Sea Scrolls, dated to have been written over the period between 325 BCE until 68 CE, it was noted that apart from the biblical books, five out of every six of the Dead Sea Scrolls are written in Hebrew. The balance are in Aramaic with a minority in Greek. Hebrew was revived by the Maccabees for nationalistic reasons, and became a joint language of the people together with Aramaic. The language ratio in the scrolls is close to 80% Hebrew, 19% Aramaic, and 1% Greek. This is based on the probability of 900 - 1,000 scrolls (complete) or manuscripts found. Some scrolls were written in a more ancient Hebrew-Paleo script, originating back to the time of King David and earlier. This script further originated and was derived from the Canaanites. The Samaritan Bible is written in Paleo-Hebrew.

Aramaic was the more common spoken language because of the Babylonian captivity. After the return from exile to Israel, it continued to be the language of the people.

It was also known and spoken at times by Jesus. Jesus' 'last' words on the cross are often recorded in the Aramaic form viz. "Eli, Eli, lamah *sabachtani*". There are many Aramaic words that are the same as the Hebrew. Thus *Eli* (My God) and *lamah* (why) are the same in Aramaic as in Hebrew, but *sabachtani* is the Aramaic for 'have you left/deserted me'. In Hebrew, it is written as '*azavtah oti*'.

Today, Aramaic is still a spoken language in some areas of Syria, Turkey, Iraq, and Iran. Ancient Aramaic is known to have dated back as far as 900 - 700 BCE. An Official or Imperial Aramaic was spoken around 500 BCE by the Persian Empire (who conquered Babylon and released the captive Jews). The Book of Daniel was first written in this language.

Even as 'late' as 300 - 400 CE, rabbinic comments in the Aramaic language were recorded in the Talmud and read and studied in its original language to this day. Some prayers used today in Judaism that are written in Aramaic include the well-known *'Kol Nidrei'* of the Atonement Service, and the daily 'Mourner's prayer' the *'Kaddish'*.

Jesus, however, most likely spoke and taught in the Hebrew language and not in Aramaic. His Jewish disciples listened and understood Hebraically. This is further borne out by the fact that over 80% of the Dead Sea Scrolls were written in Hebrew, including the many non-biblical and sectarian texts. The conclusion was reached by scholars of the Scrolls that Hebrew was the spoken language of the masses and not Aramaic as once believed, although Aramaic was spoken as well, and with Greek to a lesser extent. In the book of Acts 21:40 it is stated that Paul spoke Hebrew "...*When they were quiet, Paul spoke to them in Hebrew*". It is possible that Jesus did speak Aramaic occasionally. The fact that the Gospel of Mark contains a few Aramaic words has been responsible for misleading scholars to believe that Aramaic was the language mostly spoken and understood by the people.

Following the return of many of the Jews from Babylon after their capture 70 years previously, Hebrew ceased to be the spoken language and was replaced by Aramaic.

Paleo - Hebrew Script

Aramaic, a Semitic language, was originally spoken by the ancient Middle Eastern people known as Aramaeans. It was most closely related to Hebrew, Syriac, and Phoenician and was written in a script derived from the Phoenician alphabet.

In the Book of Deuteronomy, Abraham and his entire patriarchal family were referred to as 'wandering Arameans'.

When the Israelites arrived in the land of Canaan, they spoke a language which was similar to the Canaanites. The ancient Hebrew script, which was later replaced by the square form Aramaic script, was known as *Paleo-Hebrew* or *Canaanite* script and appears in some of the biblical scrolls. It was an offshoot of the Phoenician script.

This Paleo script was standard in the time of Kings David and Solomon, and down to the time of Jeremiah circa 580 BCE. Interestingly, the Pharisees initially forbade writing in this script. Thus the Sadducees, or those who were associated with the Essenes, may have written those Hebrew texts found at Qumran.

The paleo-Hebrew script used is similar to the script still preserved today by the Samaritans in the Samaritan Pentateuch, which itself is thought to be a direct descendant of the paleo-Hebrew alphabet (known in other circles as the Phoenician alphabet). During the Persian period BCE 559 - BCE 331), Jews used both the Aramaic and Hebrew languages and wrote in both scripts, likely the paleo-Hebrew script for biblical texts and Hebrew for administration and trade.

Fourteen biblical manuscripts fragments were found to be written in Paleo-Hebrew, including a Leviticus scroll fragment coded 11QpaleoLev. They represented all five books of the Torah. *Some* could have been brought from outside to Qumran, as Paleo script predated the Essenes by over 100 years. It still appeared however on Jewish coins during the second revolt against Rome as late as 130 CE.

In the Dead Sea Scrolls, Paleo-Hebrew is found in copies of Genesis to Deuteronomy and in the book of Job - possibly the reason being that they were regarded as the oldest books of the bible.

About fourteen different copies of Biblical texts were written in this ancient script. A version of this script is still used today by the Samaritans. In addition, some of these scrolls were written in three different *Cryptic* scripts - the oldest known form of written Hebrew. These date back as far as 1,000 BCE. In total, about 15 scrolls were written in this format.

One of the world's foremost scholars of paleography (study of ancient scripts), is Frank Moore Cross. He too is a Dead Sea Scrolls scholar. His classification of the Dead Sea Scrolls script largely follows the period in which they were used. His classification is as follows:

Archaic: 250 - 150 BCE

Hasmonaean: 150 - 50 BCE

Herodian: 50 BCE - 70 CE

The layout and technique of writing differed from today's conventional form - Instead of writing on the top of horizontal lines as done with most languages, the letters were suspended from lines drawn *above* the words, like washing hanging on a line. These lines were ruled by indentations along the animal skins called parchment. A few scrolls were also written on papyrus. The ink was carbon-based. There was no punctuation and very little paragraph indentation. In some scrolls, there was no separation between the words and often they followed a continuous stream. This is the format in which the original Torah is believed to have been received and recorded and was rather like a tickertape.

Today Aramaic still appears in the Yemenite Tanach in the books of Ezra and Daniel.

Hebrew

Hebrew was a spoken and literary language until the fall of Jerusalem in 587 BCE. It is quite likely that during the First Temple period [1006-587 BCE] there would have been significant differences between the spoken and the written language, although this is hardly something about which we can be exact. What we know as Biblical Hebrew is without doubt basically a literary language, which until the Babylonian exile [following the fall of Jerusalem] existed alongside living, spoken, dialects. (History of the Hebrew Language. A. Saenz-Badillos)

It is now recognized that Hebrew was the principal literary language for this period. The Scrolls also indicate that Hebrew was used for speech. In fact, in the late Second Temple period, the Scrolls established that Jews used various dialects of Hebrew and Aramaic - the spoken languages of the time. Hebrew as a spoken language was declining, but in their writings, a more biblical-like Hebrew style was used. The Scrolls that were written in Aramaic mostly preceded the sect. At this early stage, I need to mention that the Scrolls were not exclusive to the region in which they were found, as they were also composed of writings from other parts of the country, and so do not reflect the Dead Sea sect or Essenes exclusively, in thought and religious writings.

It is believed that most of the Scrolls written in Aramaic and brought into the region were not composed by the Essenes. This is in addition to the Hebrew scrolls script not being regarded as being written or composed by the Essenes. These Aramaic texts would already have been in circulation and were used as additional study material by them. The scroll 'Genesis Apocryphon', the Books of Enoch, and others were written in Aramaic.

The script whether in Hebrew or Aramaic now referred to as the *'Jewish script'*, which was the square Aramaic script used today and for over the past two thousand years, was brought back by the Jews following their return from their exile in

Babylon. It is also known as the 'Assyrian script'. The Talmud claims that this script was introduced by Ezra 'the scribe'. This script was primarily used for Aramaic writing and later used for Hebrew writing, particularly at the time of the Scrolls, but was scripted in various styles or forms.

"*Hebrew was the language of instruction in schools, as well as the language of prayer and Torah reading. It is probable that religiously uneducated people, who did not understand Hebrew, were conversant only in Aramaic. Although the Jewish inhabitants of the land of Israel in the time of Jesus knew Aramaic, Hebrew was their first or native language. It is especially clear that in enlightened circles such as those of Jesus and his disciples, Hebrew was the dominant spoken language.*" (Shemuel Safrai, Professor Emeritus of Jewish History, Hebrew University, Israel)

It is probable that Jesus knew the three common languages of the cultures around him during his life on Earth: Aramaic, Hebrew, and Greek. From this knowledge, it is likely that Jesus spoke in whichever of the three languages was most suitable to the people he was communicating with.

Following the return of many of the Jews from Babylon after their capture 70 years previously, Hebrew ceased to be the spoken language and was replaced by Aramaic.

Nehemiah was put in charge of rebuilding the surrounding wall of Jerusalem after its destruction and the return of the Jews from captivity in Babylon. During his time (circa 480 BCE) most Israelites as recorded in the Bible, (Nehemiah 8:8) could no longer comprehend or read Hebrew. "*They read from the scroll of the teaching of God* (Torah)*, translating it and giving the sense; so they understood the reading.*" Hence translations were necessary.

The original Hebrew Tanach was translated into the Aramaic language of the time. There no longer exist copies of these early translations, which were of an earlier dialect of the Aramaic language than that recorded by Onkelos. Today

Aramaic still appears in the Yemenite Tanach in the books of Ezra and Daniel.

The Tetragrammaton

In the Torah or Hebrew Pentateuch (Five books) Bible, God's name is written using different words: *El, El-Shadai, Adonai,* and Elohim. They all have special meanings and associations with the text. Christians also use the term 'Jehovah.' This word originates from the four Hebrew letters yud, hey, vav, hey making up the divine name that is specially assigned to God. They are all consonants, YHWH or JHVH, and are not pronounced with vowels. It is God's holy name and is pronounced *'Adonai'* when praying. When using His name in everyday speech *'Hashem',* is used - literally meaning 'the Name'. Only on the Day of Atonement, called *Yom Kippur*, did the High Priest, on entering the Holy of Holies of the Temple, use the *unutterable name* (or *Shem HaMeforash* in Hebrew) of God in true pronunciation of the Tetragrammaton. Jews ceased to verbalize the word aloud from about the third century BCE, but today this ruling is not upheld. In certain prayer books, the English translation for Adonai (God) is recorded as *'Hashem,'* Hebrew for 'the Name'. In some of the Scrolls, including the Great Isaiah scroll, the name for God is written in the Paleo-Hebrew style, whilst the text is in the 'Hebrew-Aramaic' script. In some of the Scrolls, four

consecutive dots **. . . .** were used, known as the *'tetrapunkta.'* The nearest English script format would be to spell G-d like this.

The Qumranites (those Essenes livening exclusively at Qumran) knew how to pronounce God's ineffable name, as some were ex -Temple High Priests familiar with the pronunciation. In the 'Rule of the Community' (1QS) scroll, punishment resulted for using God's holy name.

Classification of the Contents of the Scrolls

In all, there are about 930 individual now identifiable individual scrolls or scroll texts/manuscripts. They were mainly incomplete with over 100,000 pieces or fragments having to be identified, classified, and matched.

By 2002, the task was regarded as having been completed. A few of the scrolls were found almost intact, others were in small sections of the original, down to varying fragment sizes on which only a letter or part of a letter was identifiable. Some fragments appeared to be blank.

The Scrolls were written on parchment derived from kosher animals viz., goats, ibex, sheep, and calves. Some were also written on papyrus, although this was forbidden for the recording of biblical texts because it was not as stable. A simple carbon-based ink was used, with a few scrolls written in red ink.

To assist with piecing together the letters and part or completed words, a concordance was composed, photographed, and classified for the ongoing tedious detective work in matching them up. Further on, I will go into some detail about this concordance with its consequences.

Composition of the Biblical Scrolls

They were made up of about 230 scrolls and form about a quarter of the collection. The number 230 represented individual books of the bible. When collated this number approximated 10 complete copies of the bible in total. This number encompasses both those scrolls brought to Qumran and those written on-site over a period of about 150 to 200 years.

Outside Qumran, it is believed that rather than a complete scroll connecting the 5 books of the Torah and the balance of the books encompassing the *Nach*, only single copies of the books were kept at the Temple.

The table below indicates the number of fragments of books

Book	Number of Scrolls	Book	Number of Scrolls
Genesis	15	Latter prophets	10
Exodus	18	Psalms	39
Leviticus	17	Proverbs	2
Deuteronomy	31	Song of Songs	4
Joshua	2	Ruth	4
Samuel 1-2	4	Lamentations	4
Kings 1-2	3	Ecclesiastes	3
Isaiah	21	Daniel	8
Jeremiah	8	Ezra/Nehemiah	1
Ezekiel	7	Chronicles 1-2	1
Samuel 1-2	4	Judges	3

found and identified in part or more complete versions of the Hebrew Bible (Tanach).

Professor Emanuel Tov of the Hebrew University of Jerusalem calculated that had all these biblical fragments been collated to complete sections of the Hebrew Bible, they would have amounted to ten compete Hebrew bibles - not that many, considering the Essenes were at Qumran for about 150 years in total.

From the above list, we are now led into the serious business of beginning to establish, speculate and postulate what Second Temple Judaism used and regarded as the holy texts at that time, and what is now the Tanach or Hebrew Bible. The following pages will cover one of the most important revelations from the studies of the Qumran texts.

Chapter 9: Variations of the Biblical Texts

As more scroll fragments were pieced together and additional books identified, it was found that there were some variations in a number of scroll fragments pertaining to each biblical book.

Only one small fragment was found from Nehemiah, and the books of Ezra and Nehemiah are often regarded as one. The Book of Daniel's scroll fragments have been dated to only a *few decades* later than when it was believed to have been originally composed. This surprising date was clarified because of the translating of another scroll known as the *Daniel Pesher.*

The number of scrolls per book could indicate the emphasis placed on them. However, and this is where the aspect of controversy enters - how many were brought from outside the precincts of Qumran and how many were part of the Dead Sea sect's own library?

The fact that the book of Esther, or identifiable fragments pertaining to it, has not yet been found, does not imply that it wasn't used or recognized by the Jewish people or the Dead Sea sect. What was found are referred to as *Proto-Esther* works written in Aramaic, which used similar expressions and themes as in the book of Esther.

Several theories abound to try and explain an intentional absence in the Book of Esther - the omission of God or direct inference to Him in the story, and the fact that she lived with a gentile (non-Jewish) Persian king, which was regarded as sinful, even to the extent of perhaps prostituting herself for a cause.

Proto-Masoretic works were commonly found amongst Essene writings. The prefix 'proto' denotes that a work is *closely related* to the 'original' or *Masoretic* text. To some, proto means 'precursor'.

This could imply that some works of the Hebrew bible were in various stages of development. This classification or designation is covered in greater detail under the next heading.

These works were widely used by the people during the Hasmonaean (including the Essene) period. It is believed that the movement towards the complete establishment of the Masoretic biblical version had already taken place by the beginning of the second century CE. In addition to these different versions, other 'holy' writings were used by the devout that are *not* included in the Hebrew canon today. These include the books of the Apocrypha which are covered further on.

The umbrella term used to describe the collection of Jewish non-canonical (see the following heading) religious books is *Pseudepigrapha*. About 600 scroll manuscripts contained such previously unknown works. They covered Psalms, commentaries on the bible and Apocryphal works, and scrolls associated with the Jewish sect(s). Many of them carried a messianic and 'end of days' theme. They were influential in both Judaism and early Christianity and differ from Jewish prayer recited today and those from over the past 2000 years since the destruction of the second Temple.

The scrolls now fill in the gap previously left to speculation of the development of Jewish thought, prayer, and observance. The Jewish revolt that began 66 CE provided further impetus to preserve and protect their heritage.

There is the view that many of the Dead Sea Scrolls found were part of the library of the Jerusalem Temple, hidden for safekeeping. If this is correct, then the Scrolls *are* representative of *mainstream* Jewish thought *at that time*. The content of the Scrolls is therefore beyond the word 'interesting,' as they give us first-hand insight and confirmation into the development and origin of the development into Rabbinic Judaism. Further on in this book, I will detail the significance of the Scrolls in Christianity as well, which I consider being one of the most 'profound' sections of this book!

Biblical Literature, then and now

The divisions, order, sections, and contents of both the Hebrew and Christian bibles are referred to as the *biblical canon.* If we speak of the Hebrew canon, we refer to the accepted, the exclusive, the recognized, the holy (of Divine origin and or inspiration) content, forming the Bible that has not changed by even a word. The *Torah* or 'Five Books of Moses' is also known as the Pentateuch. The books of the Prophets and the Writings, including Psalms, the Book of Chronicles, Proverbs, Kings, Jonah, and so on, make up the balance of the Hebrew Bible. This balance is called the *Nach* in Hebrew. The combined collection of the Hebrew Bible is called by the acronym *Tanach* with the *'T' for* Torah preceding the *nach*. The impression when putting all the Scrolls together is that the biblical canon differed or was much more flexible during that era compared to its final Masoretic version. I much prefer the term 'Hebrew Bible' to 'Old' Testament, when the need arises to differentiate the bibles.

The Masoretic Text

We now come to another and very important aspect, namely the so-called *traditional* or exclusively accepted version of the Hebrew Bible.

Before the destruction of the Temple in 70 CE, many variant biblical texts were used in Judaism. Following the destruction, only the *Masoretic* texts had full exclusive priority. One of the criteria for the Holy Hebrew bible is the forbidding of any word, spelling, or sentence to be changed; it must remain the same from the time of its original and divine composition or dictation. This in particular refers to the Torah. The Koran has a similar foundation. In terms of the Hebrew Bible, this is referred to as the *Masoretic* or *received* Hebrew text - the *directly* transmitted text. "*Before the Dead Sea Scrolls were found, scholars were not aware that the Masoretic text existed in the same form already in the last centuries BCE*." (E. Tov).

In contrast, the New Testament has had many differing editions, recognized to have incorporated thousands of variant translations and or structural sentence changes. You will read in this book of more changes to be instituted soon.

The concept of preserving and ensuring that Jewish scriptural text remained in its original format is thought to have originated in Babylon, during the forced Jewish exile period that lasted for 60 to 70 years. Rabbinic literature also mentions men known as 'correctors' who were employed at the Temple to safeguard the precise copying of holy texts. In some of the Dead Sea Scrolls scribal dots appeared above or under letters, indicating a word or letter had been deleted by scribes where a correction had taken place. This could have been due to an alternative word having been substituted or a spelling correction.

What later became particularly attributed to the *Karaites* was their ability to establish a formal Hebrew grammar, and subsequently the final and absolute Masoretic text encompassing spelling, pronunciation, and structure/layout of the Hebrew Bible around 850 CE. Those Karaites scholars who particularly became involved in the preservation of the correct biblical text and all it encompassed were known as *Masoretes*. Other sages are who also referred to as Masoretes, originated particularly from a suburb in Tiberius and are known as Tiberian Masoretes. They lived in the first half of the 10th century and competed for their interpretations. There were also Masoretes outside of Eretz-Israel, in Babylonia. Differences between the East and Eretz-Israel also existed.

Hebrew writing is structured so that the *consonants* form the word. For it to be accurately pronounced and understood, vowel symbols forming the sounds are placed under the letters. An English example of this could be with the words lid, lad, and led. Usually, the consonant meaning is reasonably obvious, but specifically in Hebrew, the difference could be significant to its interpretation. The Masoretic text ensured the correct meaning of the words as well. The Torah as written on the parchment scroll is recorded without vowels, as are all Hebrew printed works today. Most words are thus read by 'recognition'. With the Torah however, the correct recognition of the word is critical.

This form of writing in Hebrew, particularly biblical scripture, is thought to have dated back to the time of the origin of the 'original' or earlier version. A different dimension has thus opened with the discovery of the Scrolls, and what was additionally known before that.

For in the Scrolls, we come across *many versions* of the (so-called) Masoretic text, which were accepted and used over hundreds of years during the Second Temple era. I need to add that it is believed that the Essenes seemed to have used greater variations from the Masoretic text than the Jewish community at large. All these proto works pertain essentially to the *Nach* or 'Writings' and 'Prophets'. It is also believed that an original Masoretic Torah was used at the Temple.

To further enrich or complicate opinion about proto-Masoretic texts, recent opinion collapses this concept by stating that instead of regarding some texts as being *proto*, they are in fact *original,* as they were used and regarded as the 'original' texts of the time. The universal concept of original becomes debatable and rather shows the existence of different groups of Jews practicing variations in their Judaism and having their own different biblical texts!

Was the structure of these biblical books the same as the Masoretic Hebrew Torah? In other words, was the Torah *exactly* the same then as now? The answer is a significant '*yes.*' Among the biblical fragments were those with no variation - Exceptions being some differences in spelling and synonyms compared to the Masoretic text. According to an analysis by the doyen of the Hebrew University of Jerusalem, Emanuel Tov, 46 out of 52 eligible Torah texts were suitable for analysis. The outcome was that 52% followed the Masoretic writings. About 5% of the biblical scrolls follow the Septuagint version; another 5% match the Samaritan text; 20% belong to tradition unique to the Dead Sea Scrolls and the balance is 'nonaligned.'

The Torah and other books of the Hebrew Bible today are said to be the same as those recorded almost 3,500 years ago. The (essentially) Orthodox Jewish belief is that the Torah was divinely dictated to Moses from Mount Sinai or, as some believe, was divinely dictated to leaders of the congregation of Israel 3,300 years ago. Thus 'the first edition' was about one thousand years earlier than the oldest Dead Sea Scrolls! It has been noticed that in all sites beyond Qumran, where copies of the bible were found, many conformed to the established recognized Masoretic text. It needs to be mentioned that in addition, there were *many* textual differences to the accepted Masoretic version as well. the significant 'yes' pertains to the Torah manuscripts that *did* conform.

However, in several scrolls, there were occasional variances in phrases or words. Some of the Scrolls contained additional sentences or parts of sentences, in others, there were omissions or even shortened versions of biblical passages. This pertained not only to the Books of the Prophets but also to the *Tanach*, the Hebrew Bible.

The probability exists that some of the 'Writings' of the Hebrew Bible recorded in a number of scrolls could have been either Masoretic, or 'original' in the common context of the word, or *variant* versions used during that era. This is contrary to what is regarded as the Masoretic Hebrew Bible of today and over the past 2,500 years. It was only after the destruction of the Temple in 70 CE that the rabbis *formally* closed any further considerations of what is regarded as Masoretic, including being part of the Hebrew Biblical canon. You will read further on that prior to the destruction of the Second Temple, the canon of the Tanach was essentially established. In the development of the Christian Bible, the so-called 'New Testament', there are 200,000 to 400,000 variants. This is far more than there are actual words in the NT (Charlesworth).

Two Isaiah scrolls were found in Cave 1. The longest and closest to the Masoretic is called 'A' and the shorter version is 'B'. Here again, we have two versions of Isaiah used and *not* simply an abridged version. The 'Book of Jeremiah' was also found to have two versions.

The question thus "which one do we leave out?" could be regarded as the *wrong* question. The 28 ft. (13 meters) Great Isaiah Scroll (A) found in Cave 1 was *virtually* identical to the Masoretic version. Differences are mainly in spelling and a few 'minor stylistic' changes. When comparing it to the Septuagint (which I will be covering), there is an even closer relationship to it than the known Masoretic text. Interestingly, in the Angelic praise to God 'Holy, Holy, Holy' stated in Isaiah 6:3, the word 'Holy' is repeated only twice as opposed to three times according to the Masoretic (traditional) text. Jewish readers, who are very familiar with repeating 'Holy' three times during the repetition of the *Amidah* (18 Benedictions) prayer, would appreciate how strange it would be to repeat it only twice! One can clearly see that the Tetragrammaton is (exclusively) written in Paleo-Hebrew. Other Isaiah scroll fragments were found, also showing several textual differences.

The Qumran biblical texts give us an idea of not only which books were considered authoritative, but also indicate no standardization of the Hebrew Bible in terms of written content and the canon itself. This again was one of the significant revelations to come out of the discovery of the Dead Sea Scrolls. The Biblical Scrolls found at Qumran resulted in the field of 'Textual Criticism' becoming a major subject. This is with the purpose of trying to establish the meaning of the original text. The question 'has our bible been copied accurately?' presupposes there was one original text from which all others were copied.

The Aleppo Codex

In the ninth and tenth centuries, a Karaite father and son, Moses and Aaron Ben Asher, who were biblical scholars living in Palestine, formulated the *official Hebrew established text* of the bible to ensure that no other versions were used. No other wording, spell, and importantly, and no mispronunciation of words could take place, which could occur if incorrect vowels were substituted, so leading to misinterpretation. A book or text, which has *any* deviation from the Masoretic version is not regarded as holy and is therefore not used. Masoretic also designated what was included and the order of the books of the Hebrew Bible, including the Psalms. This is known as the biblical canon. The Masoretic canon is believed to have become authoritative and finalized around 100 CE. The Karaites were considered experts in the fields of the rules of vocalization allying to biblical texts and they initiated the study of Hebrew grammar. Their texts were unanimously accepted throughout the world. The origin of the name Karaite originates from the Hebrew *'kara'* 'to read.'

Moses Ben-Asher developed and added vowels for correct vocalization to the most accurately written copy ever of the entire Hebrew Bible or *Tanach* (by the scribe Ben Boya'a). He also arranged the final and exclusive structure of the columns and verses as they appear in the Torah and the balance of the biblical books.

His son Aaron developed a series of musical cantilations or chants (trop) to emphasize reverence to the words when sung in the synagogue. This work later became known as the Aleppo Codex and is the official template for the Tanach.

A codex preceded today's books and was written on both sides of the page and bound together, unlike a scroll of the Hebrew Bible. To relate part of its history - In 1099 it was seized and ransomed by the Crusaders in Tiberius and ended up in the Fostat Synagogue of Cairo where it was stored. In

1375, it was taken to the town of Aleppo in Damascus, Syria, and stored for a further 600 years in the Aleppo Synagogue.

When the state of Israel was declared in 1948, a Syrian mob broke into the synagogue and ravaged the contents, partly destroying the codex, the remains of which were found scattered on the floor.

About one-third of the codex remained amongst the scattered pages on the floor of the destroyed synagogue after being damaged during the Arab riots in 1947. That one-third was smuggled into Israel via Turkey in a washing machine and received by former President Ben Tzvi of Israel. This codex, part of which is on display in the 'Shrine of the Book' of the Israel Museum in Jerusalem, has achieved a position of pre-eminence among Jewish manuscripts. It is widely considered to be *the* authoritative source document for the Hebrew text and punctuation of the Hebrew Bible. The whereabouts of the rest of the codex is a great mystery. Possibly they remain in the hands of the Syrian-American Jewish community. It was given the title *'Keter'* meaning crown, by none other than Maimonides, one of the greatest Jewish sages who lived in the 11th century and who *personally* consulted it for many of his writings.

Its stature was further elevated when it became known as the *'Keter haGadol'*, the *Great* Crown. Fortunately, a full exclusive copy was made from this codex two generations later in Cairo and is now stored in the Russian National Library. It is known as the Leningrad Codex.

Targum

The word Targum is taken from Hebrew, meaning 'interpretation' or translation. Its more currently used format is *exegesis* or exposition of Scripture, which means instructing one in the correct interpretation. In Hebrew, this is known as *peshat*. Targum was often applied in scroll literature by the re-writing of biblical stories and events to reinterpret or retell, for their meaning to be more clearly understood. Some of the scroll texts were changed from their original biblical narrative to provide a 'better' understanding or interpretation to a particular scribe. The related (*apocryphon*) works will be covered as we progress through this section.

Amongst the texts found at Qumran, several were classified as Targums. There were many types of interpretations from original biblical texts. Either they were completely translated into the popular language at the time or subjected to translation in an *interpretative* manner.

Most commonly they were translated into Aramaic...the vernacular of the time, and Greek, on account of the Hellenistic influence. In prayer services, a translation could only be verbalized orally and was not allowed to be directly read from such a scroll in the synagogue. This ruling could have arisen to make a distinction between a truly sacred Hebrew text and that written in Aramaic or Greek. The writing of Aramaic translation was not however forbidden. They were written for the purpose of study. Onkelos' translation of Torah into Aramaic is used to this day in Judaism for the specific purpose of gaining further clarity of the Hebrew wordings.

The Septuagint

The best known and widely used Targum even to this day is the Septuagint - also referred to in Roman numerals for the number seventy, as LXX. It is *traditionally* regarded as the Hebrew Bible translated into Greek. This translation is believed to have taken place 250 BCE. The words *tradition* or even *legend* needs to be brought in, as to the history behind its origin. Two sources account for this, namely historical tradition, and the Talmud, which records and criticizes the Septuagint in Megillah 9a.

It is the oldest Greek version of the Hebrew bible. Belief is that during the reign of the Ptolemy II Philadelphus of Egypt, (see the first chapter with reference to the Ptolemys), he requested the bible be translated into Greek. This was to be used particularly by those Jews living in the great city of Alexander in Egypt, whose only language was Greek. Additionally, he wanted to store a copy in the Great Library of Alexander.

For this task, Ptolemy contacted the High Priest in Jerusalem and requested that six Hebrew scholars from each of the twelve tribes be sent to Egypt to translate the Hebrew bible i.e., Torah, Prophets, and Writings. Tradition has it that each of the seventy-two scholars was kept in a separate cell, and miraculously translated the bible using the identical wording.

Furthermore, the works were said to have been completed in seventy-two days. This was regarded as an inspiration from God! It was said that the Septuagint, therefore, had the same holiness as the Hebrew bible. It became known as the Septuagint (70) even though there were said to have been seventy-two scholars.

For the Jews within Egypt, the Septuagint played a very important role in uniting them in their religious heritage. It also contained apocryphal writings and thus had a *wider canon* than the one used by the Palestinian Jews. It opened the Gentile (non-Jewish) world to the teachings of the Torah and became the bible of the Hellenistic Jews of Palestine, and the first bible of the Christian Church.

It is important to know that the Septuagint was not simply a literal translation of the Hebrew text, but a work on its own, and to appreciate that it *preceded* what later became the 'official' Masoretic text of the *Tanach*. It did not follow the 'authoritative' Hebrew texts exclusively. This specifically applies more to the Writings and especially the Prophets i.e., the *nach* part of the Hebrew Bible. To many biblical scholars, it represents more than a translation, as some of the so-called translations preceded the Hebrew biblical text that we read today.

All the books of the Apocrypha were also included as part of the canon. Additionally, the books of Esther and Daniel were included as supplements as well as an abridged Jeremiah text. The order of the canon also differed, and this is noted in the Talmud. Changes were later made to the text of the original Septuagint.

Psalm 145 is written acrostically. It is missing the line for the letter *nun* (N). In the Dead Sea Scrolls, and in the Septuagint translation, that line does appear. It is missing from the Masoretic text.

No complete copy of the original LXX exists. Amongst the Dead Sea Scrolls, only a few fragments from the Septuagint were found, recorded in the older Greek language. However, some of the Hebrew Dead Sea Scroll texts were more comparable to the Septuagint than the traditional works.

Only in Cave 7 were Greek texts found. This could endorse the belief that the caves in the Dead Sea region were used as a *depository* by outsiders in addition to the Scrolls attributed to the Essenes. It is doubted that the Essenes themselves used the Septuagint. The Jewish people stopped using it after the destruction of the Second Temple in 70 CE. It is however still used by the Greek-Eastern Orthodox Church today. The Septuagint is also used to convey clarity to some Hebrew words of the Torah and is even quoted in some Hebrew bibles, including the *Hertz Chumash*. In its entirety it was completed over a 200-year period.

Most of the original Christian Bible was written in the local Greek language of the time became integrated into the Septuagint. Although the Septuagint is generally regarded as a literal translation of the Hebrew Bible, in many passages the translators used terms from Hellenistic Greek that made it more accessible to Greek readers. This also resulted in subtle changes of words from the Hebrew Bible which were then used to verify the coming of the Christian messiah and the verification of all that Christianity set out to accomplish and validate.

An example of differences between the Hebrew text and the Septuagint appears in Isaiah 7:14, where in the Dead Sea Scrolls and subsequent later Masoretic texts the words *"Behold the young woman* (Heb. *Alma*) *will become pregnant and bear a son, and you will name him Immanuel"*, a divinely inspired name. Yet in the Septuagint in place of the term *'young woman'*, the words were replaced by *'virgin'.*

Christianity uses (mis)quotes from the book of Isaiah to endorse the coming of Jesus and the fulfillment of the prophecy, particularly as in this example.

According to Josephus in the preface to his work Antiquities of the Jews 1 - 4 he writes that "*only the Law (Torah) was given to translate into Greek by those who were sent to Alexandria*". Hence the balances of the books of the Hebrew bible were *freely* translated to achieve whatever interpretation or understanding.

I used several 'versions' of the Christian Bible/New Testament for research. In the 'informative' section towards the end of the 'Good News Bible Today's English Version', a heading caught my attention:

"New Testament Passages Quoted or Paraphrased from the Septuagint".

Here I read of a similar usage of the Septuagint in providing greater clarity to this version:

"The writers of the New Testament generally quoted or paraphrased the ancient Greek translation of the Old Testament, commonly known as the Septuagint Version (LXX), made some two hundred years before the time of Christ. In a number of instances, this version differs significantly in meaning from the Masoretic Hebrew text."

Pseudepigrapha

"*The Second Temple literature is often quite different from that portrayed by the rabbis and could thus have wide-ranging implications for understanding the literary heritage of Judaism or Judaisms*" (J. Neusner). There were many variations of the books of the Prophets of the bible found at Qumran, and this showed that Jews *used* these variations. Some books were shorter versions, for example, an abridged text of the book of Jeremiah. The order of chapters differed in some books, with others having supplements. Such works are classified with the addition of the prefix *pseudo*, as with *pseudo*-Daniel. It is a book, or rather part of a book of Daniel that is not the same as the Masoretic Book of Daniel found in the Hebrew Bible. Another work, the 'Song of Songs' as recorded in the Scrolls, omitted almost a third of the Masoretic version, which included wording that could possibly be regarded as erotic or sensual in its figurative description of the love that God has for Israel. Some scholarship now is beginning to deny the usage of this prefix, for their reason being that these were different versions which were used at different times!

In addition, there is an umbrella term to describe other 'important theological works' used by the Jews of the time. They are known as *Pseudepigrapha* - a collection of Jewish non-canonical religious books written during Hellenistic times. They included previously unknown works and covered Psalms, Commentaries, and Apocryphal works, with many having a messianic and *apocalyptic End of Days* theme to them.

They were filled with piety and were very different from Jewish prayer as recognized today. It is considered that the Pseudepigrapha could have provided an alternative to Pharisaism and illustrated a form of Judaism from which Christianity arose. This was proposed by renowned scrolls scholar, R. H. Charles and might be appreciated further on in the book when the possible connection between Essenism and Christianity is discussed. The writings differed from the Apocrypha, in that their contents encompassed well-known biblical persons including Enoch, Abraham, Moses, occupying a central role in the text.

Textual Differences

The book of Samuel from the Dead Sea Scrolls collection differs from the one used today. The version in *current* use has 'scribal lapses', meaning that some sections of recorded events are missing, and sometimes do not follow logically. One of the missing parts was found in the corresponding scrolls. There is now recognized to be a complete opening text to the first book of Samuel chapter 11. The missing words found in the fragment from that book, now provide a *clearer understanding* of the events that occurred when Saul (before he became king) responded to a threat from the enemy of Israel, Nachash, king of the Ammonites. The New Revised Standard Version of the Christian Bible was the first translation to incorporate this paragraph which in fact should have been the first verse of Chapter 11.

"Now Nachash, king of the Ammonites, had been grievously oppressing the Gadites and the Reubenites. He would gauge out the right eye of each of them and would not grant Israel a deliverer. No one was left of the Israelites across the Jordan whose right eye Nachash, king of the Ammonites, had not gauged out. But there were seven thousand men who had escaped from the Ammonites and entered Jabsh-gilead."

Psalm 145 was also discovered to have a 'missing verse' between verses 13 and 14, when comparing the Masoretic psalm to the same psalm in the Scrolls. Several Christian bibles have already made this correction to their latest editions.

The notion of an 'original' text was unknown to the people of this era. Each scribal copy constituted a distinct version of the text. This was probably due to composition-by-stages, as some of the scribes intentionally incorporated new material to help interpret their relevance to the text they were copying. Words could have been inadvertently omitted during transmission. This is also referred to as *textual corruption,* which may have occurred when the scribe copied from a damaged copy. Possibly some words were illegible and replaced by words thought to be the correct ones. A deliberate departure from the original by the copyist could also have occurred.

All these versions were seen as standard to that literary work. Some of these textual differences are believed to differ according to the countries in which they were copied - these being Babylon, Egypt, and Palestine. Another theory is that those who had in their possession their own accepted versions, including rabbis in the early centuries of the first millennium, influenced the Masoretic versions as more coping was undertaken. Even some minor differences have been found in the Talmud due to copying and re-editing. This took place as late as medieval times. (C Hezer. The Oxford Handbook of Jewish Studies 2002, pages 115-120)

Renowned Professor James H Charlesworth (Princeton) at a Biblical Archaeology Seminar at St. Olaf College in one of his lectures titled "Has our Bible been copied accurately?" "*This,*" he said, "*presupposes that there was, therefore, one original text,*" from which all others were copied. According to Charlesworth, there was no original or primary text. "*What we want is the least corrupt bible, i.e., the earliest version, the earliest evidence.*"

It is interesting to note that a few of the biblical manuscripts found were closer in content to the Samaritan Pentateuch than the Masoretic Bible. This is surprising as the Samaritans were regarded as having separated or estranged themselves from the Jewish people. Perhaps this further demonstrates that many, or some scrolls brought to Qumran for storage, may have been part of the library of Jerusalem and elsewhere.

It is believed they were brought to the region to be hidden for safekeeping in these caves, which could also be regarded as a Genizah. This would have been in anticipation of the possible destruction of the Jewish people by the cruel, occupying Roman force. In fact, in 70 CE this almost occurred.

Many of these scrolls could be representative of the *mainstream* of Jewish thought *at that time,* and not exclusively reflective of Essene tradition and belief. Research has now identified various Judaisms, rather than a single Judaism, at the end of the Second Temple period. The Jewish people were divided into numerous sects and parties of whom the Essenes were one of them. Each believed itself to be the true or authentic representative of the ancestral faith.

This is further demonstrated by the Judaism from Qumran, as an example of *one of* the Judaism to have been in practice. Post destruction, the Judaism is known as *Rabbinic* Judaism, is the Judaism observed to this day. It is critical that the reader comprehends this!

The Apocrypha

The name or term Apocrypha in Greek means 'hidden scriptures.' The Hebrew, literally translated, means 'the outside (*chitzoni*) or external books'.

Note: The singular of Apocrypha is Apocryphon!

They were Jewish works composed during the second and first centuries BCE, during the later Second Temple period in what is referred to as the 'Apocalyptic Period'. After the disappearance of the last prophets, and due to the times in which the people found themselves; faced with annihilation and loss of hope, there arose a need for new and inspiring literature. The books of the Apocrypha did not claim to be divine but were written to provide a revitalizing inspiration to the people. During the Hellenistic period, the Jewish people regarded these works as Holy Scripture. They were, however, eventually excluded from the Canon of the Palestinian Jews at the end of the first century CE. They were all written by Jews yet were not accepted into the canon of the Hebrew bible.

The Apocrypha did not contain apocalyptic (End of Days theme...see the intro to 'War Scroll') writings, nor were they halachic in content.

Instead, they were made up of wisdom texts, historical books such as Maccabees, and inspirational religious tales with a religious theme and prayers. The writings of the Essenes also followed some of the themes found in the Apocrypha, however, very few of these books were found at Qumran. They were most unlikely to have used the Books of the Maccabees due to their apparent fallout with the Hasmonaeans.

With the possible exceptions of the 'Odes of Solomon' and parts of 2 'Esdras', all these books were of Jewish origin and composed and written in the Greek language, except for Sirach and 1 Maccabees. These works were originally written in Hebrew or Aramaic and then translated to Greek. Prior to a fragment of Sirach being discovered at Masada under Yadin's excavations, the only record of Sirach existed in Greek. The first Hebrew copy of Sirach was found at Masada. This followed the finding of the first Hebrew version in the Cairo Geniza in 1880. This version did not however fully conform to the original Greek version in some respects. The books of the Apocrypha were an integral part of the Alexandrine Greek Septuagint, to be dealt with further on in this book.

In 382 CE, the Pope commissioned a scholar and churchman, Jerome, to make a new translation of the bible, this time into Latin. Prior to this, a Greek version was used. Jerome regarded only the books making up the Hebrew canon as authentic, and thus the additional books of the Septuagint were rejected. They included the books now called the Apocrypha. This new translation was referred to as the *Vulgate*. However, Jerome's views were not accepted, and the apocryphal books continued to be retained as part of the Vulgate. Today they form part of the Catholic bible and are known as the *Deuterocanonical books*. They are Tobit, Judith, Maccabees 1 and 2, Wisdom of Solomon, Ecclesiasticus, Sirach and Baruch. During the Reformation of the sixteenth century, they were removed from the Protestant canon. The Deuterocanonical books are read regularly in public worship in Anglican, Roman Catholic, and among the Eastern Orthodox churches. Their historical value is recognized by the Jewish and Protestant faiths even though they have been denied canonical status.

Some of the books of the Apocrypha found to be included or not, amongst the Scrolls:

Tobit	Yes
Sirach (Ecclesiasticus or the Wisdom of 'Jesus' beı Sira)	Yes
Letter of Jeremiah (Baruch)	Yes
Enoch	Yes
Jubilees	Yes
Testament of the Twelve Patriarchs	Yes
Judith	No
Maccabees 1 - 4	No
Esdras	No
Prayer of Manasseh	No
Psalm 151	Yes

Jews used the Apocryphal literature throughout Palestine during that era. To many first millennium BCE Jews, all texts were equally holy! The Book of Jubilees must have been of great importance to the Essenes since up to sixteen different copies were found in five caves. It is written as though of divine origin, and its sources are found in the 'Damascus Document,' an important Dead Sea Scroll to be covered in this book. On the other hand, the absence of books such as Judith and 1-Maccabees from the Scrolls is believed to be due to the estrangement between the Essenes and their Hasmonean contemporaries. Preservation of those works could have been seen as supporting Hasmonean propaganda.

There were different versions of scripture prior to when the official Hebrew canon was accepted, and certain books no longer were regarded as part of the canon. The general view is that during the time of the Essenes at Qumran, as early as 300 to 200 BCE, the foundations had already been laid and were generally established by the beginning of the first century.

The Hebrew canon became recognized and finally confirmed only when some of the Writings were further debated, and then finally accepted or rejected. This occurred towards the end of the century around 70 CE. The five books of the 'Pentateuch' being part of the canon were fully accepted. Canon, therefore, refers not only to the Torah but importantly to the balance of books of the Hebrew Bible. Prior to the discovery of the Scrolls, it was believed that there were three variants to the Hebrew Bible. They are being the original or Masoretic text, the Greek translation the Septuagint, and the Samara ton Bile used today used by that group. The variety of biblical scrolls found at Qumran reflected different religious groups and or sects who were the forerunners to the Masoretic text.

Tefillin and Mezuzot

Although these are not biblical works, their contents are direct extracts from the bible. Every morning, except on Sabbath and Festivals, an observant Jew binds his left arm with leather straps that are attached to a small box, inside which is a holy hand-written parchment with specific biblical passages. In a similar manner, another small box held by straps is placed on the forehead. Some special prayers are then recited. This is the fulfilment of the commandments in Deuteronomy 6:5-9 *"Bind them as a sign upon your arm and let them be tefillin* (frontlets, from the Hebrew *tefilla* meaning prayer) *between your eyes"*. These are called Tefillin.

"And write them on the doorposts of your house and upon your gates". These are the *mezuzot* (pl.), which every Jew places on the right-hand doorpost of the entrance to his house, and on all other rooms, except ablution. It contains a hand-written scroll, protected in a small tube in various designs.

About a total of 30 tefillin from various caves and eight mezuzot were found. Their written content varied from the Masoretic. Which suggests that there could have been dispute on the interpretation of the contents, and even the structure of the *tefillin,* of which there were two types. This could mean they originated from *more than one* stream of Judaism. The one set began with the words "Hear O Israel the Lord is our God, the Lord is one."(Deuteronomy *6:4)* This is the same version used today. The second version began with the 10 commandments then followed by "Hear O Israel." What was most remarkable to me when I first saw tefillin scrolls on display at the Shrine of the Book in Jerusalem was the meticulous ultra-fine print written by the scribe(s). Many people with average eyesight would need a magnifying glass to read them, let alone to write in such small lettering.

Scripture and Liturgy

Eugene Ulrich author of 'The Dead Sea Scrolls and the Origins of the Bible' writes: "*The first statement to make at Qumran is that we should probably not think of a Bible in the first century B.C.E. or the first century C.E., at Qumran or elsewhere. There were collections of sacred scripture, of course, but no Bible in our developed sense of the term.*" Ulrich explains that the term scripture implies 'holy' text, and the bible is the collection or canon of the works of scripture that made up that collection. The concept of a (Hebrew) biblical canon was not in existence at the time. There are different bibles for different religions. This is one of the most relevant statements in this book. It directs one to greater clarity of terminologies that previously had seemed similar.

Much of the scripture of the Hebrew bible viz. the Writings and Prophets was first recorded by the scribes, following the return from their Babylonian exile. The Hebrew canon began to develop and grow. These included historical works, sayings of the prophets, psalms, and proverbs. Based on the collection of biblical scroll fragments representing the various biblical books of our current bible, were circulated rather as separate books.

Then followed what could be considered as popular and 'unofficial' writings. Some were influenced by the Greek culture present at the time and later took on a strong Jewish identity during the Hasmonaean period to express their values. This is where tradition controversially separates from archaeology. <u>By this, I am referring to what is believed to be Masoretic Jewish scripture versus what the Dead Sea Scrolls revealed.</u> What you will be discovering in this book, is that the Jews used many other liturgical (a fixed form of worship) pieces. With the discovery of the Scrolls, it is now appreciated that Jewish *theology* was much more varied than previously known.

R. Davies (Univ. Sheffield) in a paper summarizes; *"Recent research in many quarters has identified various 'Judaisms' rather than a single 'Judaism' at the end of the Second Temple period and it is obviously tempting to suggest a 'Judaism of Qumran'. However, it remains far from clear that the Qumran corpus offers a systematic account of a single 'Judaism'. This is one of the very important significances that have come out of the Dead Sea Scrolls."*

How the Scrolls and Fragments are coded

After the discovery of more and more caves and the contents from each were beginning to escalate, it soon became essential to introduce a standard system of classifying and coding the fragments. This provided an important and essential method whereby pieces could be classified and identified on the basis of:

- The cave of origin.
- The identity of the scroll.
- A number, indicating the order of that manuscript relevant to others found in the same cave.

- The number of fragments being translated for the manuscript.

Examples

1QM = Found in Cave 1, At Qumran, M = Milchemah (War) Scroll.

4QS = Found in Cave 4, S = Code for scroll called Serach haYachad or 'The Rule of the Community'.

4QSa-j or 4Q255-64 Here, both codes refer to the same. The S is for Serach and the letters a-j or the numbers 255-64 indicate that in fact ten scroll fragments pertaining to the 'Rule of the Community' were found in the same cave.

These code numbers are also referred to as Corpus numbers.

You will notice when reading the scrolls [square brackets].

Example: [Then shall they gather] in the camp that n[ig]ht to rest until the morning.

The first bracket is an insert - based on the theme of the sentence and at times due to other similar sentences. These inserts need to be carefully thought out as they could make a critical difference to the meaning. An educated confirmation of the missing word(s) would be arrived at through the usage on a *concordance.* The second is usually easier. Night in Hebrew is *lailah*, as in the scroll the letter *yud* providing the *ai* sound must have been missing. Nevertheless, considering possible options, it is safe to assume that the word was meant to be *lailah.* Based on a *concordance* of words recorded from the Scrolls with their preceding and post words, this enabled reasonably accurate matches to be made.

To accurately quote from a scroll, it was accorded universally accepted numbers to sentences or themes. This enabled one to quote from designated numbered columns and further down, to actual verses. The bible is formatted in a similar manner i.e., chapter and verse. The same has been done for standardization purposes with the works of Josephus.

Chapter 10: Halachic Differences between the Essenes and the Pharisees

> ### Insight
>
> "Both schools had to determine between two halachic possibilities, and naturally chose the option that suited their general perception regarding the *adequate degree* of restriction."

Note: For the purpose of *insight,* I have linked the terms rabbis and Pharisees. The former are generally regarded as decision-makers and prime interpreters of the Law.

Under this heading, the reader will appreciate what separated the Essenes from the Jewish populous, the Pharisees, the rabbis, and the priesthood of the Temple. *Essentially, the Essenes had a far stricter approach to Halachah* (religious law) than the prevailing Pharisees. This is borne out by two scrolls in particular - the 'Temple Scroll' and the 'MMT' scroll.

From these scrolls, it is understood there was a greater emphasis on certain halachic rulings on the observation and preservation of Holiness, or the concept of the Sacred, and Purity.

Both these concepts are subject to interpretation and the *degree* to which each is recognized and upheld. Even to this day, there are certain divisions within the Jewish religious movements sometimes resulting in a bitter exchange. This today can also apply to interpretations of kashrut. What may be suitable for eating by some, may not be acceptable to others. Especially within the Sephardic and Ashkenazi groups i.e., those whose diaspora origins are from Europe, the Middle East, or North Africa.

By noting how the Essenes recorded their interpretations of Halachah, it was understood that the rabbis appeared to be *more lenient* in their interpretation. This may have resulted in the continuance of (Rabbinic) Judaism after the destruction of the Second Temple and the fading away of rigid Essenism.

It not only has given us a glimpse into these differences but also a realization that various groups of Jews and their observations of Judaism existed yet differed from each other.

This could be further borne out by the selection of the pseudepigraphal works found comprising part of the Dead Sea Scrolls collection. Many of these as mentioned earlier, came from outside the region of Qumran and thus could have been representative of certain sects of the era. It would therefore be a mistaken belief that the Essenes were the only variant of Judaism. I mentioned earlier that one of the theories as to how the Essenes originated was the core group having risen from the priestly class. Hence the reasons for these halachic differences focused on those which existed between themselves and their former counterparts in the Temple. These differences were spelled out in the 'MMT' Scroll.

Holiness

I referred to the two cardinal areas of differing interpretations viz. *Holiness* and *Purity* and I will now take this further. The innermost sanctum of the Temple where the Ark of the Covenant rested, and where God's Divine earthly Spirit was present was known as the 'Holy of Holies' - from here God's 'rays' of holiness radiated. The further away from the Temple one is, the 'level' of holiness is reduced accordingly. It is not without reason that Jerusalem is called 'The Holy City.'

The Essenes' stance on the parameters of holiness was far greater than the Pharisees in terms of the sacred space - they applied far stricter rulings to what they considered as the sacred area surrounding the Temple and declared what may or may not take place within its spatial confines.

The holiness of the Sabbath was further protected by the Essenes using the solar calendar of 364 days versus the lunar calendar used in Judaism today. They structured their calendar to avoid possible violation of the Sabbath, which could have occurred with the lunar calendar, resulting in festivals falling on the Sabbath day.

For each festival in the Torah, God declares that certain sacrifices must be performed. The Essenes believed this would violate the holiness of the Sabbath. It was their intention to ensure this would not happen, so by using the solar calendar they could make certain that festivals would always fall on a specific weekday.

Our understanding of Essene Halachah is that its holiness was very vulnerable to desecration. They strove to protect that holiness and to prevent the Divine Presence from leaving. The Pharisees and rabbis on the other hand, reduced the levels of impurity and allowed certain labors in the Temple on the Sabbath. Their apparent relative lack of attention to the danger of desecration of the holy could be explained by their having a different view as to the *very nature* of holiness.

Purity

The Essenes viewed their community as a substitute temple and believed that it would reinstate the sect in the Jerusalem Temple according to their interpretation of Halachah - in other words, the sectarians conducted their lives as if the *community* were a virtual temple. For this reason, they observed the same strict regulations governing purity.

The Essenes believed that *im*purity was an entity that threatened to desecrate the sacred, which included the spatial distance from the holy of holies, the courtyards, and sacrificial sites within the Temple itself. This neglect could cause the departure of the Divine Presence from the Temple and so as prevention, their observations of purity were increased. On the other hand, although the Pharisees followed the laws of purity, they did not see desecration taking place so easily and with such a terrible outcome, and thus, comparatively, were not *as* rigorous.

It is not difficult to understand the importance attributed by the Essenes to ensuring that this 'defilement' did not take place. Their concepts of purity differed or were stricter than the Pharisaic or associated Oral Law.

The concept of purity so important to the Essenes was applied literally, spiritually, and even morally to the individual.

Hence anyone who had broken one of the Community Laws became subject to a 'rite of purification'. This could result in exclusion from one of the 'acts of purity', for example, the daily participation of eating the Pure Meal that the graduate Essenes partook of after having attained full membership.

"Neither shall they enter the water to partake of the Pure Meal of the men of holiness, for they shall not be cleansed unless they turn from their wickedness" (Community Rule). Immersion in the pool or mikvah preceded eating the main meal before midday. (Extracted from Jodi Magness: 'The Archaeology of Qumran and the DSS')

Purity thus positively and negatively encompassed:

- Sacrifices…e.g., tainted or being carried out at the wrong time
- Food…e.g., eating of sacred food after the animal sacrifice
- Human defilement…e.g., menstruation, physical impairments
- Material defilement…e.g., one vessel contaminating another

In all of the above, there were distinct differences in the interpretation and legislation between the Essenes and the Pharisees. The point of departure was the role and observation by the priesthood of the Essenes from those of the Temple, as also conveyed in the MMT scroll.

Even these concepts of pollution and sin resulting in defilement of the holy space were spelled out in the Scrolls of the 'Damascus Document', 'Hodayot' and 'Rule of the

Community.' The Essenes saw themselves as the priestly pure - whose observation of Halachah would hasten the Messianic event and liberation of the land from its oppressors, with a return to the 'pure' form of Judaism.

The Development of Theology and Jewish Law

The Damascus Document or 'Tzadokite Work' and the 'MMT' or 'Halachic Letter' scrolls (to be covered in this book) allow us to attain a clearer picture of Pharisaic law and Sadducean beliefs regarding their attitude towards the authority of the Torah during this period. This is seen through the views of the Essenes and thus the development of Jewish law or Halachah is better understood. It needs to be appreciated that the term 'Halachah' also means 'the way', stemming from different periods and expressing differing views per time frame.

During the Second Temple era, it became a fundamental issue on how to incorporate the *extra-biblical* traditions and teachings into a Jewish legal system, *and* how to justify these inclusions theologically. The Dead Sea Scrolls incorporating the beliefs of the Essenes reflected this. The legal materials of the sect deal with *their* interpretation of the Torah. The term *'serach'* also refers to the collection of laws as found in the 'Rule of the Community'.

The Essenes divided the laws into two categories: The *nigleh* or 'revealed' and the nistar or 'hidden'. The revealed laws were known to all of Israel, but the hidden laws were known only to the sect and are revealed exclusively through their explanations or exegesis. They believed that revelations thus required 'divine' help for the members to discover their correct interpretation. As a result of the Dead Sea Scrolls, we consequently learn about the Pharisaic attitudes. The sect's criticism of the Pharisees revealed in fact what the Pharisaic law was! It has been noted within their exegesis, that they had developed their own form of legal argument. This was not dissimilar to the style and technique that is unique to the Talmudic manner of presenting a for-and-against argument.

The Essenes saw a *tripartite* division of Judaism at the time. They used the code word 'Judah' when referring to themselves, and 'Ephraim' or 'Manasseh' for the Pharisees and the Sadducees in some of the scrolls. The Pharisees were designated two code names - one being 'Ephraim' taken from Hosea Chapter 5 and the second, "the seekers of smooth things," perhaps due to their explanation of the Oral Law concerning the commandments in the Torah.

Chapter 11: The Messiah

Insight

"Central to Judaism is the belief in the coming of *a* Messiah, a time in which God's light will shine openly into the world. The Jewish apocalyptic vision is of an eternal era of peace and brotherhood *on this earth,* rather than in the Heavens."

It is appropriate to introduce at this stage the concept of the Messiah. The 'War Scroll' you are about to be introduced to describes a messianic battle. Not without reason, the messiah in this scroll is regarded as the one to redeem the world. The word Messiah means 'anointed one'. As you progress through this book you will note that the messiah will often be referred to in his representative forms. This is because the Essenes were also inter-alia, described as messianic sectarians of that period in Jewish history. The Jewish people await the coming of the Messiah who will destroy the enemies of God, usher in world peace, and gather in the exiles, the resurrection of the dead and the rebuilding of the Temple in Jerusalem.

So, I ask the questions, what is the origin of the belief in the Messiah, what are the criteria in being one and what is supposed to take place when he arrives?

Cryptic References

There is a reference to him or this concept, that first appears in the Torah in the book of Numbers 24:17, in the prophecy of Bilaam:

"There shall come a star out of Jacob, and a scepter-bearer shall rise out of Israel." The Hebrew word for scepter is translated into Aramaic as meaning 'Messiah'. See Onkelos. "...a star out of Jacob" is regarded as being a reference to King David or a King.

The Book of Isaiah, Chapter 2

Here are some extracts that will help you to understand.

Verse:

1. *"And it shall come to pass in the end of days that the mountain of God's house (Mt. Zion the site for the Temple) shall be set over all other mountains and lifted high above the hills, and all nations shall come streaming to it..."* It continues with one of the most quoted lines:

4. *"And He will judge between nations and decide between peoples. And they shall beat their swords into ploughshares and their spears into pruning hooks. Nation shall not lift up sword against nation; neither shall they learn war anymore."*

The Book of Isaiah Chapter 11 continues further:

Verse:

1. *"And there shall come forth a shoot out of the 'stump or stock' of Jesse (King David's father) and a branch shall grow out of his roots."* (You can read about this in the section dealing with the origin of the name 'Essene').

2. *"And the spirit of wisdom shall rest upon him...."*

3. *"And he shall be filled with a spirit of fear of the Lord....and he shall smite the earth with the rod of his mouth and with the breath of his lips shall he slay the wicked."*

6. *"The wolf shall dwell with the lamb and the leopard shall lie down with the kid."* (And as Woody Allen once quipped "but the lamb didn't sleep very well that night!")

12. *"And (he) will assemble the dispersed of Israel and gather together the scattered of Judah from the four corners of the earth."*

From the Book of Jeremiah Chapter 23, Verse:

5. *"Behold the days come, saith the Lord, that I will raise unto David a righteous sprout* (remember the stump)*, and he shall reign as king and prosper, and shall execute judgement and justice in the earth."*

6. *"In his days Judah shall be saved, and Israel shall dwell safely…"*

From the Book of Daniel Chapter 7:

Verse 13:

"I saw in the night visions, and behold, one like a son of man came with clouds of heaven…"

In the Book of Zechariah Chapter 9,

Verse 9:

"…behold thy king commeth unto thee: he is just, and having victory; lowly, and riding upon an ass, and upon a colt and the foal of an ass."

The Messiah is described as "lowly (humble), riding upon an ass". This is how Jesus is recorded to have entered Jerusalem on the eve of 'The Last Supper', days before his crucifixion.

And from the Book of Malachi Chapter 3,

Verse 1:

"For suddenly the master whom you are seeking will come into His sanctuary." (The Temple)

The Talmud says that he could arrive in 'grandeur', or in an 'unassuming' manner. This will depend on Israel's deemed worthiness.

Significantly, in Isaiah 45:1, the prophet states that God refers to King Cyrus, who rescued and freed the Jews from the Babylonians, as 'His anointed' i.e., Messiah. To become a king, one had to be anointed and therefore could also be regarded as a Messiah. The *Cohen Gadol* (High Priest) also had the status of a Messiah.

Isaiah might have designated Cyrus the status of a Messiah to encourage the former Babylonian captives to leave, as many enjoyed their settlement there. As a Messiah he would be linked up with God's salvation and inspire them. He was to be obeyed. Isaiah wanted the return of the Jewish people back to Israel. Here we have a reference of a human being as a Messiah, and hence the earliest concept by the Jewish people that he would come from the ranks of humankind.

Nowhere in the Hebrew Bible is it written '*the* Messiah,' but '*a* messiah'. This is in opposition to the belief in Jesus, who Christianity believes was of divine origin i.e., the Son of God, or 'God incarnate' i.e., God Himself. Isaiah 43:10 – 11: "*You are my witness,*" declares the Lord, "*And my servant whom I have chosen, in order that you may know and believe Me and understand that I am He. Before Me there was no God formed and there will be none after Me. I, I am the Lord, and besides me there is no savior!*".

It was essentially after the destruction of the Second Temple that messianic fervor really developed. The people were devastated - there was no king or messiah. The nation then entered the beginning of its yearning for a messiah that continues to the present day. The strong belief in the coming of a Messiah was profoundly present in the Essene literature and for the rest of Judaism, his coming was awaited with anticipation.

To provide greater clarity to the messianic belief of the Essenes, I quote from Prof. Gershom Scholem's paper: 'Toward an understanding of the Messianic idea'. *"The predictions and messages of the biblical prophets come to an equal degree from revelation and from suffering and (the) desperation of those whom they addressed; they are spoken from the context of situations again and again and have proven effective in situations where the End* (of Days), *is perceived in the immediate future."*

In other words, the Essenes who lived in desperate times also saw the coming of the Messiah to be 'just around the corner' and hence their preparation for his (or their) coming. This is particularly noted in the Pesher Habakkuk which you will read about further on, where the Teacher of Righteousness as a 'Prophet' interprets impending events leading to the coming of their Messiah.

Tragically, many Jews on entering the gas chambers in the Nazi concentration camps during the Holocaust, (also) sang "*Ani Ma'amin…*" "*I believe in the coming of the Messiah*". One of Judaism's 13 Principles of Faith.

There are over 40 references to the Messiah in the Hebrew Bible. All were anointed either as kings, priests, or even outsiders such as Cyrus. All were in human form and origin. They did not necessarily present as being exceptionally 'good' individuals, and some even 'messed up'.

Yet another Messianic age was just around the corner with the coming of Jesus, designated 'Christos', from the Greek word for Messiah - Anglicized to Christ. One of the prime reasons for his rejection as *'the'* Messiah by the Jewish people was that he "*did not bring peace into the world*". Christianity now awaits his 'Second Coming'.

Judaism also waits for a Messianic arrival, but *not* in the person of Jesus. This began with one of the first 'false Messiahs', Simon Bar Kochba, a century after Jesus. The Messiah is still very central to Judaism, especially within the *Lubavitch* Orthodox Jewish movement.

Jewish tradition requires that at least 10 aspects should take place or be present, for the real Messiah to be accepted.

1. He must be of Jewish descent.
2. He will be a descendant from the male lineage of King David.
3. He will gain sovereignty over the Biblical land of Israel.
4. He will gather the Jews there from the four corners of the world.
5. He will restore full Torah observance.
6. He will bring peace to the world.

7. Resurrection of the 'righteous' dead will occur.

8. He will oversee the rebuilding of the (third) temple.

9. He will have knowledge of the whereabouts of the Temple vessels.

10. He will have knowledge of the whereabouts of the Ark.

The requirement that the Messiah be a descendant from the male lineage of King David, viz. the stump of Jesse in Isaiah, is also recognized by Christianity.

Jesus is also 'coincidently' born in the same town as David i.e., Bethlehem. The Christian bible twice gives examples of the (differing) lineage of Jesus to support his authenticity in this regard.

It is a confusing matter to understand the reason for the given lineage. The question arises of how Jesus can be shown to be a descendant of David and used as 'proof' through this lineage? His father Joseph is shown to have this essential connection, yet Jesus is recorded to have been born of a virgin birth - hence Mary could not have become pregnant by Joseph. In Judaism to be the Messiah, that lineage must come from the birthfather, who in turn must be a descendent of King David.

The belief in the coming of the Messiah is an integral part of Jewish belief and is one of the 'Thirteen Principles of Faith' formulated by one of the greatest Jewish sages, Maimonides, in the 12th century. Principle #12: *"I believe with perfect faith in the coming of the Messiah, and, though he tarries (be delayed), I will wait daily for his coming."* It is also part of the Jewish daily prayer. Today among Orthodox Jews, the Hebrew word *'Mashiach'* is fervently repeated at ceremonies. There were over 30 claimants to being the Messiah from 4 BCE until 1780. Thereafter, those claiming this status have mostly been on the lunatic fringe…Waco, Texas springs to mind.

Other events that will occur will be the rebuilding of the much awaited 'Third' Temple, not only by the Jewish people but by

Christians as well…. for their own reasons. In Christianity, preceding the coming of Jesus there is a powerful belief of an 'event' referred to as '*Rapture*' based on the books John 14:3, 1st Corinthians 15:51 - 52 Thessalonians 4:15 - 17 from the New Testament and other references as well. It is a prophesied event in Christian eschatology in which selected righteous Christians are suddenly taken from the earth to participate in the Second Coming of Jesus. This belief is more prominent in certain segments of Christianity than in others.

It is believed that the Rapture will be followed by seven years of tribulation, pain, and suffering in the world with the battle of good versus evil i.e., the 'Anti-Christ.' Furthermore, the battle will be fought by the remaining Christians who 'repented'- as well as those Jews who recognized Jesus' coming.

After seven years the heavens 'will open up' and Jesus will return to destroy the Anti-Christ, otherwise known as 'The Beast.'

Following this, there will be an 'eternity' of heaven on earth, with all living under the rule of God. Evangelical Christianity recognizes an important prerequisite - that the land of Israel must be re-occupied by the Jewish people. Hence also their strong support (and motive) for the Jewish people and Israel.

One Jewish view held is that despite a 'readiness' to rebuild the Temple, this will not happen as it is believed that only the Messiah will know the details of the exact site and measurements. Another view is that he will arrive once it is rebuilt, as is implied in the prophecy of Malachi mentioned earlier. Here is an extract from the Talmud (from the end of the Mishnah tractate Sota) describing the dark days and events preceding the coming of the Messiah:

"In the footsteps of the Messiah (i.e., in the period before his arrival) presumption will increase and respect disappear. The empire will turn to heresy and there will be no moral reproof. The house of assembly will become a brothel, the Galilee will be laid to waste, and the people of the frontiers will wonder from city to city and none will pity them. The wisdom of the

scribes will become odious and those who shun sin will be despised; truth will nowhere to be found, boys will shame old men ..." and it continues on with this foreboding theme!

The 'official' Jewish belief is that the Jewish people should not wait for his arrival before rebuilding. The Talmud also states that the Messiah will come in an age that is either totally pure or totally guilty. As He did not come during the Holocaust or during many other dark days for the Jewish people and the world, Judaism currently tries to hasten his arrival by encouraging Jews to carry out as many of the commandments (*mitzvoth*) as possible. There is also a belief by some Jewish movements today that the Temple will 'drop down' onto the site (many religious Jews have a framed picture in their homes depicting this) and resurrection of the (righteous) dead will take place, a belief also pertaining to both Judaism and Christianity. Judaism also believes that the Messiah when he makes himself known will be a 'regular' human being who at the time of His announcement, will be living on this earth. His birth it is believed will take place on the 9th of the Hebrew month of Av. This is the anniversary date when both Temples were destroyed, and certain major calamities occurred to the Jewish people.

PART 2: The Dead Sea Scrolls

Chapter 12: The 'Great Scrolls'

Apocalyptic and Eschatological

Before reading about the 'War Scroll', there are a couple of important definitions and terminologies that are very relevant and seen as central to the Essene beliefs. Both the Hebrew and Christian Bibles carry similar themes in certain passages and books.

Eschatology: From the Greek *eschaton*, 'the end', and *ho logos* 'the word and or the teaching' - thus inferring 'teaching concerning the end of things', specifically the end of the world. It deals with death, judgment, and heaven and hell, all in the finality of time. In the Hebrew Bible and the New Testament, the books of Daniel and Revelations follow this theme with intimations of the oncoming of the messianic era.

However, not all the literature spewed fire and brimstone. The arrival of an eschatological figure would be an individual who would dramatically improve the situation for the people, for example, a leader who would overthrow the Roman yoke. Often such literature was based on themes of hope.

Apocalyptic: This is derived from the Greek word *apocalyptis* meaning *'revelation' 'uncovering'*, or *'unveiling'*. Apocalypse in such literature means that there is a disclosure and understanding of heavenly secrets and visions by God in the form of prophecy, with usually a powerful reference (albeit sometimes veiled) to an impending crisis.

It deals with the warring forces of good (angels) verse evil, often of a satanic nature. The theme leads to the *end of days,* culminating at times in a *messianic* event by His arrival and is presented as a direct revelation and intervention from God or an angel, who would reveal an important message to be conveyed to the people.

After the fifth century BCE, prophecy came to an end. The consolidation and redaction of the bible, incorporating designated sacred books of the Prophets and the Writings took place over the next three to four hundred years. During the last two centuries when the realization that prophetic inspiration had long come to an end, a need arose to find answers and renewed inspiration to spiritually overcome the suffering to which the nation had now become exposed. This was experienced during the cruel Greek and Roman occupation of Palestine. It gave rise to apocalyptic or pseudepigraphal literature.

Apocalyptic literature is now acknowledged as a new kind of literature having developed in Judaism during the Hellenistic and Roman periods. It sought to reveal answers to the mysteries and suffering of the world and uncover hidden knowledge, thus providing hope and understanding for a better time to come.

The apocalyptic vision was one of a cosmic struggle between good and evil ending in Divine justice being meted out. This concept is regarded as leading to *The End of Days,* during which time Israel would be purified and its enemies judged and punished. The vision and belief of this concept became the hope for national redemption and the end of individual suffering.

Many of these apocalyptic works later became incorporated into the written works that are known as the Apocrypha, comprising the books of: *Enoch, Ezra and Baruch* and the *Ethiopic Book of Enoch* and the *Assumption of Moses.* In the Hebrew Bible, the Books of Daniel and Ezekiel inter alia, and in the Christian Bible, the book of 'Revelations' is renowned for their apocalyptic themes.

The destruction of the Second Temple, followed by the defeat of a Second Revolt against Rome in 135 CE of Bar Kochba finally convinced both the rabbis and the Jewish people of the dangers of the apocalyptic imagination.

Probably one of the last books to be given recognition as being divinely inspired and canonized into the Tanach is the Book of Daniel. This book is an excellent example of a truly apocalyptic work.

Within a generation of the destruction of the Second Temple, Jews no longer composed or even used apocalyptic literature. They ceased to make speculations about God's actions or future intentions. The Pharisees, Sadducees, Essenes, Sicarii and Zealots were no longer living realities in Jewish society.

On the other hand, with the 'delay' of the 'Second Coming' of Jesus, the Book of 'Revelations' in the Christian bible continued and re-kindled this apocalyptic theme. It is widely used today to provide the message that man cannot continue doing evil in the world, and to forewarn of a false messiah that will lead Christians (the 'Anti-Christ') and others, to an impending destruction before, and when "*Jesus will come again to judge the world*".

The War Scroll

Insight

The work is a "theological consideration of a perpetual struggle between good and evil in which the opposing forces are of equal strength and to which only God's intervention can bring an end."

The War Scroll is also known *as 'The Scroll of the War of the Sons of Light against the Sons of Darkness'.*

This was one of the three scrolls first discovered in Cave 1, purchased, and obtained by Israel. It is classified 1QM, and other fragments 1Q33, 4Q491-7, and 4Q471 are regarded as shorter versions related to, but not copies of the original.

The original manuscript had nineteen incomplete columns (damaged at the bottom end of the scroll through wear) and is 2.9 meters or 9 feet 8 inches. Later the contents from another six scroll fragments were added, following their discoveries in Cave 4.

The generally accepted date that it was written, is between 50 BCE and 50 CE. Sukenik published it in 1954, seven years after its discovery.

It was the first scroll that revealed the Essene eschatological and apocalyptic beliefs that feature so prominently in many of their other works. Eschatology deals with the concept of the final days, or End of Days, in which a battle of the forces of evil (darkness), often referred to as the *Belial*, will be in battle with the righteous (light). This is referred to as Armageddon in Christian belief, and in both Jewish and Christian teachings - the beginning of the messianic era.

Rev. 16:12 "...*to bring them together for the battle on the great Day of the Almighty God*". 16:16.... "*Then the spirits brought the kings together in the place that in Hebrew called Armageddon*".

In the section under the 'Messiah', I mentioned that kings too were anointed ones and hence this could imply Messiah(s), as portrayed further on in this scroll. Armageddon comes from the site in Israel today called Megiddo, where the 'final' battle is prophesied to have taken place. Later, you will see its influence in the Christian bible, in the Book of Revelation which has an almost identical theme, in which God would intervene and conquer.

The scroll is thus a manual for the *messianic battle* anticipated by the Essenes who were to be engaged in this battle together with Angelic armies for forty years, ultimately emerging victorious. It describes a *cosmic war* between the forces of

Good and the Forces of Evil to be ultimately resolved by God. It would be a cataclysmic struggle in the world of injustice and evil

"*The sectarian (Essene) scrolls share key elements of the apocalyptic worldview. They attribute great influence on human affairs to angelic and demonic sprits and they expect both a final judgment at the end of history and reward and punishment of individuals after death*". (J. Collins on Sectarian Literature)

- As an apocalyptic sect, the Essenes saw themselves as the true form or representation of the Jewish religion.

- Their beliefs and lifestyle evolved to solve the problems of injustice in the world by totally eradicating evil.

- They were going to 'live' with God, whether it be on heaven or on earth.

These statements are cardinal to the essence of the existence of the Essenes as we understand them today.

It begins with:

"*For the Master; The Rule of War: The first attack of the Sons of Light shall be undertaken against the forces of the Sons of Darkness, the army of Belial (the spirit of evil, Satan): against the troops of Edom, Moab, the sons of Ammon, the Amalekites, the Philistines, the troops of the Kittim (the Romans) and their ungodly allies who violated the Covenant.*"

Essentially the scroll represents the struggle between good and evil and deals with it as a *spiritual* battle, as opposed to a military manual as the name could suggest. The imagery of this battle described below could have originated from the theological motifs of the Persian royal religion, Zoroastrianism. This was witnessed when Cyrus freed the Jewish captives from Babylon. Cyrus had also been designated the status of a messiah.

Column 1 speaks of the gathering of the troops of the Sons of Light to do battle and be victorious by the hand of God, with no survivors "*of all the Sons of Darkness*". This is beautifully stated in verse 8:

"*The sons of righteousness shall shine over all the ends of the earth;*

they shall go on shining until all the seasons of darkness are consumed

and, at the season appointed by God,

His exalted greatness shall shine eternally to the peace, blessing, glory, joy,

and long life of all the sons of light."

Column 2: Deals with the makeup of the army of the Sons of Light, headed by the High Priest and down through the ranks, according to their standing. It then proceeds to describe the stages over a 35-year period, and the conquests that will be achieved.

Column 3: This is further dramatized by a description of the fanfare preceding the battles, with trumpets and banners and songs of praise. It concludes with a triumphant return and recording of their gratitude with "*Rejoicing of God in a peaceful return*".

Column 4: Banners of different sizes bearing fearful words are described. They were carried by the congregation marching forward in formation. Some of the names on the banners included: "*The Order of God*", "*The Justice of God*", "*The Armies of God*", "*The Glory of God*", to name a few.

Column 5: Here we are given vivid descriptions of shields and swords of gold, encrusted with jewels and the formations of the troops as they line up in their thousands to take battle.

Column 6: Wave after wave they advance, and return to their positions, each time hurling their spears. Highly trained and unrelenting horsemen on each side of the troops support them.

Column 7: The age and purity of the troops are given as proof of eligibility to partake in this battle. The royal vestiges of the priests and their positioning during the battle are described: "...between the gap between the battle lines seven priests of the sons of Aaron, dressed in fine white linen garments, a linen tunic and linen breeches, and girded with a linen sash of twined fine linen, violet purple and crimson and varicolored design..."

Column 8: With trumpets 'shouting', thirty-four thousand warriors pursue and destroy the enemy whilst the priests in the background blow their trumpets.

Column 9: With the sound of trumpets the priests direct and control the battle.

Column 10: As Moses gave encouragement and bolstered their faith before battle, so does the High Priest to his army.

Column 13: Is filled with fire and brimstone "...The light of thy greatness [shall shine forth] [on 'go]ds' and men. [It shall be like a fire bur]ning in the dark places of perdition; (an everlasting place of punishment) it shall burn the sinners in the perdition of hell, in an eternal blaze...in all the eternal seasons." This form of expression and language is unknown in Judaism but is found in some Christian writings.

And so it continues, like battles portrayed in the movies of the US Cavalry - charging with bugles blowing, banners waving and the regally dressed officers with their swords held high leading their 'valiant' troops into battle!

The first scroll ends (Column 18) with a ceremony after the eschatological war.

As mentioned, there were in total of three *Milchemah* (Heb. for war) scrolls. Until recently, these (found in Cave 4) were considered to be part of the same as those found in Cave 1 but are now believed to be additional scrolls on a similar theme. One of them is now regarded as a Thanksgiving Hymn or *Hodayot* (Heb. pl.).

There are at least three similar passages in this scroll to the 'Book of Revelations' of the Christian bible, the 12th chapter in particular:

War Scroll: "...Today is the appointed time to lay low and to make fall the prince of the dominion of wickedness; and he will send eternal help to the lot he has redeemed by the power of the angel he has made glorious for rule, Michael, in eternal light, to give light in joy to all Israel...to exalt among the gods the rule of Michael and the dominion of Israel and all flesh."

Revelations 12:7 "And there was war in heaven. (As portrayed in the War Scroll) Michael and his angel fought against the dragon, and the dragon (Belial) and his angels fought back."

Also, with a little stretching of the imagination, from The Epistle (Letter) of Paul to the Ephesians, a similar theme is presented in Chap. 6: 10-17:

"Put on the whole armor of God that you may be able to stand against the treachery of the devil (Belial). For we are not fighting against human beings but against the rulers of darkness (Belial) in the heavenly world..."

And so, the theme continues through the 18 verses of that chapter.

The author of the scroll is unknown, but it does have similar references to the Habakkuk Pesher, covered further on, such as the mention of 'Belial' and the 'Kittim', 'Sons of Darkness' and the 'Nation of wickedness'.

In Cave 4, a collection of 10 related fragments viz. 4Q285, which were collectively designated the name 'The Rule of War' were also discovered. They appear to be related to the War Scroll.

The Temple Scroll

Insight

"In essence, then, the Temple Scroll stands alone in its literary character, at least in its presently preserved form. It is clearly a divine halachic pseudepigraphon. Will we ever know if it was delivered through the intermediary of Moses or directly to the people of Israel?" L. Schiffman.

"The Temple Scroll was probably a pre-Dead Sea Scroll" (L Schiffman)

An illustration of this scroll appears on the front cover of this book.

This scroll has its own special history. Yigal Yadin became aware of its existence in 1960 and he was the first person to be given the opportunity for its purchase. However, it was in the possession of Kando, the antique dealer in East Jerusalem who bought the first discovered scrolls from the Bedouins. Despite protracted negotiations, the deal eventually fell through. However, on 7th June 1967 with the capture of East Jerusalem and Bethlehem during the Six-Day War, the opportunity miraculously arose again

With the reunification of the previously divided city, Yadin having his suspicions aroused dispatched a colonel to confront Kando. The treasure was found hidden in a shoebox under floor tiles, and the scroll was confiscated. Ultimately the sum of $105,000 was paid to the dealer. This was the last scroll discovered. In July 2002 an intensive search for additional caves took place, using sophisticated hi-tech equipment, loaned, and funded by American institutions. Magen Broshi, director of the 'Shrine of the Book' at the Israel Museum in Jerusalem, headed the team. No other new discoveries have been revealed to the public other than two small fragments that were found by a Bedouin in the caves of

Nachal Arugot. They were offered to Chanan Eshel of Bar-Ilan University Israel in March 2005 for the sum of $3,000. The fragments are inscribed in Hebrew from the Book of Leviticus in the Torah.

The name of this most famous scroll is perhaps a misnomer. It descriptively deals with:

- Religious rulings - mainly ritual cleanliness and purity.
- Sacrifices and offerings for various festivals.
- Temple matters, design, and structure.
- Law for Israel's King and his army.
- Covenant made between God and man.
- Adultery and rape.
- Sexual relations.
- War.

The Temple Scroll was part of a rewritten Bible, together with other major compositions of the sectarian community associated with the Qumran site.

Recorded in the scroll were known biblical laws and additional laws and festivals that were not part of the Hebrew Bible. It overlaps with the biblical books of Leviticus, Exodus, and Deuteronomy, and from Kings, Ezekiel, and Chronicles, and shows a connection with the Book of Jubilees and the Damascus Document. However, fundamentally it is a work of detailed biblical interpretation (or exegesis) of those texts from the mentioned books. Examples of this will be covered further on.

Two copies discovered in 1956 in Cave 11, the scroll was designated the basic code 11QT. In that cave, another set of fragments from an additional Temple Scroll was found, which were coded 11Q20. The largest and most famous is the 11Q19. Still, some other fragments were found in Cave 4. The Temple Scroll however was the longest scroll found. In its completed form it has 67 columns and is over 13 meters (28 feet) long. The beginning of the scroll was damaged, and the first column is missing. To prevent breakage, it had to be unrolled at a humidity level of 75% because the leather parchment manuscript is less than 0.1mm thick and the scroll was only about 4 inches thick in its original rolled-up state! Yadin discovered two different handwritings in the Aramaic script which has led to speculation of there being two different authors.

Yigal Yadin, who regarded it as the Torah of the Essenes, published his work on this scroll in 1977 after 10 years of research. The copy found was dated between the late -first century BCE and mid-first century CE. Yadin believed that it originated approximately between 150-125 BCE. Although the style of writing is predominantly biblical, sometimes it reverts to Hebrew with a rabbinic style of vocabulary and syntax.

This scroll was written as though it were of divine origin, as a 6th book of the Torah, by one who saw himself as one of the designated prophets fulfilling a statement by Moses in the book of Deuteronomy 18:15 that other prophets would later arise to replace him: "*A prophet from your midst, from your brethren, like me, shall the Lord your God, establish for you…*" The intent to convey divinity was using the Tetragrammaton (YHWH) - which is not used in non-biblical scripts. The author(s) of this scroll produced a plan for the pre-eschatological Temple. It is speculated that the Teacher of Righteousness or his select followers wrote this work. This was because the Essenes believed that they lived in times of divine revelation and that their Teacher was able to receive this revelation. The debate around this scroll cannot be closed. Firstly, two questions arise concerning its origin: Was it a copy of a much older original version, likely to have then been copied in Qumran and brought there? Secondly was it unique to the Essenes? If the former, we are brought into a cascade of speculations and questions. These would include:

1.   When did it originate?
2.   Who wrote it?

3. For what purpose was it written?

4. Was it to have been regarded as divine, or divinely inspired?

5. Why was it necessary to have incorporated the given biblical texts and then add further additional text?

6. How widely known and used was this work and by whom and for whom was it composed?

7. Who are and why are the 'I' and 'Thou' referred to in the scroll?

8. Is this originally an Essene scroll or that of other sectarians?

9. Why did the author go to the trouble of presenting a blueprint for a Temple, whilst the Second Temple was still standing in Jerusalem?

10. Was there a rejection of the current Temple layout, as its design and inspiration came from Herod?

If the Teacher of Righteousness or Essene scribes composed it, its purpose takes on a different context. It becomes open to interpretation and speculation concerning the points listed below and centered on some of the following core significances:

1. There is no mention of Moses, even though large tracts cover original sections of the canonical Hebrew Bible where Moses was central to the text. By the exclusion of his name, it eliminates Moses as the intermediary of this text.

2. The scroll is frequently written in the first person, as though it was God Himself addressing Israel, and not as is in the Torah (dictated by God through Moses).

3. The Tetragrammaton is replaced by 'I' or 'Me'. 'Supplementary' Laws that do not appear in the Torah are written in the first person, endorsing their divinity.

4. The effect of the continuous usage of the word 'I' (God) and the omission of Moses has the additional impact of God speaking directly to Israel.

5. There is postulation that the aim of the redactor was to present the message of the scroll, not as an interpretation of the Bible, but as a divine revelation.

It could thus be noted that as the first column of the scroll is missing, the possibility could exist that its contents were intended to be elevated by introducing the text using the name of Moses. There are recognized parallels between the Book of Jubilees and the Temple Scroll.

The core theme is the revelation and instruction plan for the construction of the Temple that differed from the actual temple built by Solomon. Its size according to the measurements in the scroll is so great, equal to the size of Jerusalem.

Also included is a calendar for the <u>unknown festivals</u> of:

1. 'The First Fruits of Wine'
2. 'The First Fruits of New Oil'
3. 'First Fruits of Barley'
4. 'First Fruits of Wheat'
5. 'Festival of Wood Offering'

Interestingly there are two references to the 'Wood Festival' exclusively in the book of Nehemiah 10:35...

"And we cast the lots among the priests, the Levites, and the people for the wood-offering, (Koorban ha eitzim) to bring it into the house of our God, after the houses of our fathers, at the times appointed year by year, to burn upon the altar of the Lord our God, as it is written in the Law" (Torah).

Also, Nehemiah 13:31...

"And for the wood-offering, at times appointed, and for the first fruits."

Regulations are listed that pertain to these festivals and their associated sacrifices. In the MMT Scroll, to be further covered: "*The choice of calendars was a source of rivalry between communities. This scroll goes into detail about the celebration of each festival shared with most Essene groups. Several issues in this calendar brought conflict with rival groups, such as the issue of allotted days and dates. The Temple Scroll broke the months into 30-day periods with an extra day at the end of every three months, giving each year 364 days - contrary to practicing Judaism - to ensure that the festivals would always begin on the same day of the week. This was based on the statement in Genesis, that God created the moon and the sun on the fourth day i.e., Wednesday. All Torah-designated festivals including that of the New Year would always begin on a Wednesday. However, the above five would always begin on a Sunday and have exactly a 50-day interval between each one. Perhaps therefore it is an Essene scroll.*"

In the Temple Scroll, it is recorded that several festivals unique to the Essenes were celebrated. Many of the ideas found in the scroll mirrored the beliefs of the Essenes. This at first supported the acceptance of it being thus one of their works, but that belief has since been disputed. Also, there is some evidence that it preceded the Essenes.

The work is also regarded as being xenophobic as it saw an Israel devoid of foreigners, and thus had no ruling for them, which contrasts with the ruling in the Torah Leviticus 9:34 where it is written: "*The stranger that sojourneth (lives) with you, shall be unto you as the home-born among you*". Loving the stranger is stressed thirty-six times in the Hebrew bible. Here we see that the writer has combined sections from Deuteronomy and Leviticus possibly to meet his own ends. In essence, differences to the laws or rather variations are given, but essentially the laws of the Torah are followed.

Synopsis of contents in order of columns

- Cleansing tasks and laws, to be undertaken when entering Canaan.

- Detailed description of Temple architecture, structure, and furnishings.

- Description of sacrifices for various festivals, including non-biblical occasions and ceremonies. About a quarter of the entire scroll is devoted to festival offerings.

- Ceremony and sacrifices for the ordination of priests.

- Rulings for the Passover and the Omer (the counting of 49 days beginning on the 2nd day of the Passover).

- Sacrificial rulings for the Day of Atonement and the 'scapegoat'.

- Designation of the tribes to various areas of the Temple.

- Reference to animals that are permitted or not permitted to be eaten.

- Rulings pertaining to death, mourning, and unclean states.

- False prophets and idolatry.

- The duties and functions of the king together with instructions in forming an army and drawing up a justice system

- Rules for engaging in battle and the usage of the Urim and Tumim in the breastplate for decision-making as originally worn by Aaron and subsequent High Priests.

- Prohibition of abhorrent practices.

- Dealing with a body that was murdered, a murderer, a woman is taken captive in war, a rebellious child, criminals, and traitors.

- Discovery of a questionable virgin following marriage, and compensation to the false accusation in this regard.

- Laws regarding different situations of rape.

- Laws pertaining to forbidden marriages.

I mentioned in my introduction that this scroll is also an exegesis or biblical interpretation of scripture. An example of this is that the author in the third section of the scroll specifically states that on 'Yom Kippur' also known as the 'Day of Atonement', one must abstain from food and drink, whereas in the Book of Numbers 29:7, and Lev. 23:27 God instructs the people *"to afflict themselves"*. This affliction is interpreted by the Rabbis in the Oral Law, to mean *fasting*. Other examples of exegesis given by the author(s) in the scroll pertain to sacrifices made during the Temple Yom Kippur service. The *same* interpretations and conclusions were documented by Rabbis in the Mishnah hundreds of years later, as they debated or recorded the Oral Law to expound the meaning of the Torah's instruction.

A few more words on the subject, - this time for those familiar with the unique sacrifice that the High Priest carried out during the Yom Kippur service. A comprehensive explanation of how he was to sprinkle the blood onto the Ark cover is described in this scroll. Here again, hundreds of years later the exact interpretation for the same procedure as stated in the Mishnah. This custom that was instructed (Lev. 16:14) in the Torah is not clearly explained as to how it was to be carried out.

The above list can be reduced to 4 main subjects or topics:

(Source Dan Johnson)

1. *Halachot* (Religious laws).

2. Sacrifices and offerings for various festivals.

3. Details of the Temple.

4. Statutes for a King and his army.

Comments on 1 - 4:

1. This topic contains laws not found in the Torah but do appear in the Mishnah rabbinic law, and cover cleanliness, ritual purity, sexual activity, the

maimed, lepers, and containers used in the sacrifices.

2. Details on how and when festivals are celebrated. The Temple scroll followed the Essene calendar of a 364-day year compared to the Hebrew lunar calendar. It also recorded two other festivals observed by the Essenes viz. the Festival of New Wine and New Oil.

3. Nearly half the scroll focused on the furnishings and construction of the Temple. The scroll implied that this Temple would have authority over Herod's Temple.

4. It implies that the instruction for the safety of the King came directly from God. He is to have 12,000 men guarding him - 1,000 from each of the twelve tribes. Mobilization details are given. The scroll also gives details of the Kings cabinet and that he is to have only one wife, compared to some of the kings of Israel including Solomon who it is said, had hundreds!

One of the theories put forward by Dead Sea scholar Hartmut Stegeman is that the Temple Scroll is not of Essene origin but in fact, originates from a mainstream Jewish group. He believes it to be a 'lost Sixth book of the Torah' that was later rejected. By virtue of the fact that only two copies were found compared to numerous copies of other books, he postulates that it could not have been amongst the holy texts commonly used by them - no quotations from it are found in any of the Essene literature.

In addition, many of the religious laws found in the Temple scroll differed from those practiced by the Essenes. Wise on the other hand believes that the Temple Scroll had new laws for the imminent eschatological era, in other words, it was to be the book when the Messiah arrived.

Ezra the Scribe canonized the Torah after his return from Babylon in 458 BCE. This possibly means that he removed the additions and expansions to the original Torah. Included in this canonization could have been the Temple scroll which he may have rejected.

To many scholars, the architecture of the Temple together with the priestly activities recorded appears to present the scroll as a *visionary* blueprint for a future temple in a new earthly and heavenly world.

The Damascus Document

Insight

"The Damascus texts, however, comprise a coherent corpus of texts describing a single kind of Jewish organization, and offers significant clues as to its practices and the ideology that informs them."

The discovery in the Cairo Genizah of 'The Tzadokite Work' mentioned earlier in the book, culminated in one of the most important finds in Cave 4. It was very similar to the documents found in Cairo. These were subsequently called 'The Damascus Document' and known as the Tzadokite Fragments as named by Solomon Schechter after discovering the first known copy in the Cairo Geniza in 1897, and *Brit Damesek* in Hebrew.

In all, the remains of seven to nine copies of that text were found in the caves, dated to 100 BCE. There were certain textual differences and so the Cairo documents are regarded as different versions of the originals found in the caves at the Dead Sea. Neither did they fully represent the original contents nor follow quite the same order. The work found in Cairo is coded 'CD.'

That Synagogue is believed to also have been used by an established sect of Karaite Jews living in Egypt. The transcription of the document implied that it could have been a holy book to them. The variations between the CD and 4QD works are relatively minor and inconsequential. The Damascus Documents found in Cave 4 are allotted the code 4Q. Fragments of eight manuscripts of the Damascus Document were found in that cave i.e., 4Q266-273 dated from the first century BCE to the first century CE.

Karaite scholar A Qirqisani suggested that Karaites would have been particularly interested in the contents, especially the legal, marriage and divorce matters, and the lunar calendar from rabbinic law, which was opposed by the Karaites. They would have copied and transmitted the Damascus Document bringing it to Egypt.

"The rules of the Damascus Document were a strong antecedent to the Mishnah by some three hundred years. However, the Damascus Document is much less extensive and comprehensive regarding its topical and legal groupings and divisions than the Mishnah" (*Oxford Commentary on the DSS*)

At least seven references are made in these scrolls to Damascus, hence its designated name. The theory has it that it was first written 390 years after the exile of the Essenes from Babylon i.e., the return to Palestine - long before they settled in Qumran. The establishment of the community took place during a period referred to as 'the age of wrath' in the document. It appears that the Essene sect went to Qumran to establish a new covenant, *"They entered the new covenant in the Land of Damascus"* as recorded in that document. The term '*New Testament*' also means New Covenant.

The name Damascus has been under much speculation and theories have suggested that it could be:

- a code word for Babylon (present-day Iraq).
- or the more popular belief that Damascus was the name given to the (administrative) region where Qumran was situated.
- a literal reference to the city in Syria.

- a code word for Qumran. It is generally believed that the name refers to Babylon where the Essene movement may have begun - and the name later transferred to Qumran itself.

- after a staging post or resting place of the Jews returning from exile in Babylon.

Paul's conversion on the 'road to Damascus' has led to speculation that he was in familiar territory inhabited by the Essenes when he had his life-changing vision. Their works and way of life were well known to him and later used in his writings to express *his* beliefs where they could have influenced his spiritual and historical documentation in the Christian bible.

Another interpretation to that reference occurring in Acts 9:3 is that Damascus is to be regarded as an 'eschatological stopover' - as associated with the beliefs of the Essenes at Qumran. In the book of 1 Kings 18:15, God instructs Elijah *"Go return to your way, to the Wilderness of Damascus"*. The region he was sent to might have been the same as the Dead Sea area or part of the Judean desert. The word Damascus is also symbolic by its reference in the book of Amos 5:27 where the Judeans who had largely abandoned their Judaism, were threatened with exile 'beyond Damascus'.

The scroll is regarded as a composite text, meaning one which has evolved into its present state, suggesting that different sections may have been written and or composed over different time periods. It also gives insight into their interpretation of scripture. Such religious works were based on the fact that the 'Revealed' (Heb. *Nigle)* laws were known to all Israel, and the 'Hidden' (Heb. *Nistar*) laws were known only to them. Their understanding of prophecy required Divine help to confirm their own interpretations. Their works became in a sense their own *mystical* interpretations. When referring to the Nigle or revealed, it is at a 'lower level of' divine influence, whereas the sectarians were privy to the Nistar or hidden. The Pharisees spoke of laws that were unwritten or passed down by the fathers, which were not divine, for example, the 613 commandments which became subject to rabbinic interpretations.

The Damascus Document relates to those who had returned from exile *in the Land of Damascus* having gone out of the *Land of Judah* and for whom God established his covenant with Israel forever. There God would establish a *New Covenant* with them.

The work is divided into two sections referred to as: 'Exhortation' or 'Admonition' and the second section, 'Statutes' or 'Laws'.

Exhortation

When a leader passionately beseeches his followers to undertake preparation for an event, this would be known as his '*exhortation*'.

In this section, a priest or leader of the community addresses the *sons* of this community to remain faithful since God rewards the faithful and punishes the wicked. He sets out to give examples from the history of Israel. The address is given in the form of a sermon using biblical themes and he changes or re-interprets passages to put the message across.

It begins in the format:

"*Listen now, all you who recognize righteousness, and consider the works of God. When he has a dispute with all mortals, He will condemn all those who spurn him. For when Israel abandoned him, He turned away* (hid his face) *from them and His Sanctuary and delivered them up to the sword.*"

It continues a little further on with:

"*But he remembered his covenant with their forefathers* (and) *He left a remnant for Israel and did not deliver it up to be destroyed.*"

This refers to a period after the fall of the First Temple, the re-growth of Judaism by the Essenes, his faithful in Babylon. It also designates to them the term 'the returning remnant' or to give a modern concept '*Sheirit ha Pleita*' literally translated meaning the 'the rest which are saved'. It is the concept that God will never destroy the Nation of Israel. The survivors of the Holocaust or *Shoah* are also referred to by that name.

"*And God observed their deeds, that they sought Him with a whole heart, and raised for them a Teacher of Righteousness to guide them in the way of his heart.*" It took place, to quote: "*in the age of wrath,*" 390 years after the destruction of the Temple and exile into Babylon and led up to the Teacher and his followers going into their own exile in 'the land of Damascus'. This was to enter into a new Covenant before first "*groping about like blind men for twenty years*". By implication, the twenty-year time period meant that they broke away from the Jewish people at large, twenty years before the Teacher of Righteousness (Moreh Ha-tzedek. Heb.) had become their leader and inspiration.

The 390 years following the age of wrath, plus the twenty years as stated in the Damascus Document, calculates as follows:

Destruction of the First Temple 586 BCE (The age of wrath)

Plus 390 = 196 BCE

Plus 20 = 176 BCE - The date around which they settle or establish themselves in Qumran.

Note: This calculation is speculative.

Also: The Number 390 could have been derived from the Prophet Ezra, who decreed that would be the number of years Israel would be punished.

The first and more popular theory is known as the 'Palestinian Theory', purporting a breakaway from the (corrupt) Sadducean priesthood around 200 BCE, and the establishment of the Essene sectarian movement.

Here we learn that amongst the people was a group of religious Jews, formally secular Jews, and Priests, who were acutely distressed by the deviation from Judaism. For a period of twenty years, they yearned for a change in the right direction. It was this 'Teacher of Righteousness' who it is documented that God sent to guide them along the path of 'righteousness' in preparation for the *end of days*. 'Preparation' meant a return to all that encompassed God's instructions in establishing an orderly society that will be suitably prepared to meet the occasion.

'The Teacher of Righteousness' is the first and important reference to a leader who is designated this title in the Damascus Document. He is also referred to in other scrolls as 'Teacher' and 'Teacher of the Community'. He had other connotations and titles conveyed in Dead Sea Scrolls including 'Interpreter of the Law', 'the Priest' and intimations that he was a Prophet.

The understanding was that their earliest relationship with God was retained from the Babylonian captive times. After seventy years of exile, the seed group of the Essenes returned in 656 BCE with many of the Jews released from captivity, to undertake a way of life in preparation for the coming of the Messiah(s). However, not the entire Babylonian group returned to Judah. This is also referred to in the Document.

The Damascus Document has led many scholars to support what became known as 'The Babylonian Theory'. This traces the beginning of the Essene movement or sect beginning after the deportation of the Jewish people of Judea to that country, and the realization of this being a divine punishment. *"The converts of Israel who went out of the land of Judah to sojourn in the land of Damascus"* ...Damascus Document 5:4-5.

Some of them returned to Judah, specifically Jerusalem, after King Cyrus' victory over the Babylonians or at the time of the Maccabean victory over the Greek / Syrian overlords. It is possible they saw themselves as representative of the prophetic and messianic teachings of the great prophets of the First Temple period, particularly Isaiah. Much later, during the Second Temple era, the sect crystallized under the leadership of The Teacher of Righteousness - seen as supporting some of the prophecies of the 'latter' prophets including Haggai and Zechariah.

From that remaining group, about 1,300 years later in the eighth century CE, a new Jewish movement sprung up with similar beliefs, seemingly inspired by the original Essenes and Sadducees. These believers became known as the Karaites and are believed to have originated from a Mesopotamian reformer, Anan Ben David. He called for a return to the basics of Judaism and a rejection of the Talmud and sought a literal interpretation of the Mosaic Law. Their religion continues to this day, albeit a small group with a remarkable history of its own - it is estimated that over seven thousand Karaites live in Israel today. During the Second World War, the Nazis questioned rabbinical authorities on the Jewish origins of the Karaites. To prevent them from being murdered, the rabbis denied that they had Karaite Jewish roots. It is believed that the origins of the Cairo Damascus Documents came from these Karaites who were an established community in Egypt around 1000 CE. The CD scrolls were discovered in a Karaite/Rabbinic synagogue in Fostat, Egypt.

Further on, the text refers to opposition arising within the group led by the code name '*the Scoffer*,' or one who had made a *mockery* and broken away from the original group. He led his followers 'from the paths of righteousness' and removed the 'boundaries' or restrictions observed by the forefathers. He was also referred to as '*Liar*' and a '*Spouter of Lies*.'

These breakaways according to the Essenes contaminated the morality of the people and made a mockery of the rituals of cleanliness and the justice system. They had different dates allocated to the festivals and also had a decadent love of money. This angered God who then annihilated them. But the priests and the Levites and *the sons of Tzadok* were given the right to minister to God and perform sacrifices to him, as is quoted in Ezekiel 44:15.

The Document then continues to the present in which again the influence of evil prevails, as portrayed by the term Belial - when translated to literal Hebrew could mean 'without God,' or Satan. It set out to differentiate the three cardinal principles from the opposition: *Fornication*, with reference to incest, in particular, *Wealth*, referred to as acting arrogantly for the sake of riches and ill-gotten gain with misappropriated Temple funds and *defiling* the Temple in a manner of behavior and sacrifice by some of the priests. We earlier learned of other festivals kept by the Essenes that may have influenced their despair at seeing further desecration taking place. There was a predominance of the Pharisaic point of view in the list of alleged legal sins. A reference is made giving instructions to uphold an additional fast day for the members of the new covenant *in the Land of Damascus*. The word 'ta'anit also appears in other scrolls and is interpreted to mean 'fast.' Fasts were more common at that time, which were instituted for both public religious reasons and played a central role in Jewish religious life at that time.

Again, there appears the cryptic code name for an individual called '*the Man of the Lie*' and in this scroll, the phrase '*Men of Mockery*' was used. The Document records that the former adherents, who deserted to the *Liar* would experience the wrath of God in the predicted time of forty years after the passing away of the Teacher of the Community (Righteousness). The exhortations end in asking their members to be penitent so resulting in their deliverance. A reference is made to their own assumed identity name the *Yachad*, whose connotation means 'Community', from the Hebrew word 'together'.

Laws

This part of the Document covers two areas of guidance: one for the nation of Israel, and the second more specifically, laws for the Essenes i.e., their community. In dealing with the Jewish people, the presentation of the Laws remains essentially as is recorded in the Torah. Pertaining to the Essenes, it is expanded in greater detail and in a manner pertinent to the daily lives of the people. Rulings were also emphasized which were of special relevance to the author.

What is to be noted is that we see for the first time, detail, and *expansion* of the Law in a manner documented in the

Mishnah. The authors of the Damascus document saw themselves as 'the builders of the wall' - they prescribed additional laws to protect those of the Torah from being misinterpreted or defiled. Thus, Qumran law in effect carried out one of the principles of 'the Men of the Great Assembly'. Some of these expansions appeared only hundreds of years later when recorded in the Mishnah.

Although similar in layout, they were different in content and the legal solutions were contrary to those found in the Mishnah. This was a surprise to many as traditionally these Laws are regarded as part of the important *oral tradition* or Oral Laws that according to Jewish belief were given to Moses at Sinai. They are a practical interpretation of the Torah Laws which are recorded in the Mishnah and are part of the Talmud that initially began to be documented by Jehudah ha-Nasi (the prince) in about 200 CE. Peculiar to the recording of the Mishnah is the unique legal style in which the Law is written. In the Dead Sea Scrolls, this style also appears when some of their rulings were found. Therefore, contrary to popular belief or knowledge, some of the laws appearing in the Mishnah were already recorded before the beginnings of its official documentation in 200 CE in the Scrolls.

When writing on the significance of the Dead Sea Scrolls, this discovery would surely rate highly on the list. It thus also precedes the rabbinic traditions known as the Tosefta, completed in 219 CE in the town of Tzipori in the Galilee. The compilation of the Talmud, which also includes *Gomorrah*, - the rabbinic discussions on the Mishnah - took place between 200 CE and 500 CE when it was decided to bring this documentation to its conclusion. In modern terminology, it was ahead of its time by about 400 - 600 years!

It is interesting to note that as far as we know the Essenes had no concept of an authoritative Oral Law and yet attached precautionary Sabbath restrictions together with others pertaining to biblical commandments. The Laws of the Damascus Document are virtually unique amongst the Qumran scrolls found. Covering these Laws (Penal Codes) and their interpretations are rulings that they regarded as the correct interpretation of the 'Laws of Moses':

Laws that reflected the sectarian reinterpretation of the biblical commandments pertaining to:

- Leprosy.
- Behavior towards non-Jews.
- Discharges from men and women.
- Impure foods and defilement.
- Purification following birth.
- Rulings for those living in towns.
- Harvesting, gleaning, and tithing.
- Hierarchy in the camps.
- Conduct in business.
- Care for those in the camps.
- Rules pertaining to getting married.
- Punishment for breaking the community rules
- Taking oaths by women and men.
- Offerings.
- Procedures for punishing members who break community rules.
- Becoming a member of the sect.
- Disqualification of Priests.
- Punishment for spitting.
- Sabbath observance.
- Vengeance taken against fellow Jews.
- Witnesses Judges.
- Oaths

- One who sins through having become possessed

- Rules in diagnosing skin diseases
- Lost property.
- Water for purification.
- Compensation.
- Tithing for the poor.
- Purification and Ritual purification
- Rules concerning their organization of the Community.

Their Laws of Sabbath observance illustrate some of the closest connections between Qumran and the Oral Laws of the Rabbis as recorded in the Mishnah. Examples of this pertain to the law of (physical) *work* - which is not allowed on the Sabbath. Josephus cites the example of being forbidden on the Sabbath to move a vessel/object not designated for Sabbath use - this is like the Talmudic source, which also states that objects not designated for Sabbath use be banned from usage on that day. It is interesting that in the Temple the limitations of the Sabbath did not apply e.g., making a fire or physically carrying requirements for offerings.

Nevertheless, among the additional laws of the Damascus Document, there were those that were directed mainly *against* practices that were allowed in the Mishnah. Laws of Sabbath observance recorded in the Scrolls are far more strictly observed and less flexible - for example, even during the extreme situation of a man having fallen into the water he may not be pulled out with the aid of a rope or ladder. "*Any Human being who falls into a place of water…let no man bring him up with a rope or ladder or an implement*". Saving the person could only be undertaken for example, using an article of clothing designated for Sabbath attire - which could then be thrown to the poor individual! No allowance was made for the peril of life. Even defecation was not permitted on the Sabbath!

A scholar of Tannaitic literature Yaakov Epstein states that nevertheless, their recorded laws contributed to the early formation of the tractates of the Mishnah. This was despite the presence of the laws in a non- Pharisaic way.

The Rule of the Community

Insight

"The 'Rule' legislates for a kind of Monastic Society and served as something of a constitution for the Qumran Community also reflecting stages of its development."

Each time I begin an overview on one of the 'Great Scrolls', I am tempted to say that *this* is one of the most *significant* scrolls. Once again, I am introducing such a scroll which is sure to be universally regarded as a highly important work, and without which scholars would have groped in a grey world of speculation. I refer to the work known as the 'The Community Rule' and others including 'The Manual of Discipline', and by the Hebrew name *serach ha yachad*. It deals with regulations governing the life of the Essene community and with lists of rules pertaining to admission and expulsion to and from the community, promotion within the community, and its structure. It can also be regarded as the 'Sectarian Constitution'.

For the entry of a candidate to the Essenes, it was stipulated that he would have to wait more than a year before being able to participate in the *Pure Meal* - the reason being, that he was considered impure and therefore prohibited from touching the pure food and drink. This pure meal was an important daily ritual preceded by immersion into a *mikvah* or ritual bath pool before eating. The Qumranic substitution of the Temple ritual format was undertaken by the practice of immersion, corresponding to occasions and legal (halachic) requirements taking place at the Temple:

"...And when his flesh is sprinkled with purifying water and sanctified by cleansing water, it shall be made clean by the humble submission of his soul to all the precepts of God..." 1QS3.7

In my overview of the sequence of scroll discoveries and their contents, the Rule of the Community is thus designated as 1QS, i.e., on account of being found in Cave 1, with the S being the first letter of the word *serach*. The 'Rule' scrolls were originally found as two pieces, with a combined measurement of 9.5' x 6". Additional fragments were also discovered in Cave 4 that were designated as being copies of the Community Rule. They are known as 4Q255-264a-j, 4Q266-273a-h. In Cave 5 related fragments were also found and were coded 5Q11.

A complete scroll of eleven columns was found in Cave 1. Additional fragments, comprising between ten to fifteen copies in total were found in Cave 5, dated to around 50 BCE. With controversy pertaining to the exclusivity of some scrolls found identified as being Essene, here there appears to be little doubt. The fact that at least fifteen copies came from the same region indicates their importance to the Essene Community. It was also noted that this work existed in different versions.

Father Murphy-O'Connor, one of the original scrolls' scholars said that "*1QS contains an original core, a manifesto involving a group of twelve men and three priests who separated themselves from the ruling social structure around the Temple and went out into the desert. As time passed, the community increased in size*".

The manuscript makes an early reference to their identity i.e., their connection with *a* or *the* sect:

"The Master shall teach the saints to live according to the book of the Community (Yachad) Rule, that they may seek God..."

It speaks of the 'Sons of Light' and 'Sons of Darkness' and the rigorous upholding of God's word and continues with the initiation into the Yachad, taking place in the presence of their priests by a confession that they had been sinners, whereupon a blessing would follow. Their membership would be reviewed annually. As part of their spiritual enlightenment, they would be taught how the spirits of truth and falsehood, symbolized by a 'Prince of Light' and an 'Angel of Darkness', could affect their fate. Ethical, moral, and spiritual principles of the Yachad are spelled out. The structure of the organization and the different punishments that could be metered out for infringements were stipulated.

It thus begins: "[The Master shall teach the sai]nts to live [according to the Book] of the Community [Rul]e, that they may seek God with a whole heart and soul, and do what is right before Him as He has commanded by the hand of Moses and all His servants the Prophets…"

Rulings included:

The initiate could only drink the Yachad's wine after passing the second year of membership.

Dishonesty about money would mean banishment for a year from the daily special pure meals and rationing of one's bread.

Rudeness, interjection, speaking loudly, reading a 'book' during prayer.

Lying, speaking foolishly, and parading naked in front of a member, spitting, and wearing clothing with holes in it, revealing private parts.

Laughing out loud, gossiping, and murmuring against the secret teachings…

All of which had their specific deprivations, punishments, or in some cases banishment.

The messianic belief and a belief in two messiahs are also mentioned in this document. The one from a priestly background (Aaron), and the second from the lineage of David (Israel). David is representative of the Kingly Messiah who will come to lead the (apocalyptic) war and Aaron, the Priestly Messiah, who will come to restore the Temple to its proper purity. In addition, there is reference to the coming of a prophet, possibly Moses himself. The section which mentions a 'Trinity' reads:

"They will not depart from any of the teachings of the Law, through stubbornness in their hearts."

"They shall be governed by the original guideline teachings given to the men of the Community until the coming of the Prophet and the Messiahs of Aaron and Israel".

(A 'modernized' English is used to convey a simpler interpretation)

It continues in the closing two columns with teachings for the Instructor imparting rulings, teachings, and his authority on the Community. Here the same phrase is used as in the Christian bible, namely the 'Way'. This is presented…….

"…but shall impart true knowledge and righteous judgement to those who have chosen the Way."

The word 'Way' carries important relevance in the Christian Bible.

There were also warnings about guarding the tongue since speech can express the fruits of holiness or sin. A similar message appears in the Christian bible, the Book of James 3:1-12. It closes with a prayer (particularly beautifully translated and edited by Vermes) praising the majesty of God and acknowledging the unworthiness of man.

Many theories have been proposed to explain and identify the group(s), and thus bring into question 'the Essene Hypothesis' as apparently portrayed in the Rule of the Community. This is additionally covered by my observations made under the heading 'Disputing the Essene Hypotheses'. I draw on comments from a lecture by J. R. Davila to add to some of these proposals and to consider the association of the Community Rule and the Damascus Document regarding their existence:

1. We have the classic proposal that these rules apply to the Essenes - as we have been led to believe so far in this book.

2. Then we have Norman Golb's book 'Who Wrote the Dead Sea Scrolls?', in which he proposes that the Dead Sea Scrolls are the literary archives from the Jerusalem Temple that were brought into the region to be hidden from the impending Roman destruction of the city and the land of Palestine. He proposes the rulings pertained to a group of 'purity-loving brethren' such as the Chavurah/Friendship groups described in the Mishnah.

3. Thirdly, based on research by M Klinghardt, the proposal is that 'the Community Rule' is the code for a Jewish Palestinian association centered on a synagogue community, which paralleled Hellenistic associations with similar codes and structures.

Presenting these points of view to the reader highlights these real issues, and that sometimes a 'standard theory', however convenient is often far from watertight. This *may* become more apparent in the section covering the Scrolls and the Christian bible, further on in this book.

Davila continues by briefly covering the relationship between the Community Rule and the Damascus Document. I need to add that numerous papers have been presented on this. Firstly, there are some shared terminologies and overlapping legal traditions. Both use the title 'sons of light' and have the same version of the rulings or penal code. On the other hand, it is to be noted that the 'Teacher of Righteousness' does not appear in the Community Rule and that some of the penal codes although from the same source, sometimes differ in the two works. The second view is that "*the Damascus Document is the constitution of a parent group that evolved over time into the group that produced the "Community Rule*".

Rule of the Congregation - also named The Messianic Rule

In Cave 1, the two fragments found were originally copied on the same scroll as the 'Community Rule'. However, it is regarded as a complete work in itself. These documents were called 'Rule of the Congregation' and are also known as the 'Messianic Rule'. Coded 1QSa (1Q28a) - dated mid-first century BCE.

The Scrolls were given names by the person designated to them, namely the scholar delegated to comment on and translate a particular scroll. 'Rule of the Congregation' was named by D. Barthelemy when it was translated by him in 1955. Geza Vermes retitled it 'The Messianic Rule' for the following reasons:

It was intended for 'the entire congregation in the last days'.

"It is a Rule for the Community adapted to the requirements of the messianic war against the nations and refers to the presence of the Priest and the Messiah of Israel at the Council." (G. Vermes. 'Complete Dead Sea Scrolls in English')

In its essence, it lays down the rules for the 'Congregation of Israel' when they will prepare for the forthcoming and final war with foreign nations led by a messiah. This would take place at the 'end of days - in other words, the apocalypse.

This document is particularly known for details of a great and final 'messianic banquet', which I quote from in the section covering 'Christianity and the Dead Sea Scrolls'.

The rules cover the summoning of those who join up with the 'Covenant', including what is expected of them and their manner of behavior.

"... He should not [approach] a woman to know her by lying with her before he is fully twenty years old..."

"At the age of thirty he may approach to participate in lawsuits and judgements, and may take his place among the chiefs..."

"When a man is advanced in years, he shall be given a duty in the [ser]vice of the congregation in proportion to his strength."

"And no man smitten with any human uncleanness shall enter the assembly of God...no man (who is) paralyzed, blind, deaf, dumb, (etc.)... shall come to hold office among the congregation of the men of renown, for the Angels of Holiness are [with] their [congregation]."

It continues with details, hierarchy and position when attending a council meeting, ending with the famous meal and the protocols associated with it, which you will read about towards the end of this book, as I want it to appear in a more relevant setting.

The MMT Scroll

Insight

"A Qumran text, today known as the 'Halachic Letter', demonstrates quite clearly that the root cause that led to the sectarian schism, consisted of a series of disagreements about sacrificial law and ritual purity."

Now we come to one of *the* most important scrolls - described by the letters 'MMT' - an acronym from the Hebrew for *Miksat Ma'aseh haTorah*, taken from the scroll that is in the form of a letter. Popularly translated it could mean: 'Some precepts or rulings or observances pertaining to the Torah', or (Some) 'Works of the Law'. It is also referred to as the 'Halachic Letter'. Halachah is Hebrew for Jewish religious law. Its code is 4QMMT. It is a composite text comprised of three sections. It is estimated that the reconstructed text represents about two-thirds of the original document.

Their pre-emptive publication led to the publisher, Hershel Shanks and one of its reviewers being sued in court. Knowledge of this scroll was first made public at a conference on biblical archaeology in Jerusalem in 1984. Professor Elisha Qimron, a paleographer from Ben-Gurion University Israel, compiled a text from seventy fragments collectively making up 130 lines and originating from six copies of the text. He had about 60% of the original letter. The balance, at the time of the conference still had to be deciphered and understood. Qimron incidentally was the first Jewish and Israeli person to be invited to join the Scrolls team about thirty-five years after it was originally established.

The tantalizing revelation was sensational at the conference attended by leading scrolls scholars, who waited with bated breath for its complete and final publication. Qimron himself said "*Our letter is one of the most important Qumranic works. Its contribution to the history of Halachah, and of the Hebrew language, and to other fields, cannot be exaggerated*".

It took a total of eleven years and 15,000 hours to complete the draft in 1993! Copies were sent to four scholars abroad for comment. A Polish scholar obtained a copy and without permission published it in a Krakow newsletter 'The Qumran Chronicle'. A year later Shanks reprinted the article, but not in its 'raw and original' form but reconstructed and published it in his name. Hershel Shanks was the editor of the famous and highly acclaimed 'Biblical Archaeological Review' journal, or BAR, as it is popularly known. The 'MMT' was published in 1994 with a content of over two hundred pages of analysis. Legal ruling was eventually passed that only Qimron was allowed to translate the MMT, and permission would have to be obtained for using his work.

This scroll has given the world its *earliest* glimpse of Halachah, prior to the Mishnaic period when it was recorded. It showed for the first time how Halachah had been taking shape hundreds of years earlier. It is composed of twenty-four legal matters and written with the intent of highlighting these as the ones specifically being broken by whoever to whom the letter (an epistle) was addressed. It is generally believed that it was addressed to the Maccabean-Hasmonaean High Priest and other priests who had replaced the Sadducean Tzadokite priesthood. The Essenes are believed to have had affiliation or membership with them. It should be appreciated that as many as six separate copies were found and is indicative of the importance of this document. A little further on we will be introduced to a theory pertaining to the significance of MMT to the New Testament, as many copies of this document could have been in circulation during the first century of the first millennium.

There are various theories as to who wrote the MMT, which could be regarded as a manifesto rather than a letter. Possibly 'The Teacher of Righteousness' the one-time leader of the Essenes or the first breakaway Sadducees, who may have formed the original Essene sect.

This is unlikely for as is written in the Tzadokite Fragments and Damascus Document(s) that they had broken away some twenty years *before* the Teacher of Righteousness took up his leadership and therefore the letter could have been a collective plea by the sect in its formative years.

Other theories relate to Jonathan Maccabaeus or Hyrcanus II the Jerusalem High Priest 76 BCE - 35 BCE. Note earlier comments under 'The History of the Community'. The only 'identification' on the origin of the group from whom the letter came is their reference to themselves as 'The Sons of Aaron' and not 'Sons of Tzadok', which is often used in other writings of the sect. This could possibly indicate that the letter came from the early breakaway Sadducees whose roots stem from Aaron the first High Priest.

Prior to the deciphering of the MMT manuscripts or fragments, the reason for the Qumran sect separating from the mainstream was essentially based on supposition. Now for the first time it was revealed:

"[And you know that] we have segregated (separated) ourselves from the rest of the peop[le and we avoid mingling

in these affairs and associating with them in these things. And you k[now that there is not] to be found in our actions deceit or betrayal or evil, for concerning [these things w]e give[…and further] to you we have wr[itten] that you must understand the book of Moses [and the words of the Pro]phets and of David [and the annals] (events) [of eac]h generation" (Text from Garcia Martinez).

The MMT illustrates the background to an inner priestly dispute. It is a letter written to explain the differences between themselves (viz. their interpreting of Halachah) and whom they broke away from, speculated to be either their former Sadducean brethren or the Hasmonaean leader of the Temple. It was based on Jewish religious rulings that had not been obeyed. The letter is regarded as an attempt at reconciliation and to bring about a return to the Law of Moses. If once again observed, it would result in their return to Jerusalem and the Temple. They failed to bring this about and withdrew into themselves as the 'True Israel.'

To expand on the stereotyping of the Sadducees, I am also quoting from the internet site *www.Netzarim.htm* regarding comments from other writers on Qimron's interpretation of the MMT:

"Prof. Elisha Qimron has demonstrated from MMT that the traditional view was that the Sadducees rejected the Oral Law, is a misunderstanding of first-century discussions. The scroll MMT is correcting modern misconceptions on a wide scale - and revolutionizing modern perceptions of first-century Judaism - reveals that only the oral transmission of Halachah was rejected by the Sadducees. This work sheds light on the differences between the Qumran Sadducees verse the Hellenist - Roman Pseudo - Sadducees of the Temple."

My understanding of this is that the Sadducees wanted the Halachah to be recorded and thus did *not* oppose it. This is in staggering opposition to what we have been led to believe about one of the core differences between the Pharisees and the Sadducees. Perhaps then it would possibly be more accurate to delegate this belief to a *segment* of the Sadduceés. This endorses the danger of 'stereotyping'.

Prof. Qimron asserted that the popular view of the Essenes having rejected the Oral Law was in fact a misunderstanding. The scroll showed that until then, this Law which had been continuously transmitted in an *oral format* was rejected by them. They *recorded* albeit a small section (known to us) as part of their observations and codification in their own work.

It needs to be pointed out that the Oral Law, as accepted by the Pharisees and the Essenes had important differences. The Oral Law of the Pharisees (Rabbinic) is believed to be divinely transmitted from Mt. Sinai, whilst the Oral Law of the Essenes is assumed to stem from the inspired biblical exegesis of the sectarian sect. It also showed that they accepted the Halachah. (Ref. Schiffman)

Three significant revelations (inter alia) arise out of MMT:

1. It showed that the Mishnah or proto-Mishnah existed at least three hundred years before it was edited by Yehudah ha Nasi (Judah the Prince) around 200 CE.

2. It was written in a similar legalistic style of Hebrew as found in the Mishnah.

3. In Mishnaic discussions on similar matters between the Pharisees and Sadducees, they reflected the same views as those expressed by the Essenes in the MMT.

The Oral Law is an integral part of Judaism and scrupulously observed to this day. It is regarded as a second Torah in that it consists of the authoritative interpretation of the written Torah. This Law is believed to have been given by God to Moses at Sinai and passed down through the ages until its compilation by Yehuda ha Nasi.

It should be also noted that there is a continuum and correlation between MMT, and the laws as given in the Damascus Document, which is detailed in a paper by C.

Hempel of Cambridge University and can be found on the Orion website.

The disputes occurring pre- and post-Second Temple times revolved around the question of whether the Oral Law should be codified (written) or remain transmitted orally. The Essenes, it would seem argued that the oral transmission must be rejected in favor of codification. Before the recording of the Mishnah, its potential popularity was of concern to the rabbis (Pharisees) as they feared that it could rival the Torah in authority. Hence it was forbidden to put into writing and was thus elected to memory. The conveyance of oral tradition, history, and law was particularly common to all cultures at that time and subsequent eras, and remarkably retained a level of accuracy that is beyond our comprehension today.

The MMT, it was later realized, appeared to have a profound re-interpretation regarding the message of Paul and the New Testament. In my introductory paragraph to the MMT, one of the optional translations for *Miksat Ma'aseh* haTorah is 'Works of the Law'. These same words appear repeatedly in the Christian bible, specifically in Paul's letter to the Galatians. In the introduction to Galatians, I extract from the 'Good News' English Bible.......

"... the question arose as to whether a person must obey the Law of Moses (Torah) in order to be a true Christian. Paul argued that this was not necessary..." In Galatians there appears the conflict or contradiction with regard to the actual observance and disregard for the Law:

"For all who rely on Works of the Law are under a curse; for it is written, Cursed be everyone who does not abide by all things written in the book of the law, and do to them." (RSV).

In the original Greek version, the term *'ergoon nomou'* is used, which when translated means 'works of the law'. Even Jesus himself categorically stated that the Law (Torah) cannot be changed:

"Remember that as long as heaven and earth last, not the least point of the Law (Torah) will be done away with..." So

how is it possible that on the one hand the people are told to observe the Law, yet told that it doesn't apply?

In a paper by Wade Cox of 'The Christian Churches of God' Australia, he presents his view on this issue entitled 'The Works of the Law Text' - or MMT' (#104).

Cox writes: "*The Works of the Law have not been understood, and it is only now, through archaeological evidence, that we are able to understand what Paul was actually addressing. We can now demonstrate that Paul was actually talking about a body of writings, which became prevalent in Judaic sectarianism, based around Qumran.*" By Cox's implication, it was not the observation of the Laws of the Torah that were being rejected but rather the 'MMT' works, which could have been well known to Paul and others at the time. Relevance to its contents pertained to the laws of sacrifice and ceremonial purification, which had 'add on' changes recorded in the MMT and therefore could have been unacceptable to Paul.

Cox further mentions that Abegg, a renowned scrolls scholar, pointed out that the MMT "*is couched in the exact language of what Paul was rebutting in his letter to the Galatians*". In Romans 3:20 "*For no human being will be justified in his sight by works of the Law (Torah), since through the law comes knowledge of sin.*" (RSV) There also appears a contradiction here but (possibly) now with the knowledge and understanding of the MMT it may take on a completely different meaning.

I have included this view to additionally illustrate that numerous interpretations exist that so often show variance between the 'greatest minds' on scroll research, that it becomes unrealistic to follow the conclusions of even the most renown. The form I have mainly used represents scholarly views that allows for their own conclusions or research. I have tried to remain within the 'Standard Model' nevertheless.

The scrolls were discovered over a ten-year period and collated over a forty-year period. What seems to have taken place since they were first assembled and translated is that there are interpretively more variances to their texts, rather than new established breakthroughs. Be open-minded as your opinion could also be relevant.

The MMT (letter) can be divided into three sections:

Calendar

Dates for various festivals according to the solar calendar are stipulated including their sectarian festivals of 'new oil' and 'wood offerings'. These dates and aforementioned festivals do not comply with those given in the Torah. The Jewish calendar as prescribed by the Torah follows the lunar calendar.

Halachic or Religious Legal Texts

Twenty-four laws are listed herein, describing how their practices differed from those carried out at the Temple - including sacrificial worship. *"The correct conduct of sacrificial worship was the primary guarantor of their welfare* (meaning Israel). *Indeed, they regarded the sacrificial system as the prime connection of the people of Israel to God."* A number of these rulings and their presentation were identical to or had close parallels to those recorded in the Mishnah. Their recorded laws of Sabbath observation provide some of the closest approaches between MMT and the Oral Laws as discussed by the Rabbis in the Mishnah.

Ritual purity was a way of life for the Essenes. This of course originated in the Torah. To the Essenes it encompassed not only 'body, mind and spirit', but their lifestyle as well. In the Temple Scroll, it is recorded: "*You are to warn the children of Israel about every sort of impurity...*" Ritual purity was certainly not unique to them, as it was also part of the belief and practice of the 'observant' Jewish population. However, it was the interpretation and practical observance of these commandments of the Torah and Oral Law, and much later in the Mishnah that at times became 'life and death issues.

Such an example is recorded in the MMT and revolved around a dispute between the Pharisees and the Essenes. It dealt with the issue of a liquid being poured from a 'clean' vessel into an 'unclean' vessel resulting in the clean vessel also becoming unclean. The Essenes declared that this impurity arose via the upward movement of the impurity, which took place via the stream flow itself. Hundreds of years later this was referred to and recorded in the Mishnah. The Mishnah upheld the Pharisaic ruling that disputed the upward contamination.

"And concerning liquid streams we hold that they are not pure nor do these streams act as a separator between the impure and the pure. For the liquid of streams and of what receives them are alike."

Now, this may sound insignificant in the 'real world' of the Holocaust and the destruction of the Twin Towers, but it is such rulings that could be the differentiating factor between entire religious schools of thought. In this case, the rabbis in other halachic issues dealt with cookware, the Red Heifer, and by-products from unclean and clean animals. Also, laws were re-stated that prevented a person with physical deformities from entering the Temple and performing sacrifices. Even dogs are mentioned, since they were not to be brought into the 'holy camp' which was Jerusalem, to prevent them from eating any stray bones that may have derived from animal sacrifices.

Admonitions (Warnings)

It ends with examples from Solomon, Jeroboam, the Kings of Israel, and David to confirm the truth and includes warnings of separation and destruction. There is a message of the 'end of days' illustrating their apocalyptic beliefs:

"And also we have written to you some of the works of the Torah which we think are good for you and for your people, for in you [we saw] intellect and knowledge of the Torah. Reflect on all these matters and seek from Him that He may support your counsel and keep far from you the evil scheming and the counsel of Beliel so that at the end of time, you may rejoice in finding that some of our words are true. And it shall be reckoned to you as in justice when you do what is upright

and good before Him, for your good and that of Israel."
4QMMT 112-118 (Martinez).

The MMT From Different Perspectives

- Professor Qimron, who originally compiled the MMT and John Strugnell, at first considered it to be a document to have been compiled during the earliest stages of the formation of the group. It was written to persuade the current Hasmonaean leader to forsake his practices which oppose their and Jewish belief and practice at the time.

- Both Qimron and Strugnell, even before its publication, questioned whether the MMT would be better considered a proclamation an open letter as opposed to being addressed to someone specifically. Nevertheless, they continued in the assumption that it was addressed to the Hasmonaean leader. It is noted. The letter refers to a split or a schism with the Jerusalem Temple, the letter has a tone of reconciling differences.

- Professor Steven Faade of the History of Judaism, Yale University, suggested that the MMT an educational text used to train candidates and new initiates of the community for the purpose of reinforcing the process of social separation.

- Another theory proposes that the letter did not originate from the Qumran Community, but rather it was a letter addressed to the community!! This hypothesis implies that the letter did not originate from the Quarantines but could have been composed from outside

The Copper Scroll

Insight

"One of the questions that disturbed the researchers who dealt with the Copper Scroll and held up its research was the question of the scroll's authenticity."

This scroll is unique in several aspects: Firstly, it is not written on animal skin or papyrus but as the name implies, its script is hammered out with a stylus onto a copper sheet. Secondly, it deals exclusively with one subject - treasure items that are hidden in 60 or 64 sites. Then there is a third aspect - It is the only known scroll that is not part of the Dead Sea Scrolls collection in Israel, as it is housed in Amman, Jordan. The paleography or the script differs from the usual script of the Qumran scrolls and the language is closer to Mishnaic (legal) Hebrew. It could also be described as '*The Enigma Scroll*", for even until recent times archaeologists are more than divided about its purpose, interpretation, and validity. In addition, it is not known whether this scroll was of the Essene origin or was brought and hidden by an outside source. All these questions are open to speculation. The opinion is that it dates from a period after the other scrolls.

The Copper Scroll was discovered on a ledge at the back of Cave 3 in 1952 by a team of archaeologists from the Ecole Biblique Jerusalem and the Albright Institute.

It had separated into two scrolls alongside each other, having separated or broken in half with age, and was in an oxidized and in a brittle state - still in its original rolled-up form.

The first and very important challenge was to unroll it with minimal damage, and secondly to decipher it. Due to the complexity involved in the unrolling process, it was not until three years later that this task was undertaken in the department of mechanical engineering at the University of Manchester, under Professor Baker - at the suggestion of a team member from the UK, John Allegro to L Harding head of the Jordanian Antiquities Department. The publication of the scroll had however been designated to J Milik. I mention these names as they were all major 'players' in the earlier years of Dead Sea Scroll publications and not least with the politics that accompanied them.

It was eventually decided to open the scrolls by cutting through them layer by layer until eventually, twenty-three hemispherical slices resulted. With hindsight, controversy regarding what could have been the best procedure has abounded. The edges of the cuts themselves resulted in further rapid oxidation, with the consequence of letters or parts thereof being lost. It is coded 3Q15.

Deciphering the Contents, Then and Now

In 1959 and 1960, Milik and Allegro published their own books on the Copper Scroll. The scroll measures approximately 2.5 meters or 8 ft in length and 1 ft or 30 cm. wide with a total of twelve columns. It exclusively lists in cryptic format sixty-four hiding places of Temple treasures, artifacts, and a considerable amount of gold and silver.

M Lehmann in an article in BAR magazine believes that the Copper Scroll recorded the sites of Temple treasure collected *after* the destruction of the Second Temple in 70 CE, in the hope that it would be speedily rebuilt. The vast quantity of what possibly was coins could perhaps have come from the Temple funds. These funds were derived from the 'half shekel' annual dues contributed by the Jewish people as a form of tax to their Temple.

The quantity of this treasure is so huge that they would today, in weight alone be worth billions of dollars! Again, following reinterpretation, these quantities have since been considerably reduced. To further add to the enigma of the scroll, not a single item has been found despite the most intensive investigations.

The general conclusion of academia has been to label it as: 'the work of a madman', a 'forgery', 'folklore' importantly 'a charlatan who did not know Hebrew'. I need to mention that (a), the (five) scribes who so laboriously created a unique form of a scroll in beaten copper, surely must have had measured intent. It thus could be true, *or* a purposeful red herring (b), the finding of these treasure sites is solely dependent on knowing the geography *and* geology *and* topography of the terrain of Palestine and Jerusalem at the time, as each site is designated by such cryptic clues.

Lehmann, in 'BAR' writes "*Its language is also different from that of the other scrolls. While it is in Hebrew, the kind of Hebrew is closer to the Hebrew of the Mishnah*". Lawrence Schiffman stated that "*the real treasure ….is the Hebrew language in that Scroll…. there is a tremendous wealth of information in this text about terminology and language*". Subsequently the contents have undergone a renewed investigation. It has been established that there are about eighty 'questionable words' not found in *classical* or *rabbinical literature* that is used in the scroll. These have since been re-interpreted and used once again to find the items listed.

Examples of Clues

Extracted from 'The Dead Sea Scrolls in English' by G. Vermes

Col.1 3. *In the great cistern, which is in the courtyard of the little colonnade, at its very bottom, closed with sediment towards the upper opening: nine hundred talents.* (A talent is an ancient, designated weight)

Col. 2 12. *In the pond, which is east of Kohlit, at a northern angle, dig four cubits: twenty-two talents.*

Col. 3 13. *In the courty[ard of]...in a southerly direction [at] nine cubits: silver and gold vessels of offering, bowls, cups, tubes/pipes, libation vessels.* In all, six hundred and nine. (A 'libation' vessel is a type of jug used for pouring at a religious ceremony. On the Sabbath day, the sacrifice included 'a wine-libation that was poured into pipes set into the altar and water during the Sukkot service).

Col. 8 37. *In the heap of stones at the mouth of the Pottery ravine, dig three cubits: 4 talents.*

Col. 9 44. *At the sound of waters close to the edge of the gutter on the East Side of the exit, dig seven cubits: 9 talents.* ('Sound of water,' could be a waterfall).

Recently, the editor of *Biblical Archaeology Review* (BAR) - renowned authority on the Dead Sea Scrolls -published a book on the Copper Scroll. I have not yet had the opportunity to ascertain his interpretation of its origin and purpose. One must be very brave (inter alia) to be dogmatic in this field. Robert Feather, a metallurgist and 'scholar of world religions', states in his book on the Copper Scroll that it originates from Egypt and Egyptian priests "*may well have carried with them the knowledge of where some of the treasure of Akhenaten's Great Temple and treasury were buried*". Akhenaten is believed to have been the Pharaoh during the time Joseph was viceroy of Egypt.

The Habakkuk Commentary

> ### Insight
>
> "The Habakkuk Commentary deals with the fulfillment of God's prophecy regarding his elect people. The writer saw their own group history in words of scripture foretold long ago."

Before covering the following important and revealing scroll, we need to understand the word *pesher*. It is a re-interpretation of prophetic texts and psalms from the bible. The basis of pesher is to extrapolate from the original writings of the prophecy and place them as though they were written and pertaining to a then current time of a particular period in history as being experienced by the interpreter.

Pesher is found in the Qumran sectarian literature and is presented as a mystical, cryptic, and eschatological interpretation of a biblical passage. It originated through the (supposed) divinely inspired interpretation of a revealed text. 'Raz' is the Hebrew term whereby the Prophets received their revelations in dreams or visions. Pesher was applied in a similar vein.

Pesher is an Aramaic loan-word in Qumran Hebrew for 'meaning', 'interpretation' or 'explanation'. This was done with the purpose of using an author's text to give credibility and validation to its contents. Broadly speaking, Pesher can refer to commentaries on biblical works, particularly applied during Temple times. This would involve quoting a verse, followed by an explanation.

The 'divine' interpreter responsible for this interpretation was none other than the Teacher of Righteousness, the leader of those living at Qumran. This charismatic leader revealed the meaning of Scripture and clarified God's desire of them. The Qumranites thus knew that *they* were chosen for a *renewed covenant* as explained through pesher by their Teacher.

Critically we need to appreciate the following by James. H. Charlesworth who wrote: *"The pesharim are the creations of the Qumranites, who believed they were living in 'the latter days' and that the prophets, guided by the 'Holy Spirit', prophesied not (only) about their own time, but the latter days and especially about the Qumranites' place in the 'economy of salvation.' Meaning, the Qumranites perceived their own secular history through ancient prophecies now revealed pristinely by God through the Righteous Teacher."* (Charlesworth is Prof. of NT Language and Literature at Princeton Theological Seminary. I have noticed in *my* observation that at times he puts across a Christian approach or usage of language to some of his statements.)

There is a school of thinking for example, that believes the 'Book of Daniel' was written much later, with the impact being that its contents in a 'prophetic' sense were shown to be correct. Jesus' prediction or vision of the impending and post-destruction image of the Second Temple is I believe a good example of this. Examples of pesher in the Scrolls will be covered in a chapter that will follow further on. These forms of writings often had an apocalyptic theme to them. The *pesharim* (pl.) are regarded as interpretations of written prophetic texts that can be understood as the 'unraveling of mysteries.'

Sections of the Christian bible are said to contain many examples of pesher, according to certain scholars, with much having been written on this aspect.

Lawrence Schiffman in his book 'Reclaiming the Dead Sea Scrolls', writes: "*The sect inherited a method of legal interpretation we find represented in the Temple Scroll and underpinning some of the laws in the Halachic Letter*" (MMT). He also adds that the sect had its own method of Halachic exegesis that gave rise to its legal teachings. Generally, pesharim (pl.) follow a pattern whereby first a biblical passage is quoted, followed by an interpretation.

Pesher would take a section of the bible and provide its translation. It thus "*gave us a window into how the Qumran community understood their sacred texts*" (Charlesworth). They were adding the (that) text to their history. For them, the text became an understanding of a secret that they had unlocked!

The most important and complete pesher scroll is that of Habakkuk which also is the most widely quoted. However, in addition there were numerous other scroll fragments that were pesher scrolls or incorporated pesher.

Habakkuk Pesher

Habakkuk is classified as one of the 'Minor' Prophets together with Malachi, Zechariah, Haggai, and Nachum to name a few, all being part of the canon of the Hebrew Bible. The term

'Minor' is designated to those prophets because their known recorded works were not as lengthy as the works from others such as Isaiah, Jeremiah, and Ezekiel etc. They were *not* 'inferior' to the other prophets. 1QpH is a single copy that showed evidence of errors of copying by two scribes viz 'A' and 'B.' After line 13, 'B' took over and completed the copying. Both scribes remodeled some of the words and letters they thought to be incorrectly copied. An example of *scribal errors*.

In the original Book, the prophet Habakkuk delivered his prophecies circa 650 BCE in Judea. This was when the Jewish people were under threat by the Chaldeans (the Babylonians). Also, there was strife between the religious and secular. The central theme of Habakkuk is the prophet calling out to God and asking where He is whilst all this misery abounds, and whether God has the intention to bring it to an end....

"O Lord, how long shall I cry and thou wilt not hear! Even cry out unto thee of violence, and thou wilt not save!" (Habakkuk 1:2)

Habakkuk prophesies that the Babylonians or the Chaldeans, as they are referred to in the Bible, will *"come for all violence"* and *"gather captives as the sand".* Then God tells the prophet to boldly record this fact. The book has both a pessimistic prophecy and an optimistic note of encouragement and leaves the reader in fear of the immediate future but knowing that in the end the Babylonians will be overcome. The book also refers to how the wicked treat the righteous...the way the Essenes saw themselves and Israel under the Roman occupation.

In Cave 1, the thirteen-column scroll 1QpHab was discovered in fairly good condition. The scroll was dated to the first century BCE, validating the times it was written and recorded. It is regarded as one of the most important references to the origins of the Essenes viz. how they saw themselves theologically. It is in a category of its own, being part biblical and part sectarian. The book of Habakkuk was to the Essenes the exemplification of the situation in Palestine, and that in which they found themselves. In the pesher or interpretation, the writer applies biblical prophecies to contemporary events. It was written in an eschatological format and referred to the danger from the Romans, cryptically called the 'Kittim'. In the book of Daniel there is also a reference to the Kittim. They were so named because they maintained a garrison on the Island of Kittim, better known as Cyprus, today. The conflict between the observant and the wicked and the conflict between their leader the 'Teacher of Righteousness' Heb. *Moreh Tzedek* and the 'Wicked Priest' Heb. *Koheyn Ha-rasha* are re-interpreted to follow a similar theme to the original prophecy.

The Essenes saw the Teacher of Righteousness as a unique prophet, applying pesher. He took the divine revelations a step further with the book of Habakkuk by revealing the mystery of the hidden. We will read how the writer considered to be The Teacher, fulfilled his ability as the 'Interpreter of the Law.' In a Talmudic aggadah (story), God showed Moses the entire past and future. Similarly, in the current and final era then, the Teacher was also believed to possess the ability to interpret visions of the ancient prophets. Through this ability the Teacher could appreciate and understand that the time was approaching for the End of Days.

He begins with the quotation of the original words from the bible and then gives *his* explanation. Explanation is preceded with the Pesher by saying each time, 'this refers to' or 'this means.'

Examples and Extracts from the Pesher

Original Biblical Text: *"I will stand upon my watch and set me upon the tower and will watch to see what He will say unto me and what I shall answer when I am reproved. And the Lord answered me (Habakkuk), and said, Write the vision, and make it plain upon tablets, that he may run that readeth it. For the vision is yet for an appointed time, but at the end it shall speak and not lie."* (Habakkuk 2:1)

In simpler English the above <u>meant</u>: He will take up watch on a tower and wait for what God has to say. And God told Habakkuk to write down what would happen to the final generation, but he did not make known to him when that time would come to an end. The one who reads it should be able to understand the message immediately. And in the end, what will be revealed will be clear to all.

In Pesher Habakkuk this is recorded in the actual scroll as:

"So I will stand on watch and station myself on my watchtower and wait for what he will say to me and [what I will reply to] His rebuke. Then the Lord answered me [and said, Write down the vision plainly] on tablets, so that with ease someone can read it."

The scroll then continues…

This refers to i.e., "the Pesher is": (actual wording introducing that scroll) then God told Habakkuk to write down what is going to happen to the generation to come, but when that period would be complete He did not make known to him. When it says, *"so that with ease someone can read it"*, the Pesher is referring to the Teacher of Righteousness to whom God made known all the mysteries of revelations of His servants the prophets. (End of extraction).

A prophecy testifies about a specific period; it speaks of a time and alludes to no other. This means (according to the Pesher) that the 'Last Days' will be lengthy and last much longer than the prophet had said, *"for God's revelations are truly mysterious"*.

(Reference: Wise, Abegg and Cook. DSS 'A New Translation')

What the Pesher implies:

This concerns the Teacher of Righteousness, to whom God made known all the mysteries of the words of His servants the Prophets. The final age shall be prolonged and shall exceed all that the Prophets have said; *"for the mysteries of G-d are astounding…"* (Vermes)

Thus, the Teacher will understand what will be, as God has allowed him to have further insight into the original book of Habakkuk. To the Teacher has been revealed plans for the founding of the community, his rise as the Teacher and anticipation for 'the end of days.'

Original Biblical Text: *"Because thou hast spoilt many nations, all the remnant of the peoples shall spoil thee."* (Habakkuk 2:8)

Simpler Text from 'Good News Bible': *"You have plundered the people of many nations, but now those who have survived will plunder you…"*

In the Pesher Habakkuk it is recorded as: *"Its hidden interpretation refers to the last priests of Jerusalem, who gathered wealth and loot from the spoils of the people, but at the end of their days their wealth with their spoil will be given unto the hands of the army of the Kittim."*

Original Biblical Text: *"Woe unto him that giveth his neighbor (fellow) drink that puttest poison to him and maketh him drunk also…"* (Habakkuk 2:15)

Simpler Text from 'Good News Bible': *"You are doomed! In your fury you humiliated and disgraced your neighbors; you made them stagger as though they were drunk".*

In the Pesher Habakkuk, it is recorded as: *"Woe to the one who gets his friend drunk, pouring out his anger, making him drink, just to get a look at their holy days."*

This refers to the wicked Priest who pursued the Teacher of Righteousness to destroy him in the heat of his anger at his place of exile (Qumran). At the time set aside for the repose of the Day of Atonement, he appeared to them to destroy them and bring them to ruin on a fast day, the Sabbath intended for their repose. (Wise et al)

What the Pesher implies:

It would appear that after the break-up between the Teacher of Righteousness and those in the Temple going into exile, he and his followers were hunted down by his opponent, the

Wicked Priest. This confrontation took place on the holiest day of the year (Yom Kippur, the Day of Atonement), according to the Essene calendar!

Importantly, not only does the Teacher convey his divine ability to interpret, but also claimed that certain of the scripture was written with him in mind. This is based on the way he interpreted.

Other 'juxtapositions' of Pesher terminology mentions the 'Spreader of Lies' 'Man of the Lie' 'The Society of the Yachad' (Community) and the 'Family of Absalom', thought to represent a (the) Sadducean faction, as Absalom revolted against his father's rule.

Thanksgiving Hymns - The Hodayot

This collection of works covers scrolls and a collection of fragments known as Hodayot. Essentially, they are hymns of thanksgiving and reflect the lives, feelings, and period in which the writers lived. They are unique to the author('s) and those members whom they represented and thus reflect the outlook, lives, and the times in which they were written.

Hodayot were also found at Masada, having possibly been brought there by the escaping Qumran refugees.

I will for the purposes of this book, also include under this heading, Psalms and Poems.

The development and inclusion of prayer into the daily life of the Jewish people began with the Hebrew Patriarchs. They were often in a form of pleading to God on behalf of the Jewish people. The psalms of David began to form an essential part of the liturgy including his own thanksgiving songs of praise..."Give thanks to the Lord, declare his name..." Chron.16:8.

Later, the 'Men of the Great Assembly' at the beginning of the Second Temple period, composed important prayers for the nation that are said daily by the Jewish people even to this day.

Prayers were not commonly said daily by many of the observant Jewish people during the era of the temples. Of course, when visiting the Temple on the Sabbath and other festivals, prayers and prayer offerings took place. Today, set prayers are a daily part of the religious individual's life and are recorded in prayer books.

Most of the Hebrew prayers were composed after the destruction of the Second Temple in 70 CE, and later canonized into the official prayer book by the rabbis of Yavne, who were allowed to establish themselves there by the Roman emperor Vespasian.

During the era of the composition of the Dead Sea Scrolls, such prayer books or rather scrolls were certainly not freely available to the masses. The literacy level of the nation then would have been much lower than it is today. However, the Essenes formed the exception. Prayer was an essential part of their daily life.

Having isolated themselves from the Temple, a vacuum was created which was filled by their sectarian prayers. They had their own style of worshipping and praising God. This way of life flourished at Qumran. It became their way of experiencing the heavenly realm, part of their eschatological preparation and affirmation of divine law and their own sectarian rules. These hymns were shown to have drawn inspiration from the Psalms, Jeremiah, the book of Lamentations, and Job. They are songs of 'outpourings of the soul', adoration of God, of submission to the Divine will, and of God's hatred for the Belial, the evil forces. The eschatological themes incorporated hope and anguish and the thought of the imminent end of the world, future happiness, and the presence of angels.

Among the authorship theories of the Hodayot are:

- they were written by the Teacher of Righteousness.
- they were written by anonymous authors.
- the core of hymns was written by the Teacher.

The first scrolls of Thanksgiving Hymns were found in the famous Cave 1 and are coded 1QH and 1Q35. In 1952, many other Hodayot fragments were discovered in Cave 4, coded 4Q427-32. Dating them has been speculative. They appear to have been written during the two centuries preceding the beginning of the millennium. Vermes writes that there are two fundamental themes running through the whole collection: namely salvation and knowledge.

Another interpretation of the themes is presented by J. Jaffe of the Univ. of Pen., who divided the works into: "I, the humble devotee" - where the writer portrays himself in reverence and awe.

In the second section, he portrays himself as *"I the assured servant"* in other words, one who will lead the people in God's way.

There could have been a third section, where the author sees himself as "*I am a creature of clay*" as he speculates about God's influence on him.

The Hodayot provide rich theological detail and guidelines and insight into the prayers of Qumran. They have an apocalyptic theme and significantly, in several verses, there is the usage of the same language later seen in the Book of Revelations in the Christian Bible. I have extracted from Vermes' translation one of the hymns. No doubt you will be as taken aback as I was with the moving and beautiful wording below, which is only a small part of the collection. These words were first written 2,200 years ago at Qumran:

Hymn 5

[I thank]Thee, O Lord,

as befits the greatness of thy power

and the multitude of thy marvels for ever and ever.

[Thou art a merciful God] and rich in [favors],

pardoning those who repent of their sin

and visiting the iniquity (sin/evil) of the wicked.

[Thou delightest in] free-will offering [of the righteousness]

but iniquity Thou hatest always.

Thou hast favored me, Thy servant,

with a spirit of knowledge,

[that I may choose] the truth [and goodness]

and loath all the ways of iniquity.

And I have loved Thee freely

and with all my heart;

[contemplating the mysteries of] Thy wisdom

[I have sought thee].

For this is from thy hand

and [nothing is done] without [Thy will].

This scroll in its original state is estimated to have been about 3.5 meters or 10 feet long and 30 cm or 12 inches wide. When discovered, it was in two parts. One was in three separate folded sheets, and the balance was composed of about seventy fragments. Two distinctive handwritings featured on the scroll and the language was based on biblical Hebrew with some Aramaic and Samaritan influences. On the authorship of the scroll, there are two schools of opinion: the first, that it was written by the Teacher of Righteousness (TR), and the second that it was written by his disciple(s). The reason for the speculation that the author could be the TR is that the "*I assured servant*" appears to be one who is above the average man and who has been given mystical insight:

"Through me you have enlightened the face of the Many

You have increased them

Even making them accountable

For you have shown me your wondrous mysteries

By your wondrous advice you have strengthened position

And worked wonders in the presence of the Many on account of your glory..."

It is believed that this was written specifically for the Essenes themselves, based on the style of writings and references to the hymns found in the War Scroll. These hymns have been shown to draw inspiration from the Psalms, Jeremiah, the book of Lamentations, and Job.

It is interesting to read that the (speculative) attitude of the Essenes towards women is recorded in one of the psalms, which speaks of the sinner as *"some born of a woman"*, implying that man who is 'issued' from a woman, becomes 'defiled' and makes him unworthy. In Psalm 51 'of David', perhaps he too was also intimating a similar belief when he wrote in verse 7: "...*and in sin did my mother conceive me*".

The concept of predestination is expressed in Hymn 6:

"By thy wisdom [all things exist from] eternity,

and before creating them Thou knewest their works

for ever and ever.

[Nothing] is done [without Thee]

and nothing is known unless Thou desire it." (Vermes)

Also, from 1 QH column vii verses 19 and 21: *"For him, from the womb, you determined the period of approval"*...and...*"from the womb you have predetermined them for the day of annihilation"* (Martinez). The latter also accentuates the apocalyptic theme.

Nevertheless, despite inherent predestination in the scroll, the author says that God puts the man through ordeals to purify him and then restores him through punishment. In rabbinic Judaism, predestination is not a concept. Rather it is the element of 'free will' that is believed to influence Jewish destiny. Thus predestination, which is also contrary to Christian teachings, was rather unique to the Essenes and the Sadducees.

The attitude towards the Pharisees (Seekers of smooth things) is expressed by:

"I thank Thee, O Lord,

for thou hast [fastened] Thine eyes upon me.

Thou hast saved me from the zeal

Of lying interpreters,

And from the congregation who seek smooth things" (Vermes)

I end off with a short extract from Hymn 14:

"Thou wilt raise up survivors among Thy people

And a remnant within Thine inheritance.

Thou wilt purify and cleanse them of their sin

For all their deeds are in Thy truth.

Thou wilt judge them in Thy great loving-kindness

And the multitude of Thy mercies

And in the abundance of Thy pardon,

Teaching them according to Thy word;" (Vermes)

Here, you have just read only eight lines out of a 128-line Hymn. If you have the desire to praise or thank God, it would be surely most appropriate to use the text of this Hymn written over 2,000 years ago!

When reaching your next level and you begin the purchase of books relevant to the Scrolls, be sure to obtain one of the comprehensive translations by Vermes; also Wise, Abegg and Cook, or Garcia Martinez. Turn to these Hymns and begin to appreciate their power, insight, and beauty.

Qumran Psalms Scrolls

The canonized Book of Psalms of the Hebrew bible number 150 psalms and is separated into five divisions or books. They are not randomized, and each has its own designated number. The order in which they appear is also canonized into what is now called the 'Psalter'. A well-known example is a famous psalm 'The Lord is my Shepherd', known as Psalm 23. Many were said to have been written by King David although some scholars doubt this. Different composers recorded other psalms in that book.

I mentioned earlier that the Essenes religious observance focused heavily on prayer. This is further borne out by the Psalm Scrolls discovered in Caves 4 and 11. From Cave 11, the scroll 11QPs contained forty-eight excerpts from the (Masoretic) Fourth Book of Psalms which has 60 psalms in total. It is almost four meters in length has 68 columns and is one of the longest. It is dated around 30 - 50 BCE. Thirty-six of them are known Psalms, but not in the same order of the canonized Book.

In addition, it contains sectarian psalms and 'non-canonical' material. This could indicate that the Psalm Psalter had not yet crystallized both to the community at large or the Essenes themselves. These included Apocryphal Psalms, the Wisdom text known as Ben Sirach, also 'Hymn to the Creator' and 'Apostrophe to Zion', to mention some. There is still some confusion whether these additional psalms were, in fact, liturgical i.e., prayer texts, and that as such, they could be considered as a collection of hymns instead. There are several psalms in the Jewish prayer book which are very much part of the liturgy and could therefore be regarded as hymns or *piyut* in Hebrew.

I would like to quote from a 'Fragments' seminar held in New South Wales Australia in July 2000. Questions were put to leading scrolls scholars by the host, Rachael Kohn. One of them was as follows:

"*I was wondering though if a Psalter is used liturgically, whether it would undergo some shifts and re-ordering according to the congregation? But Geza (Vermes), can you comment on the Psalms Scroll?*".

Geza Vermes: "*Yes, well let's try to clarify one point. I imagine that most of our audience and the people, who are listening to us on the Internet, think that there are 150 Psalms. This is the figure that you find in your ordinary Bibles. According to the Psalms Scroll from Cave 11 from Qumran, (I'm looking at the text so that I'm not misleading you) David wrote 3,600 Psalms and 364 songs for the New Moons and feast days. In all, the songs which he uttered were 446, and four songs to make music on behalf of all those who were possessed by evil spirits. In all, they were 4,050 Psalms. Now that's a bit different from the 150 to which we are used".*

What has been noticed is that the canonized psalms recorded in the Psalm Scrolls were part of the repertoire of the Temple's liturgy. Also, even though the 'Hymn for the Creator' is attributed to the Essene composition, it nevertheless bears a close relationship to synagogue prayers today. Thus, and importantly, this scroll can be regarded as the Essene Prayer Book.

The Psalms Scrolls 4QPs from Cave 4 and other caves also contain unique Essene liturgical compositions, in addition to a selection of Masoretic psalms ranging from Psalm 5 onwards. Some were in the style of writing and grammar unique to the Essenes, whist others known as proto-Masoretic versions appeared to have come from outside the community. These proto texts were however in the majority compared to the Essene textual style. Below is an extract from what is regarded as one of the most beautiful Psalms, the 'Apostrophe to Zion'. The scroll also includes some previously known compositions, including Psalm 151 found in the Septuagint. Psalm 151 appeared in the last part of the scroll. It is considered to be a psalm of David and speaks of him as a shepherd chosen to fight Goliath and having defeated him. This has led scholars to believe that at the time, the Psalms were not yet finally canonized or that that they were prayer texts. To this day it has not been clarified.

Apostrophe to Zion

I will remember you, O Zion, for a blessing;

With all my might I love you;

Your memory is to be blessed forever.

Your hope is great O Zion;

Peace and your awaited salvation will come.

Generation after generation shall dwell in you,

and generations of the pious shall be your ornament.

They who desire the day of your salvation

Shall rejoice in the greatness of your glory,

And the beautiful streets shall they make tinkling sounds.

You shall remember the pious deeds of your prophets,

And shall glorify yourself in the deeds of your pious ones.

Cleanse violence from your midst;

Lying and iniquity, they may be cut off from you.

Your sons shall rejoice within you,

and your cherished ones shall be joined to you... (Vermes)

In concluding this section, I can only suggest that you read Vermes' book 'The Complete Dead Sea Scrolls in English' and refer to section B, 'Hymns and Poems' to do justice to the vast liturgical works found and the compilation of the Dead Sea Scrolls

Songs of the Sabbath Sacrifice

Insight

"The songs evoke angelic praise and elaborate on angelic priesthood, the heavenly temple, and the Sabbath worship in that temple. They are also known as the Angelic Liturgy."

It is also referred to as: 'Songs for the *Holocaust* (holocaust from the Greek meaning *sacrifice*) of the Sabbath' and 'Angelic Liturgy'. Classified as one of the 'Mystical Texts', it is made up of nine scrolls in all: Eight fragments from Cave 4 and a large fragment from Masada. Later, another fragment was also found in Cave 11. It is thus coded 4Q400-407 or 4QShirShabb. 'Shir Olah ha-Shabbat' in Hebrew.

Interestingly, both the Songs of the Sabbath Sacrifice and the Book of Revelations from the Christian Bible reflect the same priestly and mystical background. Revelations was composed between 50 and 70 CE. The question then arises as to whether there was a connection or influence from Jewish sectarian groups or the Essenes themselves in the composition of the book.

Whether it is exclusively Essene or whether another sectarian terminology is used, is still open to question. Dated around 75-50 BCE and written in the Herodian script, it covered worship over a period of thirteen Sabbaths of the first quarter of each year…13 x 4 = 52 weeks - recalling that they used the solar calendar. Some scholars regard these texts rather be contemporary Jewish writings. This is also based on the discovery of a large fragment having been found at Masada, which could suggest that it circulated among Jews of various backgrounds. Some of the phraseology and terminology is similar to other texts from Qumran believed to be of Essene origin. Even if the Essenes did not compose those Masada scrolls, the discovery of eight manuscripts there could indicate acceptance within the Essene theology and liturgy.

The text's composition is divided into thirteen different sections, one for each Sabbath of the year's first quarter. They are the hymns of angelic priests. Possibly each weekly composition was recited together with the burnt offering that took place every Sabbath at the Temple. "*The time when the Sabbath sacrifice was offered was a sort of divine window of opportunity, a time when prayers were especially effective. The songs intended to unite the worshiper with the angels worshiping in heaven*" (Wise et al). Each begins with its designated number:

"For the Master. The song of the sacrifice of the seventh Sabbath on the sixteenth of the month..."

They covered the angels praising God, angelic priesthood, the Heavenly Temple, and worship in that temple. Inspiration for the wording was heavily drawn from the Bible, the Book of Ezekiel, for some of these weeks. As in Ezekiel, there are references to God's throne-chariot, known as the 'Merkavah'. The Merkavah also appears in the Apocryphal book of Enoch and has mystical connotations. Hence these collections of scrolls are also classified as 'mystical', in view of their ethereal content and presentation in themes related to the apocalyptic community. The settings are either earthly, to which angels are invited, or the heavenly realm, to which the people ascend for their Sabbath worship.

Allow me to extract from Vermes' translation of scroll 4Q405 which portrays two theological themes: the heavenly sanctuary and the throne-chariot:

"The [cheru]bim prostate themselves before Him and bless.

As they rise, a whispered divine voice [is heard], and there is a roar of praise.

When they drop their wings, there is a [whispere]d divine voice.

The cherubim bless the image of the throne chariot above the firmament,

[and] they praise [the majes]ty of the luminous firmament beneath his seat of glory.

When the wheels advance, angles of holiness come and go.

From between His glorious wheels, there is as it were a fiery vision of the most holy spirits.

About them, the appearance of rivulets of fire, in the likeness of gleaming brass,

And a work of ...radiance in many-colored glory marvelous pigments, clearly mingled.

The spirits of the god[like] beings (Wise et al) *move perpetually with the glory of the marvelous chariot."*

Extremely beautiful words! You should read the entire text using both the Vermes and Wise translations for further inspiration.

The purpose of this book is also to introduce the many wondrous texts currently known as the 'Dead Sea Scrolls'. It is the briefest insight to this vast library of scrolls, written with the purpose of opening a 'new world' of information which hopefully will lead to a more detailed study of the subject.

Chapter 13: Additional Scrolls

By mid-2002, the Dead Sea Scrolls and fragments were established to be close to what would have comprised 950+ individual scrolls. These scrolls or scroll texts were published over a period of 50 years. Many, in particular the biblical and some of the sectarian scrolls, had a number of duplicate copies made. The biblical scrolls alone accounted for just under a quarter, or about 230 of the collection. Of these, about 50 other copies or duplicates also existed - thus 50 + 230 = 280, leaving about 700 not covered in this book. My arithmetic may not be spot on but helps to give an idea of the vastness of the found collection. Of these, around 700 very small fragments remained, which could have been part of some longer and more profoundly revealing scrolls. How tantalizing is that!

A full complete translation now exists recorded in Vermes' 'The Complete Dead Sea Scrolls in English.' Martinez's 'The Dead Sea Scrolls Translated' and 'Dead Sea Scrolls' by Wise, Abegg and Cook - also available on microfiche.

The most cited reference (serial) works are called 'Discoveries in the Judean Desert', also known by the letters 'DJD'. The DJD are the primary references, translations and commentaries and official series on the Scrolls presented by the world's greatest scholars, or those who were granted privilege to contribute to these works. They are individually numbered: DJD I, DJD II up to currently #39 and are published by The Oxford University Press. The first edition was published in 1955 and the most recent in 1997.

List of Scroll Titles

Other works of varying length include the following allocated titles - their names may differ at times according to various scholarly titles. Nevertheless, the names of the Scrolls largely indicate their composition. I will be listing only some of them to give the reader an idea of the variety of the compositions and will give insight into some of them, the more significant and widely known scrolls. Thereafter I will be summarizing a selected few and leave the balance to be further investigated by you, the reader.

The breakdown of the speculated 1,000 individual scrolls is approximately as follows:

One-quarter biblical books -Tanach

One-quarter sectarian, pertaining to Qumran

Balance of known and unknown Jewish literature, including works of the Apocrypha

Pesher Nachum

Testament of the 12 Patriarchs

Pesher Psalms

Rule of Benedictions

Ritual of Marriage

Wiles of the Wicked Woman

Testament of Naphtali

Visions of Amram

Sapiential (mystery) Work

Florigium (anthology)

Prayer for King Jonathan

Daily Prayers

Words of the Luminaries

Purification Rituals

Aramaic Apocalypse

Messianic Apocalypse

Pesher Isaiah

Horoscopes

Coded Horoscope

The Book of Giants

Various biblical commentaries

Laws for Purification

The Book of Secrets

Apocryphal Psalms

The Vision of Daniel

The words of Moses

Words of a Sage to sons

Aramaic Deed of Sale

List of False Prophets

Astronomical works

Prayer for Mercy

Beatitudes

Leviticus in Paleo-Hebrew

Wiles of the Wicked Women

Work Containing Prayers

Meditation on Creation

Calendrial Document

Zodiology and Brontology

A Discourse on the Exodus

Admonition of the Flood

Visions and Interpretations

A Vision of the New Jerusalem

Marriage Ritual

Apocryphon of Levi

Unidentified Greek Fragments

Laws of Gleaning

The Vision of Amram

Sermon on the Flood

Priestly Service on New Year

Aramaic Text on the Persian Period

Redemption and Resurrection

Songs to Disperse Demons

The Coming of Melchizedek

Commentaries of Psalms

Tongues of Fire

The Parable of the Bountiful Tree

Words of the Archangel Michael

The Words of the Heavenly Lights

The Seductress

Commentary on Genesis

Words of Moses

Book of Giants

Apocryphal prophecy

Wisdom Apocryphon

Liturgy of Three Tongues of Fire

New Jerusalem

The list continues, together with numerous commentaries on various biblical works, poems, prayers, and psalms. Despite these intriguing titles, we are unable to have the rendition of those complete works. This leads one to imagine the original extent of the collection. Whilst this collection was not in competition with 'The Great Library of Alexandria' destroyed by fire, it could well have upturned the religious beliefs of the day. Perhaps it is just as well that not too much has been revealed, and that speculative interpretation and opinion results from what has been found and interpreted, and maybe this is all we are meant to know.

Book of Jubilees

The Book of Jubilees, also called the Little Genesis, is a pseudepigraphal work not included in any canon of scripture. It most notable for its chronological layout, by which events described in Genesis on through Exodus 12 to 24 are dated by jubilees of 49 years, each of which is composed of seven cycles of seven years. The institution of a jubilee calendar supposedly would ensure the observance of Jewish religious festivals and holy days on the proper dates and set Jews apart from their Gentile neighbors. A jubilee also relates stories explaining the origin of Jewish laws and customs.

The Jubilee Book, in its final form, was likely written about 150 - 100 BCE, though it incorporated much older mythological traditions. Its isolationist religious spirit and its strictness led the Essene sect of Jews at Qumran in Palestine to quote extensively from it in the Damascus Document, one of their major works. Jubilees was also closely connected with the Genesis Apocryphon, which also parallels Genesis and was favored by the Qumran community. (Encyclopedia Britannica)

The author of this book presents his work as a revelation from God, through an 'Angel of the Presence'[*], that is, one who serves God's presence. He in turn tells it to Moses, who writes it down. The book is largely the retelling of biblical stories from creation until Israel arrives at Mount Sinai and Moses ascends the mountain to receive God's words (Exodus 19 and 24). The writer uses the biblical text in which he applies his own views on theological and legal matters.

[*]Hebrew: *Mal'akh HaPanim*, or **Angel of his presence/face** (Hebrew: *Mal'akh Panav*, refers to an entity variously considered angelic or else identified

with God himself. Alternatively, it could also be regarded as 'Gods special agent'.

This book creates the impression that most of Israel's important laws, even those revealed at Sinai according to the Torah, already existed during the era of the patriarchs and matriarchs; thus, the antiquity of Jewish laws can be sustained from Jubilees. (John C Endres)

The Book of Jubilees claims to present the division of the days of the Torah, dividing them into year-weeks, and jubilee-years, as was revealed to Moses by angels while he was on Mount Sinai for forty days and forty nights. The chronology given in Jubilees is based on multiples of seven; the jubilees are periods of 49 years (seven 'year-weeks'), into which all of time has been divided and supported the solar calendar. Hence it had authoritative status at Qumran by the Essenes - 14 copies were found in five of the Qumran caves. Jubilees is considered one of the apocryphal books by Roman Catholic, Eastern Orthodox, and Protestant Churches. It is not considered canonical within Judaism. Its basic code is given as 4QR.

The Torah instructs certain laws to be applied during a *Jubilee* year, which is every seventh year of the calendar. Included in these laws is the instruction not to plant new crops during that year and allow the land to lie fallow. During this year, previous debts were also to be annulled. Today one is able to purchase a complete copy of the original book.

The Genesis Apocryphon

Apocryphon ('secret writing'), plural Apocrypha, was a Greek term for a genre of Jewish and Early Christian writings that were meant to impart 'secret teachings' or gnosis (knowledge) that could not be publicly taught.

Before it was unrolled, this scroll was known as the 'Lamech Scroll,' after Noah's father. You will recall that it was one of the seven scrolls first discovered in Cave 1, with later additional fragments found in Cave 4.

This relatively lengthy work is regarded to have preceded the Essenes and probably formed part of the vast non-canonical literature used by the Jewish people. This particular scroll is dated as though it had been copied in the first half of the first century but is believed to have originated in the second century BCE. It was incomplete, written in Aramaic, and was a retelling (hence Apocryphon) of parts of the book of Genesis. It was the last scroll acquired by Yadin, who published it together with Nachman Avigad in 1956 and coded 1QapGen. There were substantial sections missing from both the beginning and the end of the scroll.

It recounts various (anecdotal) episodes in the life of Noah - who is believed to have resulted from a relationship between his mother and an angel.

In the early part of the actual book of Genesis, there is a fleeting reference to the Nephalim or, translated from the literal Hebrew, 'the fallen ones'. These are regarded as 'fallen angels,' having come to earth as giants to breed with humans. This occurred before the flood. They too were regarded as being responsible for the evil in the world at that time, resulting in God 'destroying' humankind and starting up again with Noah and his family.

It continues with its own version of various episodes of Noah's life, including his 'own first-hand account' of the flood. After which Noah 'says':

"… Then I Noah went out and walked on the earth through its length and breadth…delights on her in their leaves and in their fruit. Then I blessed the Lord of heaven who made splendid things".

A few visionary symbolic activities and events experienced by him, together with their interpretations are thereafter described.

This is followed by Abraham and Sarah's lives in some detail up to the time God promises that Abraham's wife will give birth to an heir. Here again, a significant visionary dream is experienced by Abraham.

The work could be described as a 'layman's' description in an abridged version of the biblical events covered. It does not propagate bias but rather attempts to provide some 'inside' information in a novel and interesting manner.

A Poetic Composition: 'Bless My Soul'

Titled 'Bless My Soul,' on account of the opening words, *borchi nafshi* in Hebrew. I have once again selected this example because of its sensitivity and beauty. It was written over 2,000 years ago. Although it probably draws the similar opening words from Psalm 104, its content and liturgy differ.

I have used Geza Vermes' translation:

Extract from: 4Q434 (Below, 9 out of 43 lines)

Bless my soul, the Lord

for all His marvels forever,

and may His name be blessed.

For he has delivered the soul of the poor,

and has not despised the humble,

and has not forgotten the misery of the deprived.

He has opened His eyes toward the distressed,

and has heard the cry of the fatherless,

and has turned his ears towards their crying.

Original Scrolls on Display at The Shrine of the Book

The following scroll fragments and or sections of the original manuscripts can or could once have been viewed at the Shrine of the Book in Jerusalem:

- Community Rule fragment 4Q258

- Community Rule 1QS columns 8 - 12

- The Temple Scroll 11Q19 columns 31 - 37

- The Temple Scroll 11Q19 columns 38 - 40

- The Thanksgiving Scroll 1QHa columns 1 - 4

- The Thanksgiving Scroll 1QHa columns 13 - 16

- War Scroll (also titled: 'Scroll of the War of the Sons of Light against the Sons of Darkness') 1Q33 columns 1 - 4

- War Scroll 1Q33 columns 5 - 10

- New Jerusalem Scroll 4Q554

- The Words of the Maskil to All Sons of Light 'Dawn Scroll' 4Q298

- Exodus Scroll 4Q22 written Paleo-Hebrew

- Isaiah Scroll 1QIsa columns 23 -30

- The Psalms Scroll 11Q5 columns 25 - 28

- The complete Isaiah Scroll which is a copy, in the center of The Shrine of the Book.

- Two original pages from the Aleppo Codex.

- Song of the Sea (recently added): This is a scroll fragment from the 8th Century. A rare Torah manuscript from the 'silent period', lasting some 600 years, sometime between the 3rd and 8th centuries, from which almost no Hebrew biblical manuscripts have been found. Apparently written in Egypt, this scroll fragment contains a section of the book of Exodus, including one of the earliest and most beautiful examples of biblical poetry - the Song of the Sea. The manuscript's text is strikingly similar to the traditional Masoretic version familiar from later Bible codices (dating from the 9th century on). It constitutes a link between these medieval manuscripts and more ancient texts from the late Second Temple period that were found in the Judean Desert. This special exhibit is on loan, courtesy of the Rare Book Department at Duke University, North Carolina. (The Israel Museum, Jerusalem Newsletter).

Chapter 14: Christianity and the Dead Sea Scrolls

On September 11, 2001, the Times Newspapers Ltd UK released the following brief, from which I have extracted relevant information:

>Begin excerpt<

"VATICAN ALLOWS SCROLLS CHANGE"

"The Vatican is to abandon decades of secrecy and obstruction to allow changes in the Bible based on revelations in the Dead Sea Scrolls…

… the revised version of the New Jerusalem Bible will take five years to complete."

Father Gianluigi Boschi…said *that "some of the changes would be radical".* He predicted that the changes would be *"surprising and innovative".*

>End excerpt<

Then on 13th September 2001 on Channel 7 Israel News, the following announcement was issued:

" NEW, NEW TESTAMENT"

"Vatican scholars are in the preparation stages of an amended version of the New Testament, with changes based on new information revealed in the DEAD SEA SCROLLS. The scrolls were discovered in the Dead Sea region in 1947. A Dominican monk, one of the leading world experts in the field, told the Italian newspaper La Stampa that an international committee is working on the new version. An official announcement to this effect is expected at the end of the month by Prof. Etienne Nodet, author of 'The Origins of Christianity'. He is one of the few people privy to the changes. The researchers are also preparing a multi-media edition of the New Testament" (Arutz Sheva News Service www. Israel National News. com)

Then on 14th October 2001 in the South African edition of the 'Sunday Times' in their 'Lifestyle' supplement, the following was published:

"NEW TESTAMENT"

"Vatican scholars are preparing to rewrite the Bible, incorporating new revelations from the Dead Sea Scrolls.

A team of theologians and historians are gathering in Italy to start the potentially explosive task of inserting new details of the life and times of Jesus Christ. It is thought that the radical Jewish groups who wanted to overthrow Roman rule are likely to feature in the new version, supporting the views that:

Jesus was a revolutionary who fought political repression.

The Bible is based mostly on manuscripts written centuries after Jesus lived, but the 900 plus Dead Sea Scrolls, which were discovered by shepherds in 1947, have been dated to just decades before and after his crucifixion".

It's unlikely, though that the Vatican would ever allow any sensational discoveries to come to light. Dr Martyn Percy, a theologian at Sheffield University, in the UK, warned that the results might be less than dramatic.

"There has never been a settled definitive version of the Bible (Christian). It has been an evolving book, which has gone through many translations. Only fundamentalists think it came in a fax from God."

I wonder about the sources for these changes. Are they from the Scrolls already known to us, or from 'other' scrolls in the possession of the Vatican? No doubt the impact of this was lost to the world, following the tragedy that became known as 9/11 - the most horrific event that occurred on the very same day!

At the time of this book going to print, the world has heard nothing further. One can only speculate about the reason. However, some of the recently produced bibles now have footnotes that justify a change from the traditional text by saying *"following the Dead Sea Scrolls"*.

It is my belief and hope that it will be used to purge the New Testament of the subsequent hatred, prejudice, and inaccuracies that have implicated the Jewish people in the death of Jesus.

Would this be part of an ongoing process that the Vatican has undertaken in its (eventual) recognition of the discrimination and persecution of the Jewish people in the past? It is recorded as Jesus had said in his dying breath "*Forgive them for they know not what they do.*" (Luke 23:34). This forgiveness was never granted to the Jewish people. I quote from 'Constantine's Sword' (recommended!) by James Carroll, a former Catholic priest, "I remember how the question was finally put to our professor one day: *"Either the Jews are guilty or the Gospels falsify history - which is it? Our professor could not answer us."* Carroll, who asserts himself "as a Catholic Christian", in his book writes*: "The New Testament, that is, was made by the Church; the Church was not made by the New Testament."*

I investigated the Vatican Internet website and confirmed the scholarly credibility of Prof. Nodet but was unable to obtain more information pertaining to this announcement. Support of this impending change can be found by 'Googling': "Richard Owen/Rome scrolls change bible"

Perhaps by now, you are not as surprised. For surely, let's face it this is a rather dramatic, albeit cryptic news release! In this chapter there will be no intimations from my side, but rather than focusing on the possible and probable connections between the Essenes, the Scrolls, and Christianity as proposed by Scroll scholars.

Following on the earlier years when sensationalism preceded the serious business of inter-relating the Scrolls, many more heavy-weight scholars have become available to challenge opinion. In earlier years, the word 'threatened' was bandied about more often. Both Judaism and particularly Christianity were seen to be under threat. Judaism had to defend current Masoretic biblical works and the possibility that Christianity was the 'natural' course of development from an 'abandoned'

Judaism, and Christianity also came under threat when the uniqueness of Jesus and the writings in the Gospels were under serious consideration. In the same breath, the more apparent strong Jewish roots in Christianity have been brought out into the open.

The Dead Sea Scrolls have pointedly shown Jewish origins of the New Testament, in that they have contributed significantly towards its understanding and interpretation. At the end of the book, I have listed a bibliography of reference books and suggested reading. At this point I wish to draw attention to one of the books, 'Jewish Sources in Early Christianity' by David Flusser - winner of the 'Israel Prize', the nation's highest honor, for his knowledge in this field. Flusser has also gained recognition by the Vatican for having written the most authoritative book on Jesus, which is in excess of 600 pages.

James Charlesworth (Prof. of New Testament Princeton) writes in 'BAR' Sept/ Oct 2007: "*Moreover, the model of an orthodox and monolithic Judaism was evaporating. In Jesus' time there were as many as 24 groups and subgroups of Jews, the Baptist groups and, of course the Palestinian Jesus Movement. The early Jesus movement should also thus be considered as one of the subgroups of the Jewish stream.*

After the destruction of the Temple in 70 C.E., only two types of Judaism survived - a type of Pharisaism that became modern Judaism (which later became known as 'Rabbinic Judaism') and Jesus' group that became Christianity. We now know, especially from the Dead Sea Scrolls, that the formation of Christianity was originally a form of Judaism."

In the section below you will become acquainted with possible Christian connections and their origins from Essenism.

Some of these were:

- They were both organized into biblical patterns.

- Their (Essene) communities were organized into twelve tribes led by twelve chiefs, whilst the Nazarenes or early Christians were led by twelve apostles.

- Both considered themselves as recipients of the divine promises recorded in the bible and regularly used quotes to demonstrate this.

- Both believed that prophecies from the bible became fulfilled in their time.

- Both had the eschatological expectations about the (return) coming of a messiah(s).

- As neither messiah arrived within an expected time, both gave their own reasons for the delay. In Christianity, this is referred to as the 'Second Coming.'

- Both had similar organizational hierarchies except different title names were used e.g., 'mevaker' vs. bishop.

- Both the writers of the Scrolls and the early Jewish-Christians saw themselves as the meek and poor, also referred to as the eb'ionim (Heb.). These Eb'ionim formed the earliest members of Christianity.

- Both saw themselves as the 'true Israel.'

- Both judged outsiders as men of iniquity (sin) or sons of darkness.

- Both believed that their founders, the Teacher of Righteousness and Jesus, were the correct interpreters of divine revelation and thus exclusive conveyers of the will of God.

- Both believed in "preparing a way in the wilderness."

- Both believed that they were separating themselves from the ungodly and raising up a holy people.

- Both believed that they were the "New Covenant."

- Both practiced water purification by ritual immersion.

- Both were against the Temple which they saw as curript.

- On the joining up of both groups both individuals gave theit material wealth to the group

This list could be greatly expanded but serves as an introduction and continues in this section.

It would be a reasonable question to ask why there is no obvious reference to Jesus or the early development of Christianity in the Scrolls. Several authors in their books deal with this and I shall refer to them further on in this chapter.

On the Google site for the Dead Sea Scrolls, there are thousands of web pages, leading to tens of thousands of additional articles with almost half of them dealing with the Scrolls and Christianity. This indicates how relevant these postulations are. Most of the books published on the Scrolls have a significant proportion of the contents devoted to this, with a high proportion of books dealing almost exclusively with Christianity. This has occurred particularly over the past ten years due to the availability of material to scholars and the public. Many of the articles are quite absurd and highly imaginative. This applies to some books as well.

Below are some book titles on the Dead Sea Scrolls directly associated with Christianity. These titles, out of 30 listed are taken from the 'Amazon.com 'Best-selling' list of books on the Dead Sea Scrolls:

- James the Brother of Jesus… R Eisenman
- Jesus the Man…B Thiering
- The Dead Sea Scrolls and the Jewish origins of Christianity…C Thiede
- The Dead Sea Scrolls Deception…M Baigent and R Leigh
- The Library of Qumran…H Stegemann and E Tov
- Scrolls and Christian Origins…M Black
- The Messiah Before Jesus…I Knohl and D Maisel
- Jesus and the Dead Sea Scrolls…J Charlsworth

- The Dead Sea Scrolls and The First Christians...R Eisenman

- The Dead Sea Scrolls and the New Testament...G Brooke

Above are only a few of the scores of related and similar book titles.

And more recently (2008) following a spate of related books including: 'Jesus the Wicked Priest'...How Christianity was born of an Essene Schism, by M Vining.

When undertaking an online search through 'Questia', which advertises itself as "The world's largest online library", I searched for: 'The Dead Sea Scrolls and Christianity'. Questia listed in detail 356 books devoted to that subject.

Three books need to be mentioned, all major bestsellers, each one dealing universally with this aspect and being most controversial: 'The Dead Sea Scrolls Deception', 'Jesus the Man' and 'The Dead Sea Scrolls Uncovered' also by R. Eisenman.

The main purpose of my writing this book as I previously mentioned, is to bring about insight to the subject. With the background you have now gained, you will be able to read these and other books far more objectively.

Having now appropriately conveyed to you the worldwide belief viz. the related connections, I shall now briefly cover these apparent and recognized associations.

It is possible that Jesus was familiar with the Essenes and their beliefs. He too was highly critical of the Temple management, as were the Essenes. He may have adopted several their concepts previously unknown to Judaism and these will be further illustrated:

At the Essene communal meal, the priest blessed the bread and wine, as Jesus did at the Last Supper. This is found in 'The Rule of the Congregation' scroll or 1QSa, also known as the 'Messianic Rule' and could have been a blueprint for the 'Last Supper'. It reads as follows:

......"And all the heads of the [households of the congrega]tion, their sag[es and wise men,] shall sit before them, each according to his importance. [When they] mee[t at the] communal [tab]le, [to set out bread and wi]ne, and the communal table is arranged [to eat and] to dri[nk]the new wine, [no] one [shall extend]his hand to the first (portion) of the bread and [new the wine] before the priest. Fo[r he shall] bless the first (portion) of the bread and the win[e and shall extend]his hand to the bread first. Afterwards,] the messiah of Israel [shall exten]d his hands to the bread first [and] all the congregation of the Community [shall utter a] blessing, [each man in the order] of his dignity". (Column 11:15-20)

Both Jesus and the Essenes refer to the term 'new wine' at a meal. Both Essene and the Gospels refer to a 'messianic banquet,' which will take place.

The Essenes and Jesus differed in their acceptance of the physically 'handicapped' on entering within a certain proximity to the Temple. The Essenes abided by the ruling as given in the Torah, whereas Jesus reached out with compassion to the crippled, blind, the deaf, and those who were maimed - and accepted them.

There was a strong and unique mutual belief between Jesus and the Essenes in their attitude towards divorce. In the Christian Bible, it is mentioned four times in the Synoptic Gospels and again in Paul's epistles: *"Every man who divorces his wife and marries commits adultery."* The Essenes took a strong view against divorce as they too saw marriage as a sacred union in which two people became one. Remarriage was permitted, however, but only after the death of a spouse. The Damascus Document speaks of those who are "*caught in fornication twice by taking a second wife while the first is alive*". In Temple Scroll a prohibition is even placed on the king: "*And he shall not take upon her (his first wife) another wife, for she alone shall be with him all the days of her life. But should she die, he may take unto himself another (wife) from the house of his father from his family.*" Possibly coming to mind would be King Solomon and his many wives, which was against God's Law in Deuteronomy 17:17 *"Neither shall he* (the king) *multiply wives to himself…"*

Nevertheless, recent research has shown that divorce was not an Essene absolute but was very rare and probably made it difficult to take place. Jesus too allowed divorce in cases of sexual unfaithfulness, as stated in Mathew 5:31 and 19:9. The opinion is that Jesus was influenced by the Essenes' stance on marriage being a holy union. The Essene doctrine did in many respects differ markedly from the Jesus movement. Jesus could have been viewing the Essenes as 'pious simpletons.' In Luke 16:8-9 he says: "*For the sons of this world are wiser in their generation than the sons of light.*" Were these the Essenes he was referring to?

The Essene definition of poverty being a positive virtue was unique to them and was not part of Jewish belief. Later, in early Christianity, this belief became part of the Christian way of life. To this day the 'Vow of Poverty' is still practiced by some Christian monks.

In the Hodayot, their contemptuous attitude towards wealth was expressed*: "The soul of thy servant has loathed [riches] and gain, and he has not [desired] exquisite delights."* In the Gospels, one of the most famous sayings of Jesus is: *"It is easier for a camel to go through the eye of a needle, than for a rich man to enter the kingdom of God."* In the Beatitudes, Jesus says *"Blessed are you the poor, for yours is the kingdom of God."* And in Luke 6:24 *" But woe to you who are rich, for you have received your consolation."*

Jesus, as did the Essenes, criticized the Temple for becoming too caught up in materialism and deviant from its Divine purpose and activities.

Both Jesus and the Essenes were opposed to the taking of oaths…Mathew 5:34 and the 'Rule of the Community' 15:1-3.

Conversely, in Mathew 5:43 it states that Jesus said *"You have heard it said 'love your friends, hate your enemies'…".* Nowhere in the Hebrew Bible, or in rabbinic literature is this said. However, in the 'Rule of the Community', there is the instruction to *"hate all the sons of darkness each according to his guilt"*. Could this be a reference contrary to the command issued to the Essenes? There were however important differences about Mathew's recorded observance of the Sabbath, compared to those of the Essenes.

I have already mentioned that John the Baptist is widely believed to have lived among the Essenes for several years. Having grown up in the wilderness, it is believed that this region may have been in the vicinity of Qumran. Other parallels are that he was also preparing for the coming of a messiah in that wilderness and that together with the Essenes he berated the Temple Priests and demeaned the rulers of the land as puppet kings. The practice of baptism is thought to have originated through the ritual immersion baths, used as a daily part of the purification belief of the Essenes. Nevertheless, subject to interpretation is the following quotation from the 'Rule of the Community' (4Q255 [qpapsa] Fragment 2 1Q111, 7-12 I:

"And by his holy spirit which links him with his truth he is clea[nsed of all] his sins. And by the spirit of uprightness and humility his s[in is atoned. And by the compliance of] his soul with all the laws of God his fle[sh] is cleansed [by there being sprinkled upon it] cleansing waters and being made holy with the waters of repentance, and [by the st]eadying of his steps in order to walk with the perfection on all the paths of God..." (G Martinez)

This concept is however speculative as the Essenes immersed themselves as part of a purity ritual, whereas baptism in Christianity is an initiation rite, albeit to (also) remove impurity. Both John and the Essenes used the quotation from Isaiah...*"Prepare a way in the wilderness, the way of the Lord, and make straight the paths for our God"*. Both he and the Essenes stressed that the Day of Judgment was imminently approaching.

Jesus told his followers to sell their possessions and distribute the money to the poor. Later, in the early days of Christianity, his followers lived in religious communities sharing and supporting each other. This form of communism was very similar to the system under which the Essenes lived.

Acts 4:32 "The group of believers was one in mind and heart. None of them said that any of their belongings were their own, but they all shared with one another everything they had." (GNB)

Another unique similarity was the introduction of celibacy to the early Church. This could have been an adaptation from the Essenes' belief in abstinence as being part of their acetic and monastic way of life. This is very contrary to the Jewish religion.

Like the Essenes, the early Christians attempted to create a utopian community.

There was a sense of alienation from the rest of society, expressed in their calls to repent together with an eschatological zeal within those groups.

The association that John had with the Essenes ended with a schism in that: The Essenes in the 'Rule of the Community' state that their members must "bear unremitting hatred towards all men of ill repute...", whereas John called on these men of ill repute to "Repent, for the Kingdom of God is offered" (Mathew 3:2)

Important differences held by the Essenes were in their isolationist and xenophobic attitudes compared to the all-embracing views of early Christianity, as well as their strict adherence to the 'Laws of Moses'.

Both the Scrolls and the New Testament were critical of Temple desecration. Both understood the concept of a Spiritual Temple in that they each envisaged themselves conceptually as the true Temple. This is recorded in the 'Rule of the Community' Column 8 verses 5 and 8:

"When such men as these come to be in Israel, then shall the society of the Yachad be established in truth, it shall be an everlasting plantation, a Temple for Israel...it shall be a House *of perfection and truth in Israel that they may establish a Covenant..."*

Both saw themselves as having entered a 'New Covenant' with God, fulfilling the 'old' Mosaic covenant. The Essenes regarded themselves as the people of the new covenant because of their breakaway from the Temple which they saw as unclean.

In column 3:6 of the same scroll, 'cleansing by the Holy Spirit' is also conveyed: *"For only through the spirit infusing God's true society can there be forgiveness for a man's ways..."* This precedes the Christian belief that the acceptance of Jesus will also result in forgiveness.

Another area of scholarly dispute was the comparison of the meal and its format held by the Essenes. This is seen to be similar to the 'Eucharist' also called 'Communion'- a ceremony in the Christian church during which people eat bread (in the form of a wafer) and drink wine in memory of the last supper that Jesus had with his disciples.

At this stage I wish to introduce and record a few relevant quotes from renowned Christian and Scroll scholars:

- *"Christianity is an Essenism that has largely succeeded"*
  (A Dupont-Sommer). He also said, "*The Teacher of Righteousness was in many ways the exact prototype of Jesus"*

- *"For myself, I must go further and confess that, after seven years, I do not find my understanding of the New Testament substantially affected. Its Jewish background is clearer and better understood, but its (NT) meaning has neither been changed nor significantly clarified"* (M. Burrows of Yale)

- *"Nothing has been brought to light in the Qumran Scrolls that contradicts anything that Christians hold dear"* (Father Joseph Fritzmeyer in 'Responses to 101 Questions on the Dead Sea Scrolls')

- "*At the heart of Essenism rested elements of intolerance, rigidity, and exclusiveness. This, perhaps is why it vanished, whereas the flexible and dynamic Judaism of the rabbis and cosmopolitan Christian were able to live on*" (G. Vermes)

- "*As Christians who trust the Bible to tell us the truth, both about God's plan for his people and about how he worked that plan out among the first Christians, we have nothing to fear from the Dead Sea Scrolls. This is not because we reject the false teaching of the scrolls regarding Christian belief, but precisely because the scrolls say nothing about Christian belief*" (Alistair Wilson)

- "*For those who see Christianity and Christian doctrine as something entirely new and unrelated to its Jewish milieu (background), the scrolls are threatening*" (Hershel Shanks)

- "*What we do mean is that specific sayings and actions attributed to Jesus in several Gospel passages may now reasonably be viewed as authentic, since similar sayings or actions are recorded in certain key scrolls that predated him*" (Vanderkam and Flint)

- "*In short, I think anyone who has accepted claims of the discontinuity between Christianity and Judaism uncritically or has been brainwashed by the perennial tendency of the Christian pulpit to compare Judaism unfavorably with Christianity, may be shocked and may have to rethink his faith*" (Frank Moore Cross in conversation with bible scholar Hershel Shanks in 1994)

Covenant, Connections and Coincidence

The word 'covenant' often appears in the writings used to describe God's re-establishment and recognition of the role given by Him to the Essenes. They saw themselves as 'Sons of the Covenant' and those joining their sect as entering a new covenant. The word 'covenant' is believed to have been taken from Jeremiah 31:30-32. *"Behold, the days come, saith the Lord, that I will make a new covenant with the House of Israel, and the House of Judah..."* The word 'testament' originates from the Greek, *testos*, meaning covenant. The 'New Testament' refers to the Christian Bible (but excludes the Pentateuch, Writings and Prophets) and was later compilated and redacted in addition to the Hebrew Bible.

Usage of the term 'Old Testament' for the 'Hebrew Bible' is by implication, a severing of God's relationship with the Jewish people and the Laws He designated to them.

'New Testament' then implies that God (having abandoned the Jewish people) has now chosen the Christians to carry out His word in place of the Jews. This is referred to as 'Replacement Theology,' which teaches that the church has replaced Israel in carrying out God's plan. Adherents of Replacement Theology believe that the Jews are no longer God's chosen people, and God does not have future plans for the state of Israel. Replacement theology implies thus that the many promises made to Israel in the Bible are now fulfilled by the Christian Church.

The Essenes 'entering a New Covenant in the land of Damascus' (CD 6:19), is not the same as the 'New Testament', meant to replace the 'Old' Testament or Hebrew Bible. I once saw painted on the side of a building in the city of Durban (South Africa) a large slogan which read: "The Koran - the Last Testament."(!) Perhaps in place of the word 'Old Testament' it could be referred to as the 'Original Testament.' I prefer and generally use the descriptions 'Hebrew Bible' and 'Christian Bible.'

Certain phrases and wording appearing in the Scrolls, which could be called 'Qumranianisms', have largely contributed to the belief that they are remarkably like those used in the Christian Bible.

They include:

- 'the pierced Messiah'
- 'and by his name will be designated...Son of God'
- 'He will be called great'
- 'He will be called the Son of the Most High'
- 'Sons of Light'
- 'Revenge on the body of his flesh'
- 'The Way'
- 'Angel of Satan'
- 'Living water'
- 'Belial'
- 'He that walks in darkness'
- 'a book sealed with seven seals'
- 'the human temple of God'
- 'the righteousness of God'
- 'Works of the Law'

These words do not appear in the Hebrew Bible or other Hebrew texts. 'Belial' appears only once in 2 Corinthians 6:15 "*What harmony is there between Christ and Belial*" and once in 2 Samuel 22:5. In that verse, it is translated as 'ungodly men'.

It becomes even more striking when one reads similar counterparts such as found in 'The Sermon on the Mount' also called the 'Beatitudes' of Mathew 5:1-12 and Luke 6:20-23.

Scroll 4Q525 reads:

"Blessed the man who has attained wisdom and walks in the Law with the Most high [blessed is he who speaks truth] with a pure heart and does not slander with his tongue...Blessed

is he who seeks [wisdom] with pure hands and does not go after her with a deceitful heart."

Nevertheless, this scroll message could simply reflect Jewish teachings, which was the basis of Jesus' belief.

Scroll 1Q28a/1QS *"this is the assembly of famous men, [those summoned to] the gathering of the community council, when [God] begets the Messiah with them."* Here we read of the sectarian expectation of a divine Messiah. This impending show of a savior could possibly have been a common desire or belief, particularly in view of the cruel times the people lived in.

Paul (?) also proffered the concept of predestination which appears in the Scrolls and is not part of Judaic belief.

"Predestination is a Christian doctrine according to which a person's ultimate destiny, whether it be salvation or damnation, is determined by God alone prior to, and apart from, any worth or merit on the person's part. In some cases, it is claimed that God only determines those to be saved; in others, that he determines those to be saved and those to be condemned. The latter teaching is called double predestination." (Rom. 8:28-30 and 9:6-24). The writer William S Babcock continues his brief adding *"The doctrine of predestination became important in the late medieval period and passed into the theology of the Protestant reformers…"* (http://mb-soft.com/believe)

The Christian concept of Messiah is similar to the Essene messiah as also noted from the War Scroll...*"one who brings you good news is the one anointed* (Messiah) *with the spirit…he shall make them wise in all areas of wrath".*

Scroll 4Q521 speaks additionally of the Messiah:

"The heavens and earth will listen to His Messiah…he will glorify the pious on the throne of the Eternal Kingdom, He who liberates the captives, restores the sight to the blind, straightens the bent…For He will heal the wounded, and

revive the dead and bring good news to the poor" (Translation: Vermes).

The Books of Luke 7:22-23 and Mathew 11:4-5 records:

"Go and report to John what you have seen and heard: the blind receive sight, the lame walk, the lepers are cleansed, and the deaf hear, the dead are raised up, the poor have the glad tiding preached to them."

There are also significant differences in messianic concepts. I have focused on certain examples to the exclusion of counterargument, as this is not within the scope of the book. I leave it to you the reader, to advance in this field and draw your own conclusions.

Neither is it my intention to alter any belief, but rather to create the opportunity for a new perspective. This also relates to Judaism. Christianity did not necessarily begin with the birth of Jesus - rather similar concepts were already established for at least one hundred years or more before his birth. Hence some of the analogies presented to show the influences conveyed from Qumran and other sects of that period which may have been of influence on the writings appearing in the Christian Bible. This is a core statement!

The early Christians were known as 'Jewish Christians', i.e., those Jews who saw Jesus as a Messiah but still upheld all the Jewish laws and festivals. This segment of Christians remained for at least 150 years after the death of Jesus until the final parting of the ways became established. I mentioned earlier that Christianity also grew out of other societies and beliefs including the Pagans and those in general terms called 'Gentiles' who came under Paul's influence.

I shall now continue to provide some more examples of the considered connections and other scholarly points of view.

In the New Testament, some readers may have difficulty with Jesus' title as the Messiah i.e., Christ and or 'the Son of Man' or 'Son of God'. As a result of the discovery of the Scrolls, there is no doubt of a clearer understanding of the Jewish societies from which Christianity developed. Martinez writes that ..."*the new texts expressed not only the hope of an eschatological salvation (but) introduced into this hope, the figure of a Messiah using technical (specialized) terminology.*"

Divine Associations in the Scrolls

The first line of the second column of scroll 4Q246 reads:

"He will be called Son of God, and they will call him son of the Most High"

The Gospel of Luke 1:31-33 reads:

"You (Mary) will be with child and give birth to a son, and you are to give him the name Jesus. He will be great and will be called the Son of the Most High"

It is unclear to whom the writers in the Scrolls were referring to - possibly a messiah who would arrive at the 'end of times'- as was so thematic in their writings. Nevertheless, this could well have influenced Luke's writings.

Although remarkable in its similarity and considering that the scroll was written 100-150 years before the book of Luke, it is not regarded as significant by E Cook, author of 'Solving the Mysteries of the Dead Sea Scrolls'. He writes that "*they both appear in different contexts*". In conclusion to apparently similar quotations, I extract from scroll 4Q541 known as "The Suffering Servant at Qumran:

"He will atone for all the children of his generation, and he will be sent to all the children of his [pe]ople. His word is like a word of heaven, and his teaching is in accordance with the will of God. His eternal sun will shine, and his light will be kindled in the corners of the earth, and it will shine in the darkness. Then the darkness will pass away [fr]om the earth, and a thick darkness from the dry land..."

"...and do not afflict the weak by wasting or hanging...[Let] not the nail approach him..." In this latter quote, it is recognized that it is not necessarily the same individual being referred to as in the two former extracts.

"They will speak many words against him and they will invent many [lie]s and fictions against him and speak shameful things about him. Evil will overthrow his generation...His situation will be one of lying and violence [and] the people will go astray in his days, and be confounded..."

Almost universally, to a greater or lesser degree, scholarly opinion believes that there appears to be a connection. "*To say that Essenism is the 'mother of Christianity' or has its roots there is taking it too far*" says Vermes.

We now realize that the ideas identified with Christianity existed much earlier within Judaism, which was richer and more varied than we realized. Essenism represented one of the mainstreams of Judaism that was opposed to Rabbinic Judaism.

Historian Sir Martin Goodman states in a chapter titled 'Jews and Judaism in the Second Temple Period': "*Perhaps the most productive development has been the widespread (but not yet universal) recognition by specialists both in the New Testament and Jewish studies, that the history of Jewish Christianity is part of the history of Judaism.*"

Hence the plethora of studies, papers, and books on 'Jesus the Jew.'

In his book published in 2008, 'Jesus the Wicked Priest' by Marvin Vining, a recognized biblical scholar ordained by the United Methodist Church, he writes on "*How Christianity was born of an Essene schism*".

The connection between the development and foundations of Christianity, Jesus to a lesser degree, and the content of the Scrolls continues to take prominence in the debates amongst most scholars today. Remember that the term 'Wicked Priest' is used in the Scrolls to identify the one who opposed the Essenes and their leadership.

Vining postulates that some of those Essenes who broke away from Essene theology included Jesus, together with some who became his disciples. Earlier in my book, I referred to the possible connection with the disciples Paul and John the Baptist, and their familiarity or associations with the Essenes and their teachings. Vining continues to provide a further argument for additional connections to the disciples James, Peter, and his brother Andrew.

Interestingly he suggests that the notorious flagellation of the Pharisees in Mathew 23 as presented in the first part of my book, in fact does not refer to the Pharisees but to the Essenes themselves, from whom the breakaway occurred.

A core element of his book is that around the 50 or more references to the 'scribes' in the gospels refer to Vining having identified them as Essenes. Hence the supposed dialogue between Jesus and the scribes referred to them, and sometimes they were also coupled with the Pharisees.

An example that is used to endorse a direct connection is the introductory phrase 'You have heard it said' - this phrase is used many times in the book of Mathew preceding a teaching. For example: "*You have heard that it was said, 'Love your friends, hate your enemies*" Vining writes, (and this has also crossed my thoughts during my studies), "*There seems to be no doubt that Jesus was referring to the Essenes*," I read his bold, lucid, and outsider theories with a relatively open mind and with interest.

Overall, mainstream scholarly opinion acknowledges that there is an association with the Scrolls - not only from those speculated to be Essene - and the Christian bible. It has been well noted that copies of the biblical books most frequently found amongst the Scrolls, viz. Deuteronomy, Isaiah, and the Psalms are the ones most frequently quoted in the Christian Bible.

Importantly, the Scrolls have further endorsed that the origins of Christianity were strongly tied to Jewish thought, culture, and religious ethics, particularly in its formative years. Only later, when the canon of the present Christian bible by the time of the Council of Nicaea in 325 under Constantine concluded its redaction or compilation and final editing, was the separation between the two religions finally established. It was at Nicaea that the concept of the "Trinity" was voted in.

Chapter 15: Significance of the Dead Sea Scrolls

(In no specific order of relevance)

- The knowledge of belief, history, and customs of the Essenes themselves.

- The most important contribution to the Hebrew Bible is that many of the Scrolls support the Masoretic text.

- That many of the 'biblical' texts used then do not support the biblical text used today. I have avoided using 'Masoretic' this time, in view of comments appearing in this book under that heading.

- That many other 'Holy Texts' were used in addition to those formally known prior to the discovery of the Scrolls.

- That the canon as we know it today was largely established by about 300 - 200 BCE as opposed to the belief that it was 'finalized' in Yavne, also known as Jamnia, after the destruction of the Second Temple.

- That some of the Oral Laws recorded in the Mishnah, supposedly for the first time, already appeared in writing 300 - 250 years earlier.

- If the 'Works of the Law' as designated in the 'MMT' are the same as those appearing in the Christian Bible, then a serious review of its meanings will need to take place.

- They are the oldest collection of biblical manuscripts ever found. Prior to their discovery, the oldest biblical work known was dated 895 CE known as the Cairo Codex of the Prophets - more than a 1000 years later!

- There were variants in the belief and practice of Rabbinic Judaism, which has been practiced over the past 2,000 years.

- Jewish theology was much more varied than was previously known.

- In the scholarly belief that Christianity and some of the writings in the New Testament were probably influenced (to a greater or lesser degree) by the Essene movement.

- That the Judaic roots of Christianity are more firmly entrenched than was previously appreciated.

- The Scrolls provided a greater understanding of the religious history of that era.

- A new field of scholarship was created.

- A better understanding of the Hebrew Bible, Christian Bible, and Apocrypha together with non-biblical Jewish religious literature.

- The Hebrew language was far more widely used during that era than was previously believed.

- The Apocrypha and its works were far more widely used than previously thought. Apocryphal works such as Judith and Enoch were written in Hebrew.

- What has been discovered could possibly be only a small part of what was hidden. What were in those nine empty jars in Cave 1, that I wrote about earlier in this book? Furthermore, what have we been deprived of and what would their impact on the world have been?!!!

- Every book of the Hebrew Bible (Tanach) except Esther is represented in the scroll collection.

- 80% of the Scrolls are in Hebrew, 19% in Aramaic, and 1% in Greek.

- The Dead Sea Scrolls "*are a point encounter between Jews and Christians and were written during a period of great interaction between the Greek culture and Jewish culture*".

- New scientific techniques have been developed in the field of archaeology that were applied to the Scrolls.

- The Scrolls have enormously increased our knowledge of ancient Jewish scriptural interpretation and the history of ancient Jewish law.

- Messianism was as important a belief to some Jewish sects then, as it is to some Jewish 'sects' today. This perpetuation is also found in Christianity.

- The Essenes could have been the forerunners of the Karaites.

- They have shown us the rich variety of approaches to Jewish law and theology.

- We now have a greater appreciation that the Rabbinic Judaism of today originated from the Pharisees.

- The texts of the 'Prophets' and 'Writings' of the bible we read today are not necessarily identical to their 'original' or earliest compositions. Some have undergone changes or omissions while recopying by many scribes, with possible changes to the text being made by the scribes themselves.

- All Scripture texts were equally authoritative in ancient Israel, except to those who perpetuated and followed the Masoretic texts.

- Some of the Oral Laws that were verbally transmitted by the Pharisees were themselves independently arrived at and enforced by the Essenes, who arrived at them by their own inspired biblical exegesis. This is confirmed in the MMT scroll.

- An additional 25 biblical scrolls that were found outside of Qumran at various sites, were all noted to be Masoretic and thus identical to today's Torah.

- The fact that there were found to be non-Masoretic scripture texts found at Qumran, implied that these variations were also regarded as equally authoritative in ancient Israel. The concept of Masoretic scripture had not yet been fully established.

Further additions can be made to this list. Hopefully, you can do so, as you recall the contents of this book and further your knowledge on this wonderful subject.

(Disputing) The Essene Hypothesis

Before it may appear that I am now embarking on a path leading towards discrediting all that I have set myself to convey about the Essenes, and their possible impact on society and religion during and following their era, I need to clarify why it can be considered a 'hypothesis'.

When presenting this subject and all that relates to it, to be credible to myself and the readers wherever possible and necessary, I have avoided dogma and presented as many relevant views as possible that I could draw upon to declare optional opinions. Even when referring to certain cardinal aspects pertaining to own religion, I have tried to bear this in mind.

All that has ever been written surrounding the association and content of the Dead Sea Scrolls has been essentially based on the broad opinion that there was such a sect and many of the Scrolls (at least those regarded as sectarian) originate from them. It needs however to be appreciated that all or much about what we think we know about the Essenes remains, hypothetical. There ain't no absolute proof! There are certainly many theories as to the origins and different pathways have taken by the Essenes, the Groningen Hypothesis as related earlier is an example.

But if one took this concept to another level, the actual existence of the Essenes could be brought into question, or at least to a marked dilution in this belief. I will undertake to succinctly present some views which could bring into question the credibility of the Essene hypothesis.

Most of what appears to be factual and informative regarding the Essenes is based on the writings of Josephus. In an article appearing in the 'Biblical Archaeology Review' magazine November/December 2008, there appeared a feature article captioned 'Did the Essenes Write the Dead Sea Scrolls'? It was further sub-titled 'Don't rely on Josephus'. It was written by Steve Manson, a leading and respected authority on the works of Josephus. Manson states that "*if the scrolls were written by the Essenes, that (fact) cannot be demonstrated by Josephus.*"

The basis for his point of view is that all of Josephus's works were aimed at 'redeeming' the Judean national character, by presenting one of the Jewish sects as courageous, showing a contempt for suffering, living a simple life in piety, and in essence reflecting virtues the Romans most admired.

He also portrayed the Essenes as an exceptional order who were much disciplined and essentially also deprived themselves of sexual relations. This would be in opposition to a stereotyping image negatively reflecting the Jewish people humiliated by the destruction of their Temple and the outcomes. These characteristics were not reflected in the Scrolls believed to be Essene writings. Although there are parallels between Josephus's Essenes and the 'scroll community' these customs were also "*common to other groups with utopian aspirations*". Thus, implies Manson that "*there is little or no resemblance between Josephus's Essenes and the scroll community*".

In a recently published book (February 2009) in Hebrew by Prof. Rachel Elior of the Hebrew University of Jerusalem, titled 'Memory and Oblivion: The Mystery of the Essenes'. she suggests that the Essenes never existed. She writes that Philo, Pliny, and Josephus were all "*fascinated with the ideal of a holy community*" and one which represented an ideal peaceful society in Utopia.

This virtuous society was in marked contrast to the (real) struggle between what she portrays as a struggle between a Tzadokite priestly society that had had lost the sacred sovereignty of the Temple worship and an emerging class of rabbis. These rabbis presented different beliefs which gave 'human' reason and laws for the shaping of the (Jewish) religion.

This power struggle is also given prominence in this (my) book, but within the context of the Essene Hypothesis. Elior writes that it was the priestly class who for centuries had used a solar calendar which emulated the pattern set by God. The week of seven days, the Jubilee (shmita) year was the conclusion of a cycle of seven times seven years. There are many other occasions within the Jewish religion directly relating to the seven-day cycle. This was contrasted to the rabbinic favoring the lunar cycle calendar. The scrolls, which she writes were from a Priestly Tzadokite library representing a conflict between themselves and the Hasmonaean priestly leadership. Interestingly, Manson used the term 'scroll community'.

The Pharisees who were strongly in opposition to this solar observing Hasmonaean priestly dynasty had their opportunity to take over the reins of the religion following the destruction of the Temple in 70 CE. The rabbis as they later became known following on from the Pharisees, according to Elior, favored a lunar calendar, because they saw it 'symbolically' freeing the nation from dependence on a closed priestly class observing the solar calendar and claiming divine authority.

This conflict was further exemplified by the eventual and final establishment of the Hebrew biblical canon used today and the excision of other scripture including Apocryphal works, by these rabbis. Elior speaks of a 'reinvention' of Judaism by these rabbis. This took place after the destruction of the Temple at the religious canter for the re-establishment of Judaism by a group of rabbis in the then Palestinian town of Yavne. She further states that at these clandestine meetings, certain biblical passages were amended to minimize references to the solar calendar. The final establishment of Rabbinic Judaism, concluding correspondingly with the first major compilation of the Mishnah, the great collection of early rabbinic laws recorded circa 70 - 200 CE.

Prof. Norman Golb Univ. Chicago

Author of "Who Wrote the Dead Sea Scrolls"

"According to the new theory, no sect lived at Qumran, and the Scrolls themselves are in fact testimony to a previously unknown, yet highly significant episode of the Jewish revolt against Rome: they are the writings, not of a small sect, but of many different groups of the Jews of Palestine – part of a vast collection removed from various libraries in Jerusalem and stored away, along with other items of value, in sundry hiding-places in the Judaean Wilderness in response to the Roman siege of Jerusalem in 70 C. E. We will call this the Jerusalem theory.

Unhappily, at the present time, Scroll scholarship is divided into two opposing camps grouped around the two theories, and this situation has resulted in a not-too-edifying power struggle among scholars internationally. Exhibitions of the Scrolls, which are controlled by traditional Qumran scholars, as well as presentations made during official guided tours of the Khirbet Qumran site, always champion the traditional Qumran-Essene theory, omitting any reference to artifacts or texts that contradict that theory. "

Ongoing Cave research

Each year in the winter months about 5 plus volunteers together with 3 archeologists and 1 geologist work on a project digging and scouring the caves along the Dead Sea for contents and artifacts. So far up to cave number 61 has been explored. That amounts to an additional 50 caves since the last revealing cave number 11 in the early 1950's was investigated.

Only caves number **53** and **61** have revealed anything of significance.

Beginning with cave **53**, in 2017 a blank scroll was found in a jar in a hidden room of the cave. There were indications that this cave was used as a scriptorium i.e. a place where scrolls were prepared and written on. Judging by the large quantity of olive and date pips that were found there, indicated that a number of people worked on these parchments scrolls.

Numerous clay oil lamps were lying around further indicating the likelihood of people living there. It is interesting to learn that prior to the Greeks arrival; olive oil was exclusively used for lighting and not cooking. Amazingly a group of tourists illegally wandered in to the vicinity and found a complete beautiful jar just outside the cave which had been overlooked! Also found was a unique beautifully decorated metal jar, painted in green.

Cave **61** was situated 60 meters above the Qumran settlement and cannot be viewed from the sea ward side. There were found oil lamps dating from the First and Second Temple era.

A hand dug tunnel measuring about 100 meters long which forked towards the end, remains a mystery as to it purpose. The tunnel supplied no clues as to its purpose. The search continues each year, and it is estimated that scores of caves remain to be investigated.

One of the accepted theories as to the reason for the storage of the scrolls in these caves is that they were to be a library. People had easy access from the road below to peruse these scrolls in many of these 11 caves.

With acknowledgement to Dr.Oren Guttfeld current head of excavation Qumran cave exploration project.

Chapter 16: Conclusion

About one-third of all the Scrolls had never been seen before, although some have been mentioned in other sources. I, and many others, firmly believe that many of these scrolls were spirited out of Jerusalem and the Temple for safekeeping before their destruction, prior to the approaching Roman forces in 70 CE. I have read of scrolls from the Dead Sea region being in the hands of private collectors. It is almost like having the 'Mona Lisa' but not being able to share it with anyone! As difficult it is for some to accept, Judaism *did* evolve. We have learned from the enormous amount of popular material used to understand the Tanach. Now we have a greater understanding by way of the vast material discovered at Qumran. Some surely must have been known and used by many outside the Essenes community?

Many of the 'Orthodox' Jewish community who are so disturbed by other divisions currently in Judaism (Reform, Conservationism etc.), could perhaps regard this trend, particularly over the past 150 years as being rather threatening. Now, one can also look back and note that even within Temple times, much interpretation among the populous existed as well. But the *big* lesson to be learned is that these divisions certainly weakened the nation and significantly contributed towards the Jewish Revolt in 66 CE, leading ultimately to the destruction of the Second Temple.

In Israel today, there exists a religious segment described by the popular press and others, as the 'extreme' or 'ultra' Orthodox. Some describe them as being isolationist, fanatical, and out of kilter with the established Orthodox Judaism of the past hundreds of years.

Many, including those in the *Shas* religious party in Israel and particularly their leaders and mentors, have issued statements that may have been likened to that segment of Pharisees, referred to in a derogatory manner in the Book of Mathew. This is a problem well recognized, and unfortunately used by the secular population as an example for negating religious Judaism, citing those reasons for their non-observance and criticism. Should peace ever come to Israel, this will be regarded as one of the *important* challenges to that era.

And what could be learned about the Christian bible and Christianity itself from the Scrolls? Firstly, the adage 'As true as Gospel' becomes somewhat outdated as we begin to understand more about the Christian bible's redaction and compilation. Insofar as we have understood Essenism to be a cult of the times, the early development of Christianity and the later *selected* editing are of the Christian Bible leave one open-minded as to what truly took place, and what was really recorded between 50 CE and 350 CE.

One wonders if there is a 'missing link' scroll(s) that was destroyed, maybe still hidden, or in fact, has been suppressed - which could answer some of my questions. The Nag Hammadi Gnostic Gospels were found in Egypt after WW II and encompass a vast amount of very ancient 'Christian' works. The 'Gospel of Judas' is a recent and very controversial example of a Gnostic Gospel, all of which adds some further insight to what is considered original. Faith and belief should not be questioned - rather its imposition on others, particularly when in a violent or suicidal manner!

I am a firm believer in the adage "Tell me who your friends are, and I will tell you who you are." This can also be applied to religion. One need not be compelled to know the contents, for example of the Koran or the New Testament, before commenting on that particular religion. One only must observe how the people of those religions (have) *tolerated* others to conclude whether it is divinely inspired or reflects a beneficial and contributory belief towards *all of* mankind. In this regard, to draw a quick and simple conclusion, watch the TV news, read your history books and today's press for the answer.

In this book we covered the only known and widely recorded details of a type of fundamentalist within a sect, and even the fanatical practice and interpretation of Judaism. Yet what is markedly noticeable by its absence is the total lack of physical violence in the name of Judaism, or the need for imposition of its belief onto others.

I interpret the significance of this as Judaism being a unique example of a truly non-violent religion that does not forcefully impose itself on others. This is in marked contrast to Christianity (in the past), attempts at conversion in the recent past, and Islam (both past and present).

One of the important questions I would have liked to ask the renowned Dead Sea Scroll scholars, would be "How has your research affected your faith?"

In an article published in the March 2007 edition of Biblical Archaeology Review titled 'Losing Faith' with the sub-heading '2 Who Did and 2 Who Didn't', Hershel Shanks, the editor, questioned four such renowned biblical/archaeological academics on the very issue that had plagued me for years. They were Bart Ehrman, James Strange, William Denver and Lawrence Schiffman. Those whose faith remained unchanged were Lawrence Schiffman and James Strange.

In my opinion amongst the most dynamic speakers and intellectuals in their fields I have ever been privileged to hear and whose works I have read, are Schiffman and Ehrman. Both specialist professors in their fields at leading universities.

Prof. Schiffman, a former New York University professor of Jewish studies and a giant in the scholarship of the Scrolls is also a very orthodox Jew. He is now vice-Prost of Yeshivah College. Bart Ehrman Distinguished Professor of religious studies at University of North Carolina, a former fundamentalist Christian gradually changed in his vies and now regards himself as a 'non-believer.'

Whilst this is not the place to debate this topic, nevertheless having been so involved over the years in compiling this book and subsequently having studied umpteen books and articles, listened to umpteen lectures on *YouTube,* I can only reiterate that which I wrote earlier in this book: "*You believe what you want to believe, but don't impose it on me*".

From the first-time mankind gazed into the heavens and selected whatever to believe in, billions have died, been massacred, tortured, and discriminated against in the name of religion. Some have rationalized their reasons for these occurrences and others refer to it as 'man's inhumanity to man.' I am now waiting for scrolls to be discovered that will put an end to all this hatred that pervades our societies, beginning with ISIS and the source of their beliefs. But don't hold your breath!

Bibliography

The Illustrated Guide to the Bible	*JR Porter*
The Complete World of the Dead Sea Scrolls	*P Davies G Brooke P Callaway*
The Meaning of The Dead Sea Scrolls	*J Vanderkam P Flint*
Reclaiming The Dead Sea Scrolls	*L Schiffman*
The Stones Cry Out	*R Price*
Understanding the Dead Sea Scrolls	*H Shanks*
The Hidden Scrolls	*NA Silberman*
The Dead Sea Scrolls Deception	*M Baigent R Leigh*
The Complete Dead Sea Scrolls in English	*G Vermes*
The Coming Last Days Temple	*R Price*
The Dead Sea Scrolls Uncovered	*R Eisenman M Wise*
The Oxford Handbook of Jewish Studies	*M Goodman*
Josephus and the New Testament	*S Manson*
The Dead Sea Scrolls Today	*J Vanderkam*
An Introduction to the Complete Dead Sea Scrolls	*G Vermes*
The Secrets of the Dead Sea Scrolls	*R Price*
A History of the Jewish People	*H Ben-Sasson*
Who Wrote the Dead Sea Scrolls?	*N Golb*

References from the Internet and Other Sources

All listed email sites and downloaded notes are on file with the author. In some instances, the given site may have changed since their downloading.

Crash Course in Jewish History Series	*Rabbi K Spiro of Aish.com*
Orion Center for the Study of the Dead Sea Scrolls	*Hebrew University of Jerusalem*
Second Temple Judaism: A Brief Historical Outline	*B Fisk*
A History of Jerusalem	*Alick Isaacs*
Timeline for the History of Judaism	*Jewish Virtual Library*
Divrei Torah: Parshat Pinchas	*DR Shuman Institute*
The Oldest Jewish Dynasty	*David Einseidler*
The Laws of the Damascus Document	*Joseph Baumgarten*
Public Fasts in the Judean Desert Scrolls	*Noach Hachman*
The Damascus Document from the Cairo Geniza	*Stefan Reif*
The Judaism of the Damascus Sect	*P Davies*
The Linguistic Study of the Damascus Document	*S Fassberg*
The Damascus Document: A Centennial of Discovery 3rd. Orion Int. Symposium The Dead Sea Scrolls Fifty Years On	*Geza Vermes and Richard Bonney*

Who were the Pharisees and the Sadducees?	*Brian Huie*
The Essenes and the DSS at Qumran	*GoodNews Christian Ministry*
An Introduction to the Classical Descriptions of the Essenes from the Accounts of Josephus	*Chad Salyn*
Joseph Flavius	*info@jewishpeople.net*
Hellenism and Judaism	*Encyclopaedia Britannica*
Frequently asked questions	*The Temple Institute*
The Mishnah	*Mishnah.htm*
Second Temple Times	*Lambert Dolphin*
The Maccabean Revolt	*Al Maxey*
The Hasmonaean Dynasty	*Al Maxey*
Greek Rule - The Ptolemys and the Seleucids	*Al Maxey*
The Roman Era	*Al Maxey*
Second Temple and Talmudic Era	*The Dinur Center - Heb. Univ. Jerusalem*
A Jewish View of the Messiah	*Rabbi Chaim Richman*
Extracts from 8th, 9th and 10th Orion Symposia	*Orion Web Site Heb. Univ. Jerusalem*
Fifty Years of the Dead Sea Scrolls	*Lehrhaus Judaica*

Made in the USA
Columbia, SC
29 April 2023

15854075R00157